Tap Dancing on a Hot Skillet

a memoir

gabrielle brie

poetica
PRESS

TAP DANCING ON A HOT SKILLET
Copyright © 2021 by Gabrielle Brie

This is a work of creative nonfiction. The events and conversations are portrayed to the best of the author's memory. While all the stories in this book are true, some names and identifying details have been changed to protect the privacy of the people involved.

Attributions for photographs and songs can be found at the end of this book.

Paperback: 978-1-7351359-2-2
Ebook: 978-1-7351359-1-5
Library of Congress Number: 2020924558

First paperback edition published March 2021.

Published by Poetica Press
Austin, TX 78704
www.poetica.press
www.GabrielleBrie.com

Edited by A Hunter Sunrise
Cover art & book layout by Marico Fayre
Cover photograph by Laura Fuhrman

This book is dedicated to my children,
Judah Shalom Conlon and A Hunter Sunrise.

You taught me the truest meaning of unconditional love.

"What is REAL?" asked the Rabbit one day, when he and the boy were lying side by side in the nursery. "Does it mean having things that buzz inside you and a stick-out handle?"

"Real isn't how you are made," said the Skin Horse. "It's a thing that happens to you. When a child loves you for a long, long time, not just to play with, but REALLY loves you, then you become Real."

"Does it hurt?" asked the Rabbit.

"Sometimes," said the Skin Horse, for he was always truthful. "When you are Real you don't mind being hurt."

from The Velveteen Rabbit by Margery Williams

Tap Dancing on a Hot Skillet

a Hot Skillet

a memoir

gabrielle brie

Prologue

Me and Dad

T HIS IS A story about me and my Dad so, in a way, it's his story as much as mine. And even in his death, though forty-five years have passed since he crossed from this world to the next, his presence continues to loom over me. He lives on in my memory as he did when he was on this earth—larger than life and a force to be reckoned with.

His influence as the lead character in my childhood has informed my life in many profound ways. He was someone I loved and hated. He could elicit adoration and utter fear. To say that he was, at times, damn-near impossible to live with would be an understatement. It is only the passage of many years, coupled with becoming a parent myself, that has made it possible for me to write about our relationship at all.

He was, as you will learn, Dear Reader, what they call "a true character." And though he spent a lot of time being recalcitrant, it is his *joie de vivre*, not the crazy, I remember the most.

A wise person once told me, "We should forgive our parents so one day our children may forgive us."

My desire in writing this book was to gain a clearer understanding of all that happened back then, to uncover the stories and family secrets seldom shared, and to extend some measure of honor and forgiveness to both my father and myself.

The information, learned late, that my father brought a heavy load of troubles into his marriage with my mother has also helped me to understand his behavior, which for many years I had written off as him simply having an innate need for routine hysteria. As a child, I could only make sense of things through a narrow explanation—that he thoroughly enjoyed spending a significant amount of time making the lives of his wife and children miserable.

The baggage my father brought into his marriage held both secret heartaches and hard-won wisdom—wisdom which he generously shared with me, and for which I am eternally grateful. My hope in writing this book is that, together, we can unpack the stories of this most brilliant and impossible man.

Dad once told me a story about a little mouse who lived on a farm. Every day, after the animals were fed, the mouse would visit the horse stall. One day the mouse was standing there as usual, busily picking the corn out of the horse manure, when the barnyard animals gathered around him. Laughing, they chattered to one another about how disgusting this mouse was because he was picking the corn out of the horse pies. The geese, chickens, rooster and pig were all getting a kick out of making fun of the little mouse. The mouse just stopped, looked up, smiled, and said, "It might be shit to you but, it's my bread and butter."

If ever there was a man who could make Shinola out of shit, it was my father. My hope is that this book turns out to be Shinola for you as well.

Gabrielle Brie, San Miguel de Allende, Mexico, 2021

The Silvery Moon

The four of us kids

IT WAS ANOTHER unbearably hot Friday afternoon in Florida when my burly, balding, father ran through the back door calling our names through the halls of the house. He peeled his clothes off, sweaty shirt hitting the floor, and the pencils in his front pocket flew everywhere.

"Come on, Redheads, let's celebrate! It's the end of the week and we can finally get back to working on our act!"

We knew the drill, so we ran tumbling after him, undressing as we went.

Dad always saw his children as a vaudeville performance group in the making. From the time I was a baby he'd spend his early mornings in the woods practicing his clarinet, or what he called the "licorice stick." He adored big band music—Benny Goodman was his idol. Dad's dream was that he and his children would eventually form a touring family band. So, I started playing the accordion at age six.

To Dad, rounding up his little chickens, jumping past the mermaid-etched shower stall door to teach us song-and-dance routines was his reward for working all week at a thankless commercial art job. Dad, whose professional art training was in New York at the prestigious Pratt Institute and The Art Students League, hated the Florida crackers he worked for. I heard him say more than once, "They wouldn't know the difference between a Rembrandt and a macaroni wreath."

In our musical household, little Benny, the youngest, just past two, started singing, "Skidamarink a dink a dink" before he could walk. Chunky Benny and my four-year-old sister Paulina took after the Polish side of the family. Paulina, with her round face and Buster Brown haircut, looked like a real-life version of a Raggedy Ann doll.

Mom said Harvey and I favored the Hungarian side of the family because, like her, we're fine-boned. Mom was small and birdlike, with tiny, deep-set, watery blue eyes that always seemed bigger when magnified by her horn-rimmed glasses. Like Mom, Harvey had one crossed eye and wore glasses, too. I figured that was why he was her favorite—because they made him look like a little professor, and the parents concluded he'd one day be a great success story as the lawyer or doctor in our family. Harvey, eighteen months younger than me, was wiry and athletic with thick, orangey-red hair cut in a flat top, that all the old ladies loved to run their fingers through.

Mom was always in a hurry. It seemed to me that she was in such a rush to get to the next thing that she rarely enjoyed what she was doing at the moment. At pretty much every meal, she'd eat too fast, which caused her to choke. This sent Dad into a tizzy fit and he would jump up from the table, red-faced and worried, to perform the Heimlich maneuver. It's my contention that Mom learned to eat fast when she was growing up with five foster kids during the Great Depression, competing for every morsel.

And me? I was a gangly ten-year-old with a strawberry-blonde pageboy hair style who fantasized about becoming a movie star one day because the kids at camp nicknamed me "Rhonda" after the actress, Rhonda Fleming (also a redhead).

In our small performance space of the family shower stall, the choreography was simple: all five of us marching around in a circle, stopping only when it was our turn to sing under the microphone (showerhead). Whenever it was my turn, I did a couple of my fancy tap steps—the shuffle ball change.

Our favorite show tune was, "By the light of the Silvery Moon." Dad began by singing "By the light," and each of the three oldest kids would echo, "By the light, by the light, by the light." Then we'd sing, "... of the silvery moon," in unison.

Benny would chime in a few bars later with, "yeah moon," holding his arms out in true Al Jolson fashion. Because there were only three "by the lights" and four kids, the echo, "yeah moon," was his part.

Then Dad sang solo, "I want to spoon to my honey. I'll croon love's tune."

Then we'd sing in unison, "Honeymoon, honeymoon, honey-moon, keep a-shinin' in June," and so on.

Dad's nickname for Benny was "Fishhook, end-of-the-line!" So it was only fitting that at the end of the song he got to sing the last few words, "... of the silvery moon," which were sung twice, slowly.

Once the water began to run cold, Dad blasted through the door in his towel, leaving a trail of water into the kitchen while Mom screeched, "Max, get some damn clothes on!" in her signature Brooklyn accent as he danced around the room.

Mom's job, as she saw it, was to hand each of us a bath towel while commanding us to get into our pajamas. We begrudgingly obeyed, going to our bedrooms then emerging in the kitchen in our PJs, ready for dinner.

Mom once told me that her mother Gussie, who died when she was three, used to bathe her and her brother in cold water to "toughen us up for the world." It seemed to me that Grandma Gussie's plan worked because Mom did turn out to be a tough cookie but, sadly, her chance to be a child went down the drain with the water.

Dad was the fun parent.

We never saw Mom naked—and she certainly would never have danced in the shower with us, or even thought up such a thing. After Grandma Gussie died Mom was sent to live with a no-nonsense Austrian foster mother named Mrs. Kravitz, who didn't think play had any value. Later, when Mom was eight, Mrs. Kravitz threw away her only toy, a doll, telling her that she was "too old to play with toys."

My job was to set the table and make a salad while Mom stood at the stove making our Friday night special, "peppa steak"—her version of Chinese food. Also, a way to stretch a bunch of meals out of half a pound of top round. She sautéed small pieces of beef with onion, green pepper, and soy sauce, then served it over a generous portion of Uncle Ben's rice.

As she stirred the pan, she glanced over her shoulder at Dad, clearing her throat and exhaling with a forceful "harrumph" in an attempt to get Dad to realize he needed to put on some clothes.

Her hints were wasted on Dad, who'd be so absorbed in some creative pursuit—on this night, carving a bust of Venus de Milo out of a bar of ivory soap—that he wouldn't notice her. Truth was, it looked to me like Dad didn't really give a rat's ass if dinner was late. Her final plea was always, "C'mon Max, you're setting a bad example for the kinder" (Yiddish for kids). Mom and Dad used Yiddish to talk about things they didn't want us kids to understand—in this case it was an obvious translation.

Finally, Dad, not one to give up easily, jumped up from the kitchen table and sidled over to Mom crooning, "Five foot two, eyes of blue," and dropped to the floor for dramatic effect, kneeled on one leg, and continued, "But oh what those five feet can do."

Then, he rolled his eyes in the style of Yiddish theater, hopped back up on both feet and offered Mom his hand.

"C'mon Ruthie, let's dance."

"Max, get some damn clothes on for Christ's sake." She replied, giving Dad a scowl while she ushered him out of the kitchen with a wave of her hand. "And, hurry up, supper's getting cold."

"Yes, ma'am," Dad said dutifully, then headed to their bedroom to change out of his towel, winking at us kids on the way out of the kitchen.

It was damn near impossible to make Mom laugh, no matter how hard we tried, so taunting Mom for the sake of comedy became a recurring theme in our house.

Another Friday, after a dance through our shower stall watery funhouse, Dad headed into the kitchen in his bath towel, plopped himself down at the table, grabbed a raw turnip and began whittling miniature creatures.

"You know, daughta," he said to me in his deep, slow Yankee voice, "If I had a few more turnips I could make an entire set of the animals in Noah's ark."

He held out his huge palm—in the center were four perfect white turnip half-moons.

"Ya want a piece?" he asked.

I took a couple of the slices and crunched into white root. The taste was almost as sweet as the feeling that Dad and I were sharing a special ritual between just the two of us.

Guess in this way I'm lucky, I thought. *The other kids aren't crazy about turnips.*

Dad and I also had a persimmon rite that we shared. When they were in season, he'd buy four of the luscious fruits and put them on top of the refrigerator. It'd take about a week for them to ripen. Each day we'd both give them a gentle squeeze and venture a guess as to how many more days until they'd be ready. Once they softened up and felt just right, Dad would place them in the refrigerator in the morning, and by evening the two of us would sit in the kitchen after the little kids had gone to bed and eat them with a spoon like pudding. I loved those perfect, fleeting moments when it was just Dad and me hanging out, making memories.

At the age of ten, I thought Mom's inability to join in with the fun was only a temporary problem, imagining that one day she would figure out how to tease him back and, more importantly, learn how to bust out with a genuine belly laugh.

But poor Mom grew up in a home where she was repeatedly told, "children are to be seen, not heard." Her foster mother's edicts succeeded in squelching any chance she might have had at learning the gift of banter. And there she was, married to the likes of my Dad. It was perplexing, but she seemed just as charmed as she was frustrated by this wildcard of a husband she'd picked.

I once asked Mom why she married Dad, a man she had only known for a week.

"Well, we met at a dance in New York when I was twenty-two and still living in the foster home," she said. "The next day, smitten, he invited me to lunch," she said in her Brooklynese, then paused, smirked, and finished, "I took one look at his hands and knew I was going to marry him."

"But what did his hands have to do with it?" I asked, dumbfounded.

"Well, I knew I was going to have two boys and two girls," she continued, "And I didn't want my sons to have tiny hands like my father."

Simple as that: Mom put in her order with God, got the husband, the four kids, and joined the great baby race of the postwar era.

As zany as Dad could be, he still managed to be both the breadwinner and the parent who tucked us in at night, massaging our little fingers and toes. He made up games, drove us to music lessons, and took us fishing, while Mom seemed to be always in the background, making sure we got our dinner on time and looked nice. And though she wasn't the least bit funny, she did create a certain sense of stability in our home, whereas Dad vacillated from being the most loving and entertaining half of the duo to an irrational lunatic at the spin of a dime. I wondered why it was so dang hard for Dad to control his anger.

One night I was awakened from a frightening dream.

In it, Dad was kneeling next to my bed sobbing, muttering, "I'm going to die, I'm going to die, die in a car." I couldn't stop the words banging around my skull until I forced myself awake.

For weeks after, I couldn't shake the feeling from that dream, of Dad, panicked and scared. Of him lost at the edges, coming to me for comfort. I wrestled over the significance of that dream, believing that maybe, if I could translate the meaning of his words and find the answer, I could figure out a way to help him. Maybe I wouldn't worry so much about him or feel so protective of Mom and my younger siblings.

But I couldn't do a damn thing to stop him when his battle with "crazy" was winning. So the family and I learned to enjoy him when he was in a good mood, and tread lightly when he came home from work wearing the wild-eyed expression of someone whose hatches were not battened down.

My Earliest Memory

I was a handful

THE MORNING SUN slices through the crack in my pink seersucker curtains, and I am startled from the careless deep sleep of my five-year-old dreams—practicing my tap dance routine to "Oh You Beautiful Doll" in Mrs. Bagley's recital hall—when the sound of Daddy wailing pulls me awake. He's kneeling next to my bed, sobbing hysterically, one jerking fit giving way to another and another. When he pauses to breathe, I sit up, thinking he's gonna stop, but instead he lets out a sharp howl the way my dog Blackie did once when I stepped on his foot by accident. Frightened, I gather my pink bedsheet to my neck and reach for him. He grabs my hand, desperately, like a drowning man.

"Daddy, you're squeezing my hand too tight," I yelp.

His chest shakes as he lets go, sighs long and hard then swallows me into his cavernous caramel eyes. His eyes speak of remorse;

gut-wrenching and deep, coming from a place where words do not exist.

I say to him, "Daddy, what's wrong?"

He shakes his head then hugs me close, making my flowery batiste baby doll nightie wet from his elephant tears.

Later that day in the kitchen I ask Mom, "What's wrong with Daddy?"

She walks away without a word.

The next day, Daddy puts on his work clothes but doesn't leave the house.

He hasn't picked up Harvey in two days. He's only three and must miss his daddy.

There's no giggling at supper. It's as though nobody wants to disturb the unwanted guest. A ghostly gossamer silence hovers over our table, enveloping our family. I reach for Mom again, question marks in my eyes, but she looks away.

After dinner I ask, "Are you a-scared of the pirate, Daddy?"

I figure, like me, Daddy's afraid to go to work on account of the man who moved into the Thompson's house a week earlier. Whenever I see him, black patch over one eye, I fly running into the house. This has to be the problem, 'cause he surely scares the heck outta me.

"Well, is that it?" I ask again.

Without looking my direction, he shifts his head from side to side, signaling *no.*

What else could it be? I wonder. Maybe it's those huge red and black devil's horse grasshoppers that the Thompson's youngest daughter, Charlotte, torments me with every afternoon.

"Better run or they'll sting you and you won't be able to move or talk," she yells as she picks up the pitiful creatures with clothespins and flings them at me.

I'm trapped, I thought. *I don't want to go outside because of the pirate and the grasshoppers, or be inside, afraid that Daddy's tears will drown me.*

I don't know what to do to help him.

I stretch my arms as far around him as I can to give him a hug, pat his head and tell him the words he says to me, when I'm feeling sad, "It'll be okay, Sugar Plum."

The next frame...click.

A few days later, Daddy comes home from work and brews up a pot of sassafras tea. The fragrant cinnamon scent fills me with hope. He picks Harvey up and totes him around and tickles him. I feel joy.

The day after that, Daddy walks through the back door holding a pile of cardboard boxes. It feels like he has stepped out of a thick grey fog, and brought it with him into the kitchen. My eyes search for the end of the fog and find a ghost standing just outside the door.

"Daddy, can you push us on the swings?" I ask.

"I'm sorry, Sugar Plum, I have to pack. We're moving."

"C'mon Harv, I'll push you instead," I say, grabbing his tiny hand as we walk outside.

When we come back in, I ask Mom, "What's moving?"

"We're taking our things to Grandma and Grandpa's house."

"But where will they live?" I ask, confused.

"They died."

My feet freeze to the floor. I want to scream, to run to—I don't know where. I can't move or breathe. I am Dorothy in *The Wizard of Oz*, tangled and spinning in the center of a cyclone, watching my house whirl by. I reach for it, but it's moving way too fast and I can't grab on.

The Red Brick House

Mom and Dad at the red brick house

I T WAS SATURDAY morning and Harv and I, five and seven, were sitting on the living room floor watching cartoons. Two of the little piggies were dancing joyfully around their straw and stick houses while the third piggy, his face twisted in a grimace, labored to finish his brick house.

"The big bad wolf is gonna huff and puff," said Harvey, seconds before the wolf showed up threatening to blow the house down.

Harv looked over the top of his lopsided glasses and smiled proudly at me, then asked, "Do you think Grandpa read the story of the Three Little Pigs when he was young and that's why he built his house out of brick?"

"Sure could have, little brother," I say, unable to match his enthusiasm.

I felt like one of the happy pigs until the Angel of Death showed up at our house, I think, but keep it to myself. That Dad sometimes seemed like the wolf also crossed my mind, but I didn't mention that, either.

It'd been almost three years since Grandma and Grandpa died and Dad still had days where he came home from work crying, put his fake teeth in the glass of water on his nightstand and fell asleep without dinner.

The house that we inherited from the Grands was much bigger than our old little old two-bedroom, one-bath, rental down the block and looked rather stately sitting back from the street on its double corner lot. A brick walkway wound up to a set of round steps that led to a big screened porch with slatted glass jalousie windows. A majestic dogwood tree graced the front yard and a pear tree peeked out around the side of the porch.

For Mom—who grew up sharing her fifth-floor walkup apartment in the Bronx with eight people—living in our big brick three-bedroom, two-bath house was more than she could've imagined.

I shared the biggest room with Paulina, just a year old, and six years younger than me. Harvey had what Mom called "the boys' room" even though he wasn't sharing it with another brother, yet. But Mom always said she wanted two girls and two boys, so he'll share his in about three years when our youngest brother Benny pops into the family.

The Boys' Room was originally built as a pantry with a swinging door into the kitchen—a tiny room barely big enough to house a set of bunk beds and a small dresser. Worse, he was lulled to sleep each night by the humming refrigerator motor on the other side of the wall, making the room hot like a pizza oven. It did have one thing going for it—the heavenly perfume of night-blooming jasmine growing outside the window.

Mom and Dad's otherwise unremarkable bedroom also had something special about it—the small bathroom with a naked mermaid etched into the shower door where we did our family song and dance routines. I loved sneaking the Southern Baptist neighbor kids into the bathroom to watch them cringe over the sinful thing.

Our parklike yard was filled with a heavy-duty swing set, monkey bars, sandbox, and a playhouse that Dad had custom-built for us. The many fruit trees, along with the nine pines, helped cool the relentlessly hot house trapped by the Florida sun. Most days after school and in the summer neighbor kids played on our swing set, ran through the sprinkler, or swung badminton racquets, sending shuttle cocks flying.

Even with so much to play with, we were always inventing new games.

"Tree Dodge," one of our favorites, was when someone held a stopwatch while blindfolded kids took turns riding around the yard on their bicycles to see who could stay on the longest without hitting a tree.

Most afternoons were grand, ending only when the neighbor kids, most having witnessed Dad's temper at least once, scampered off at the sight of his car pulling into the driveway.

One afternoon, Dad asked me to go bring Paulina's tricycle in off the street.

"It idn't mine," I responded.

Dad smacked me across the face.

"The word is *isn't* not idn't," he said, pointedly.

Another time, he arrived home from work in one of his bad moods and asked Harvey a question I couldn't quite hear. Well,

Harv didn't respond quickly enough, because the next thing I heard was Dad yelling at him to hit the ground and do twenty-five pushups.

Another time, provoked by something silly and insignificant, Dad pulled his belt out of his pant loops, made Harvey bend over and wailed on him in front of a couple of the neighbor kids.

Dad had only spanked me with the belt once, but I always wondered when it would happen next. We never knew what would set him off, or when it might happen. Because he was fun and engaging so much of the time, Harvey and I were always caught off guard.

Dad was a farm boy at heart. Each evening after dinner, he'd roam among the pear, kumquat, and grapefruit trees. I adored watching him inhale the lovely scent of the blossoms, giving each fruit a "squeeze test" to see if any were ripe enough to pick.

Our house wasn't as glamorous as the two Georgian revivals that sat at opposite corners on our street, nor was it one of the largest, but it certainly had more style than what Dad called the "cracker shacks" lining the side streets. Those small bungalows were originally built during World War II as temporary housing for the families stationed at Jacksonville Naval Air Base nearby. But after the war many of them stayed put, continued working for the military, and joined the great baby race. And the two-bedroom, cheaply built wood-frame homes strained to house the large Catholic families who stayed busy being fruitful and multiplying.

Dad sectioned off part of our brick double-car garage for an art studio, where he spent evenings at his drafting table working on paste-up ads for grocery stores. On the side of the garage there was a tiny bathroom built for "the help," which the neighbor kids used until our nanny, Wilhelmina, came to work for us.

Prior to moving to Florida, Dad was a successful artist working for Warner Brothers in Manhattan. Mom, a fashionista, worked in the garment district for six years before she met Dad. Now, they and their four flamed-haired children found themselves smack dab in the middle of a neighborhood comprised of Catholics and Southern Baptists—spitting distance from one of the Deep South's largest Ku Klux Klan conclaves in the U. S. of A. And us the anomaly, as one of only three Jewish families on our side of town.

As to why my grandparents chose Jacksonville rather than a more multi-ethnic city farther south like Miami, the way the story goes is that Grandpa Ben had been running a numbers racket out of the small grocery store he owned in Harlem and owed money to a bunch of creditors. This would explain why as soon as he and Grandma hit Florida, they dropped anchor in the first place they came to.

To make a fresh start Grandpa Ben dreamed up a new goal which was to have a business there, in the hot Florida sun, where his three sons and his only daughter's husband could work together to make their fortunes. And, since Florida was experiencing a building boom while New York buildings were being demolished, Grandpa reasoned that a plumbing business would be a shoo-in. He could ship the salvaged bathtubs, toilets, and sinks from the teardowns from New York to Florida and sell them for a pretty penny, along with new pipes and tools to install the fixtures. Dear ol' Gramps was certain that in two shakes of a lamb's tail the family would be neck-deep in dollar bills.

Mack Plumbing was born.

Along with helping out in the store, Dad was put in charge of the newspaper and radio advertising. Once, he was asked to come up with a jingle and so coined the phrase, "If water runs through it, we have it."

One day a sassy woman called the company and said, "I know something water runs through that you don't have."

The slogan remained, though it became the butt of many a joke.

Dad's parents bought a triple lot to build a house for the two of them and a smaller brick house next door for Dad's sister, our Aunt Rudy, her husband, Harry, and their three kids. When Dad's younger brother, Uly, who was living with the Grands, married our Aunt Frances, he built a brick house several blocks away. In the early days, with the exception of the oldest brother, our Uncle Sid, who settled on the south side of town, the tight-knit family lived within a few blocks of each other and shared all the Passover Seders and other Jewish holidays.

But once the Grands passed, Aunt Rudy and Uncle Harry sold the house next door and moved themselves and their three kids, cousins the same ages as us, to the south side of town—where most of the other Jewish families lived. And after a while, Uncle Uly and his family followed.

It didn't take long before Dad realized that his position at the plumbing company wasn't a good fit. While he enjoyed the art portion of his job, he had no inclination for scurrying into the back room to fish out a particular plumbing part. So, when I was eight, he bid farewell to the pile of toilets, sinks, and bathtubs and started freelancing until he could find a permanent commercial art position.

Soon after Aunt Rudy and Uncle Harry moved, we got our first television set. Aside from cartoons, the comedy "Topper" became my favorite. It depicted a young, good-looking married couple named George and Marion Kirby and their Saint Bernard dog, Neil. The theme of the show was that the Kirbys had died in an avalanche on a ski trip while they were celebrating their fifth wedding, anniversary. Now they were ghosts who continued to live in their home, which had since been purchased by a cranky Englishman by the name of Cosmo Topper and his wife, Henrietta. Because Cosmo was the only one who coulc see them and their martini-loving pooch, every show became a comedy of errors with the Kirbys pulling stunts that made Topper look crazy to everyone around him.

If there are ghosts living in Cosmo Topper's house, maybe Grandma and Grandpa are still living with us, I thought.

At times, I was sure that I saw my grandparents out of the corner of my eye, and I was certain there were a couple of other ghosts lurking just below the surface of what the grownups considered "real." I knew nobody would believe me, so I never told a soul, not even Harvey.

Harv and I were never without something fun to do. We spent the long hot days running through the sprinkler, swilling down lemonade, digging for doodle bugs, and playing with the gopher tortoises that showed up in our sandbox. We were enchanted by the many creeping, hopping, or crawling creatures—chameleons being my favorite—that filled our yard.

One day after school, a raggedy, one-eyed, grey-brown cat ambled up the round steps to our front door. The poor thing had a bloody eye socket. Before my parents got wind of it, I hid him in the playhouse and used peroxide and water to clean up his wounded eye. Harvey, thinking the cat was a boy, named it Jerry. I couldn't wait to get home from school each day to see the scraggly creature I'd fallen in love with. One happy day, Jerry had a surprise for me—a litter of ten tiny kittens. This discovery marked the beginning of the rest of my life of rescuing and caring for animals. We dubbed the playhouse, "The Gabrielle Rose Rescue Shelter."

Mom complained about the kittens—but Dad saw how much animals meant to me. One Sunday he picked Harv and me up from Sunday school and drove us to the Humane Society to get a dog. At the time, it was commonly believed that a neutered female dog who'd already had a litter of puppies was the best choice. I'm pretty certain this notion was an old wives' tale—but it didn't matter, because I was getting a dog and couldn't wait to pick one of the pooches clamoring against their cages looking for us to notice them. I struggled, as I walked the rows, realizing we could only choose one dog to take her home with us. But when I saw Tippy, I was smitten and, as importantly, Harvey seemed to like her, too. She was a nine-month-old, medium-sized Labrador mix, mostly black, with a white tip at the end of her tail. As much as I loved Jerry, a dog was a different story. Tippy was bigger and sturdier. I didn't have to worry that I might squoosh her by hugging her close. Plus, Harv and I could take her with us on our many adventures— my best friend in a fuzzy suit.

With Tippy in tow, Harvey and I took to tromping around the neighborhood looking for a secret hiding place to call our own. Lucky for us, the swamp was just six blocks away. Though it was relatively close to home, it felt a world unto itself and soon became our private, sacred hideout. The swamp was only the width of an average city block, but deeper in length, and had a creek running right through the middle of it. We knew that no parent would ever enter the goopy mud that you had to cross to get to the winding trail along the creek, which led to the dark woods in the back. On the hottest days, the swamp enchanted us. It was cool and damp inside and filled with the delightful sounds of twittering birds and the croaking of thousands of tiny frogs—a magical place for us to escape when Dad transformed into the Big Bad Wolf.

Our New Friend

Willie believed if her photo was taken it would rob her of her soul

ONE MORNING, I walked into the kitchen for breakfast to find Mom talking to a skinny, smiling, chocolate-brown woman wearing a raggedy dress.

"This is Miss Gabrielle, my oldest." Mom introduced me.

I got to wondering if she might be "the help" Mom had mentioned to Dad she would need once her fourth child was born.

"Do you have any children of your own, Wilhelmina?" Mom asked.

"Yes, Ma'am, two boys—Raymond and Marvin."

Raymond, five, was close to Paulina in age and Marvin, who was only three, would, in time, become Benny's favorite playmate.

Wilhelmina Jordan, who I was sure was about to become our most beloved friend, continued, "I would need to bring my boys to your house in the summer since school's out." Then a brief pause. "Would that be alright, Miz Mack?"

Wilhelmina was raising her boys alone.

"That'd be just fine," Mom replied.

She offered Wilhelmina fifteen dollars a week and "car fare." In New York this meant subway money but here, in Florida, it was for bus transportation. Wilhelmina agreed, they shook hands, and the deal was made.

I glanced into her sparkling brown eyes, and in that moment hoped that Willie, as we would come to call her, was going to bring some of the joy back into our home that had been missing since Grandma and Grandpa died. As we stood together in the kitchen smiling at one another, I felt a warm spirit wrap itself around me.

After that first visit with Willie, I hurried to finish my cinnamon toast and ran into Harvey's room, where I grabbed his hand and pulled him outside to play on the swings and share the good news.

Humiliation

Gabrielle, age 7

A FEW DAYS after Willie came to work for us, a neighbor girl, Bonnie Piehl, pranced into the yard like a banty hen, wearing what Mom called a "cat that ate the canary" look on her face.

"Hey, hey, hey, I've got a game for us to play," Bonnie said, "C'mon, let's go over to Dottie's."

"What kinda game?" I asked.

"It's a surprise," Bonnie answered, clever enough to use a word that piqued my curiosity—*surprise*—the best bait she could toss out to get me ambling along behind like a sheep being led to slaughter.

Other than Charlotte Thompson throwing those horrible grasshoppers at me when I was five, I'd never met a mean-spirited kid, so in blind expectation of something wonderful, I followed her out of our yard.

Though Bonnie's house backed up to mine and I'd seen her palling around with her brother, Jeff, I didn't really know her. We were in the same grade but different classrooms and this was the first time she'd ever singled me out to play.

Dottie Welch, blonde and adorable, was another third-grade neighbor who I really liked, so I jumped over the fence and followed Bonnie through her backyard and down the strip of dirt that ran along the side of her house to Dottie's garage. When Bonnie pulled up the metal garage door Dottie was sitting on a small pillow on the cement floor. Two other cushions were placed around a cardboard box with deck of cards in the middle.

I said, "Hi, Dot."

"Hey, G," she bounced back.

"Well, girls," said Bonnie, "are you ready to play a special game of poker where the winner gets this here fifty-cent piece?"

"Sure," we agreed, in unison.

Bonnie, who had two rowdy older brothers, did her fancy shuffle on the cards, a skill I could never seem to master, and then dealt.

"Listen up girls, this is how it's gonna go. Each person gets three cards. When it's their turn they'll draw a card from each player, and then take one from the stack until we all have a total of six. If you get any pairs—two cards with the same suit or numbers on them—or a full house, you can set those cards aside. Then you add up the remaining cards in your hand to see who has the highest number. Deuces and Jacks are wild."

Bonnie drew her cards from us, then Dottie did, then me.

"What's a suit?" Dottie asked, looking to Bonnie.

"I'll tell you later," Bonnie quipped.

"It's when you have a set of the same kind, Dot, like four hearts or four fives," I told her.

I'd played a little poker with Dad, so I knew a bit about the game, but the rules Bonnie explained weren't anything I'd heard before.

We drew our remaining three cards from the deck, set aside our suits and pairs, then quietly counted up the numbers in our hand. I had a pair of kings that I set aside and still had a two, six, eight and an ace left.

"Isn't my two a deuce?" I asked Bonnie.

"What's an ace worth?" followed Dot.

Bonnie ignored us.

"It's worth one, Dot," I said.

Dottie had a pair of Jacks, an eight, four, five, and a ten.

"So, I set this pair of Jacks aside, right?" asked Dot.

"How does this work, Bonnie?" I asked, urging her to catch us up to speed.

"I forgot to tell you that single cards of the royal family count as ten each," Bonnie added.

I piped in, "I've gotta' go home for dinner soon."

"Well, let's see whatcha' got, girls," Bonnie retorted, and totaled my cards, then Dot's.

I noticed that Bonnie had laid down three sets of pairs, she was left holding nothing.

I had a total of thirty-seven points, including ten each for the kings. Dottie, forty-seven, if it included her two jacks. But I wasn't sure if it did.

I looked at Bonnie across the table. She wore an expression I couldn't name, but it reminded me of that saying I'd heard about looking like the cat who ate the canary.

"Remember, I told you that the person with the highest total number was the loser?"

"Uh," I said, not remembering, but not sure enough that she hadn't mentioned it so I chose not to argue.

"Sorry, losers!" Bonnie piped. "Since I beat the two of you I get to give out the punishment."

"What? Dadgum, Bonnie, what are you talking about?" I asked.

"Yep, it looks like the two of you just found yourselves smack dab in the middle of a game of Strip Poker," she continued. "Now, each of you losers takes off a piece of clothing."

Dottie, the obvious loser of this round, obediently removed her shoes.

I whispered to Dot, "Don't worry, we'll beat the pants off her on the next round."

Laughing at the idea of Bonnie without pants, Dottie smiled and whispered back, "That'd be something, alright."

We played and played and played. And kept losing. How it was that Bonnie kept coming out on top, was a mystery. But we were determined to turn the tables and show her what it felt like to be on the other side of the coin, so we kept playing each hand dealt.

As the game drug on and we stripped down further, Bonnie took to putting each piece of our clothing underneath her until she was sitting on the concrete floor on top of our outfits. At the close of each losing hand, when we gave her another piece of clothing, she'd let go a laugh, "Ha ha, damn losers!"

I felt protective of Dottie because she was younger than us, and more naïve. With each passing round, I got angrier, until I couldn't stand it anymore. We were down to our skivvies and whatever game Bonnie was playing was surely a cheat, even if we couldn't be sure how.

"C'mon Bonnie, give us our clothes back," I pleaded.

She just sat there with that same shit eatin' grin, ignoring my plea, basking in her victory.

Now, I was furious. "Well, say something! At least give Dottie her dang clothes, she's sitting here buck ass naked!"

If Harvey had tried to pull a stunt like this on me, I would have stopped him in his tracks. But because these were girls my age, in the name of being polite I allowed Bonnie's sham to go on way longer than I should have.

Suddenly, from the big door behind us, the sound of metal-on-metal pierced the silence. I jumped. Like a smack in the face, blinding sunlight streamed in and cut across our naked bodies as Dottie's mother lifted the garage door.

Dottie and I scattered, diving behind some empty boxes in the back of the garage.

Bonnie flew out the door.

By the look on her face, Dottie's Mom was gobsmacked.

"Get in this house this damn minute, Dottie," said her mom tersely, and Dot scurried after her in all her naked glory.

I grabbed my clothes from the floor and bolted out the door. Once safely in the side yard, I clumsily got dressed, then I ran home and tore through the back kitchen door. Now inside, without reason, I started half-muttering, half-singing aloud, "Damn, damn, damn, damn, damn, damn."

I looked up, and turns out, the whole family was sitting at the kitchen table, listening to the cuss words roll right out my mouth.

Without a word, Dad's huge arm swooped down and tightened around me, lifting me off my feet to the kitchen sink, where Mom promptly slammed a bar of soap into my mouth. I wriggled loose, ran into the hall bathroom and shoved toothpaste into my mouth to try and wash out the bitter taste of Boraxo, then ran into my bedroom in tears.

It would be another couple of years before the word betrayal found its way onto my tongue but, when it did, it would remain there all the years I'd know Bonnie Piehl.

We Flew Under the Radar

Mom and her four kids at miniature golf

ENERALLY SPEAKING, HARVEY and I tried to keep being Jewish a secret from our friends at school, and, for the most part, it worked. We were able to fly under the radar for several reasons. First, we were Ashkenazi Jews from Eastern Europe. Unlike most of the Sephardic Jews, who tended to be olive-skinned with dark hair, Mom and all four of us kids had red hair and freckles. The few Gentile folks who thought they knew what a Jew looked like assumed that Jews were all dark and swarthy like the Sephardic. And, second, because our last name was Mack, most folks assumed we were of Scottish or Irish lineage.

We also blended in because, like our Christian neighbors who went to church, we too left the house early on Sunday to attend religious school at our synagogue. And while we loved kosher deli food, participated in Passover and Chanukah at home and the high holy days at the synagogue, there were Southern traditions that Mom and Dad enjoyed as well. Mom, who didn't keep a kosher home, occasionally baked a beautiful ham with pineapple slices pinned to the top with cloves.

Whenever Mom sent me to fetch something for the main course, it went a little like this:

"Gab, can you run down to Winn-Dixie? We need something for dinner."

"Yeah, sure. What do you want me to get?" I asked.

She'd point her ice blue eyes at me, smirk, and say, "Buy the mostest for the leastest."

Sometimes this meant calf liver, sometimes round steak, but occasionally the forbidden meat, pork, was on sale and that's what I got. For Mom, it had more to do with buying what was cheapest; she didn't spend much time thinking about it being a sacrilege.

Pork, usually in the form of hog jowls, along with black eyed peas, found its way onto our dinner table at least once a year. This was due to the Southern belief that each pea a person eats on New Year's Day will bring a dollar in the upcoming year.

Dad would start the peas soaking in a big pot of water a couple of days ahead. "This way," he told me, "we won't miss out on all those dollar bills waiting for us on the other side of this old year, see."

I never knew of another Jewish family who celebrated New Year in this way, but I was glad for any tradition that gave me an excuse to suck on those juicy ham hocks and eat those delicious peas.

Mom and Dad had a tight grip on the Yankee philosophy, "The less those neighbors know about your business the better," another reason Harvey's and my Jewishness went undetected. Since Mom and Dad weren't interested in getting to know the parents of the neighbor kids, in most cases, our neighbors had no idea we were Jewish, and Harvey and I preferred it that way.

This was not an era of multicultural awareness. Most people didn't know what Jews were, other than the horrible rumors spread by the Ku Klux Klan that all Jews were sinister rich. *If only that was true*, I thought, considering my parents' near-constant financial struggle. The preposterous notion that Jews controlled all the banks in the world made me furious. As did the other things I'd overheard like when the KKK called us Jews "nigger lovers" and "Christ killers." But, I supposed, the crackers were right about the first part because we were certainly taught from an early age to be compassionate toward other persecuted people.

My guess was, most of our neighbors had never met a Jewish person. The fact that their Christian Messiah was a Jew certainly didn't seem to count. We knew that we were different. Still, all we really wanted to do was to fit in. So, unless we became really good friends with a neighbor kid, we didn't tell them.

Still, despite our best efforts, sometimes our secret leaked out around mid-December.

As Christmas season rolled around, unlike our neighbors with their glittering tree gracing the living room picture window, we had a menorah. Dad called it a candelabra but ours was small and simple and a far cry from the elaborate accessory Liberace displayed on his grand piano.

Chanukah chronicles an event that happened in 167 BCE. The story is, ultimately, about Jewish persecution and involves a character named Antiochus the Fourth, who issued a decree forbidding religious practices. His troops desecrated the temple by slaughtering pigs on the altar, throwing their blood all over the synagogue, then destroying the temple. Our Chanukah hero, Judah Maccabee, and his sons, fought for two years to regain the freedom to worship, after which the Jews began rebuilding their temple. They were making great progress but, even working twenty-four hours a day, needed another week to complete the structure when they realized that they only had enough lamp oil for one more day. They prayed to God and He granted a miracle: the oil lasted the eight days needed to finish the temple, which is why Chanukah is called the "Festival of Lights." And as awesome as the Chanukah story is, contrasted with the birth of the son of God, Jesus, who came to forgive all the sins of his followers and give them a free pass into heaven, Judah's lamp oil miracle seemed insignificant.

Truth was, the little menorah looked puny next to the giant, jolly, fat man in the red velvet suit along with the beautiful tree with its flashing lights and colorful ornaments.

Even our presents paled in comparison. In an attempt to round out what we knew would be meager gift-giving, Harvey and I would save our allowance for weeks so we could go to the five-and-dime and the ninety-nine cents store to buy presents for the little kids—five-year-old Paulina and two-year-old Benny—and for Mom. I always worried about Mom because, in my young life, I'd only ever seen Dad give her a gift once: a jewelry box.

We'd buy the little kids a new bag of marbles, a set of ball and jacks, or some Silly Putty, which would only set us back about fifty cents each. Both stores carried a nice selection of gift-boxed rhinestone costume jewelry for a dollar—that took care of Mom. The only expensive gift we bought was for our beloved nanny, Willie. Each year we got her a gift-wrapped gold box with purple satin lining that held two cobalt-blue bottles of Midnight in Paris cologne, and despite our repetition, she always acted surprised. Whatever money was left over after Willie's gift, Harv and I spent buying each other a little something.

Each Chanukah season, for eight nights after dinner, Mom would throw the dish towel onto her head and light the candles as the entire family recited the prayer in Hebrew together.

Baruch atah, Adonai Eloheinu, Melech haolam, asher kid'shanu b'mitzvotav v'tsivanu l'hadlik ner shel Chanukah.

Blessed are You, Lord our God, King of the universe, who has sanctified us with His commandments, and commanded us to kindle the Chanukah lights.

Then, she'd hand us our presents. But this part of the ritual only lasted two nights, because, after that, she'd have nothing to pass out.

I'd try to avoid looking at Dad, who'd sit at the table silently seething. The little kids wouldn't notice the crazy as it began to wash over Dad's eyes the minute they started unwrapping presents. But I noticed Dad's patterns and each year it was always the same. With each passing second of the unwrapping process, Dad's neck would start by turning pink, and after a while, begin inching upward toward his face like a thermometer, reddening as it rose. Harvey and I'd be ready. We agreed ahead of time that we would hand out our gifts quickly so as to try and outrun Dad's rage monster. Knowing that Dad's red face often resulted in a heavy swing of his huge hand, I'd take this as my cue to slowly back my chair away from the table. Harvey followed along.

Mom, in an attempt to include Dad, would cheerfully hand him a wrapped box with something terribly practical inside—a new cotton work shirt or a pair of socks. Then Dad would begin to speak, slowly, each word louder than the last, punctuated by the pounding of his gigantic clenched fist on the dining room table.

"Ruth. Didn't. I. Tell. You. Not. To. Buy. Me. Anything. Dammit. I don't want it." Mom would shudder but try to look unfettered. "Next time, save your money, see," he'd shout. Then he'd push the unopened box across the table toward Mom, jump up and thunder out of the dining room.

For one long, ugly minute, I'd look toward little Benny and Paulina, whose sweet spirits had been crushed to smithereens, and wait for the crying to begin. Then, I'd say, as cheerfully as I could muster, "Get your presents and come with me, kids! I'll push you on the swings." Mom must have felt worse than we did, though she never said.

Every year, without fail, I found myself wondering: *If we are really God's chosen people, how come we get the socks and the sweater and the neighbor kids get the nice dad, a new bicycle, and the roller skates?*

Neighbor Kids

Paulina and Benny in Daytona

MOST OF THE neighbor kids' fathers were in the military and most of the military families were Catholics or Southern Baptists. Some kids were in Jacksonville because their father was in training at the big base, Naval Air Station, nearby. They'd only be around for a year or so, then move to another base and another town someplace else. But some of the other kids' dads would get permanent positions and live in our neighborhood for years.

One such Catholic military family who had a long history of working at the naval base seemed to have taken the scripture, "Be fruitful and multiply," literally.

The Crottys were a family of twelve blonde-haired, blue-eyed kids all with names beginning with the letter J. Combined with the first letter of their last name, their initials were the same as their Lord, Jesus Christ.

Every evening just before dinner time, eight-year-old Harvey, five-year-old Paulina and I would hide under the kerosene tank behind our house to watch Mrs. C., a bone-thin, emaciated baby machine, walk out onto her front porch and yell for her little chickens to come home to roost for the evening.

"Janet, Jerome, Jack, Janelle, Jerry, Jimmy, Julia," and so on, "get in this house."

When she started shouting those J names like a limerick, it was all we could do to keep our uproarious laughter from traveling across the street.

Each weekday morning, for years, the Crotty kids filed out of their house in their green and red plaid Catholic school outfits like a little Irish Army. We knew their names but didn't play with them because they mostly kept to themselves, but for one exception, a few years later, when Harvey befriended Jimmy, the oldest son.

One evening, sitting on the pine needles under the oil tank waiting for Mrs. Crotty to call her brood in for supper, Harvey bragged, "Hey, Gab, I got myself a gen-u-ine business opportunity."

"How so, Br'er Harv?" I'd given him this nickname taken from the Uncle Remus bedtime stories we were reading.

"Well, I got Jimmy to sell me a couple of his dad's magazines for a dollar."

"Isn't that a lot to pay for some old magazines?" I interject.

Well, turns out Harvey had discovered that Jimmy had a stack of French girlie magazines he'd stolen from his dad, who brought them back from his tour of duty in France.

Harvey gave me a look and continued, "Anyway," he said, "I cut out the pictures of the naked ladies and I'm selling 'em—my friends are payin' me fifty cents apiece!"

For the next few weeks, I'd walk with Harvey to the corner nearest the junior high school and watch as the horny prepubescent fifth grade boys lined up.

After he ran out of offerings, he jokingly told me, "I'm sure many a kid went without lunch buying 'em. How 'bout if I treat you to the movies on Saturday?"

We never stopped to ask ourselves whether the neighbor kids were good "friend material" or not. We simply choose who was there. Mostly because we needed a certain number of kids to play games like tree dodge and badminton, or to be members of the clubs we invented.

One of the short-lived clubs was formed when Katie Barry, another sixth grader like me, found a dead bird in her yard, and nailed it to the back of her garage. The primary duties of The Dead Blue Jay Club were to meet each summer day at noon in the swamp where we shared the L&M and Salem cigarettes we'd swiped from our mother's purses. Mostly, we swapped neighborhood gossip, told jokes and caught frogs until we ran out of smokes. After the other kids left, Harv and I would stay behind in the swamp to get a head start on one of our moneymaking schemes.

First, we'd dig up what was known as "cypress knees"—roots that live above the water line at the base of the indigenous cypress trees. Then, after we yanked the knees out of the wet soil and threw them in an old pillowcase, we took them home, boiled them, and peeled off the bark. We sold them for fifty cents each to a couple of the neighbor kids' fathers, who used them to make lamps. It was an easy way to earn enough money for a long afternoon in the air-conditioned movie theatre, never mind having a secret.

The cool dark movie theatre was, to me, a holy place. Waiting expectantly for the theatre lights to dim, I felt giddy with anticipation, as though I was about to unwrap a present. When the MGM lion finally roared, I knew I was in for a treat.

As native New Yorkers, Mom and Dad had great respect for actors, and they often took us to see live theatre performances. They particularly loved musical theatre. It was a Jewish rite of passage to go the theatre or, better yet, to be employed by the theatre or the film industry. Dad liked to remind us that the owners of the major film companies were Jewish.

The tradition of storytelling began long before the diaspora through Ellis Island at the turn of the twentieth century. Yiddish theatre was all the rage from the moment the eastern European Jews stepped off the boat, so it was no surprise that a group of people who had a religion based on storytelling continued to position themselves in the entertainment business in their new home. It was simply another evolutionary adaptation of storytelling on screen and stage.

Whenever we went to the movies with our parents, they scanned the film credits to see if they could spy a Jewish actor who had changed their name—Tony Curtis, Paul Newman, Kirk Douglas, Michael Landon, or Harvey Keitel, to name a few.

Dad would always say, "Ah, there's a Jew Boy," or "He [or she] is a member of the tribe."

I remember being surprised to find out that Lauren Bacall and Claire Bloom were Jewish, and being proud that Marilyn Monroe, Elizabeth Taylor and Sammy Davis Jr. had converted to Judaism. It felt good be proud of something having to do with my religion, which was predominantly misunderstood or hated by most folks in our southern neck of the woods.

I learned early on that if a person was Jewish it was pretty much a requirement to be able to converse intelligently about the latest important films. There is an element of truth to the line often repeated among Jewish people: without the Jews and the gays there would be no Hollywood film industry, or New York theatre scene for that matter.

Still, we lived in Jacksonville, Florida, more than nine hundred miles from 42nd Street, so the more easily accessible alternative was films. I adored live theatre but, for every play I saw, there was time to see a dozen movies in between. Some of the plays were even made into movies, especially if they were musicals. So, Harvey and I did everything we could to scare up matinee movie money.

My best friend was Marsha Kraus, a Catholic from a Navy family. She had three brothers, Johnny, Kip, and Joe, and was the only girl in the family. Her father, who she called "Pops," was about twenty years older than her mother and would soon retire from military life.

I adored Marsha's mom. Mrs. Kraus had rosy cheeks and laughed constantly. Her entire wardrobe consisted of shapeless cotton muumuus covered with flowery designs. She was the fattest person I ever knew, and also the sweetest. She had a fanny which stuck out like a shelf—so big you could set an entire place setting on it and still have room for a teapot. She had the best sense of humor of any adult I'd ever met and always got a kick out of us kids.

One time, Mrs. Kraus invited me over to help decorate the family Christmas tree. Having no idea that there was a technique to hanging tinsel, I proceeded to pick up handfuls and just throw clumps of silver at the tree. She laughed and laughed. Then taught me to hang the silver strands delicately one by one on the very ends of each limb. I was the only kid she'd ever met who didn't know something as basic as that, which tickled her to no end. For years after, she told that story sending herself into stitches of laughter. The only time I ever sat on Santa's knee was the year Mrs. K. took Marsha and me to May-Cohens department store.

Having my picture taken with the jolly man in the red suit was a thrill I never forgot.

Because Marsha was the only girl in the family and they didn't have "help," she got stuck doing the lion's share of the housework and most of the cooking for the family. I can't recall her brothers ever doing a dang thing to help. She was also expected to wait on her mom, who was always saying, "Marsha, can you get me..." this, that, and the other thing—most of the time it was booze.

The first time I ever heard Ray Charles sing was at their house. Mrs. K. had all of his albums. My parents loved Sammy Davis Junior but Mrs. K. was the only Christian white person I ever met who liked listening to a Black man sing.

It never occurred to me, at that age, that Mrs. K.'s jovial nature came from imbibing alcohol all day. Even if it had, I wouldn't have much cared because she was always so sweet to me.

Bullies

Harvey the jock with Paulina

BONNIE AND JEFF Piehl were a couple of those 'friends of convenience' simply because they lived nearby. Jeff, at age fourteen, had a sinister streak and was always looking to do something designed to make Harvey or me look stupid. Still, we needed a certain number of kids to play games so we continued to include them, despite the fact that Bonnie teased me relentlessly.

At the age of ten, I had a slight overbite, which I was very insecure about. I'd asked my parents to buy me braces more than once. Their reply was always the same, "The dentist said your teeth will straighten out naturally as you get older!" Truth was, they lacked the money to buy them.

Bonnie had x-ray vision when it came to spotting a person's vulnerabilities. Seeing that I was self-conscious about my teeth, she immediately nicknamed me "Bucky Beaver"—after the cartoon beaver that advertised Ipana toothpaste on TV. And whenever she saw me on the school grounds or around other people, she'd start singing the jingle, "Brusha, brusha, brusha," at me with her teeth sticking out. She was jealous of my close friendship with Marsha and did whatever she could to try to create discord between us.

People gossiped that Bonnie's mother was crazy and that her oldest brother David smoked opium. It was rumored that the family were atheists or communists, both of which sounded strange and scary. Since none of the other neighbors, or my parents, were about to deal with Bonnie's parents given all the rumors, she and her brother got away with murder half the time.

Mrs. Piehl didn't work outside the home. She wore a faded housedress and never seemed to leave the house for any occasion. She always had a sink full of dirty dishes floating in water with soaking wet dishtowels over the top of them and seemed to have a phobia about germs and bugs, especially roaches. Bonnie once told me that her mom swore that leaving the dishes under water kept the palmetto bugs from showing up to eat the leftover food stuck on the plates. I resisted asking if her mom had ever considered that the roaches might get thirsty? I also wondered why, if she was slouching around the house all day instead of working, she didn't just wash the dang things, dry 'em and put 'em away.

Mr. Piehl, tall and lanky, wore a suit to work at the shipyard and did something administrative. He never gave any of us kids the time of day.

Harv was nine on a beautiful summer day that found him marching around our backyard proudly waving his new quarter-sized American flag. Far as I could see, he deserved to be proud—he'd saved his allowance for weeks to buy it. His sheer, unbridled joy was interrupted when Jeff and Bonnie walked into our back yard.

"Watcha got there, Harv?" Jeff asked, and Bonnie giggled.

"Oh, it's a flag, uh, I just bought it, been savin' my allowance for it," Harv replied.

"Is that so...Can I see it?" Jeff asked.

"Sure," said Harvey, smiling proudly.

Jeff, older and much taller than Harv, started throwing the flag up into the air and catching it. This went on for more than a few tosses, when Harvey finally piped up and said, "Okay, Jeff, give it back."

"Sure, here ya' go," he said, throwing the flag it high in the air.

Harvey ran to catch it, missed, and the flag fell to the ground.

As Harvey scuffled to pick it up, Jeff said, "Uh, oh, you know what we have to do now, don't you?"

"Uh, no?" replied Harv.

"Well, I'm surprised that you don't know this, young man. It is government law that if an American flag touches the ground it immediately becomes defiled and must be burned—give me that thing,"

He snatched the little flag out of Harvey's hand, pulled his zippo lighter out of his pocket in a swift motion, and lit the flag on fire.

Harvey burst into tears and ran crying into the house.

I ran in fast behind him.

"What happened?" Mom asked us once inside.

"The Piehls' are always mean to us. Jeff just burned Harvey's flag and Bonnie sticks out her teeth and sings the Bucky Beaver jingle whenever she sees me at school. What should we do?" I pleaded.

"I'll tell you what you should do," Mom said, without missing a beat, "Next time she does that, tell her to kiss your ass in Macy's window on the noon hour."

As funny as her advice seems in retrospect, at the time, it made me furious. The visual image that Mom's retort provoked would have been wasted on Bonnie, Jeff, or damn near anyone else I knew because most had never seen or heard of the huge department store on the bustling broad boulevards of New York. But the naiveté of youth, coupled with the fact that I'd seen Dad act mean and crazy then get ahold of himself and be nice again, caused me to believe that Bonnie and Jeff would come to recognize the error of their ways, change, and treat us better in the future. So, I continued to give them second chances.

Until another day, some months later, when I stormed through the back door upset, again, over Bonnie teasing me. This time, though, Willie had some worthwhile advice.

"Child," Willie said, "You gotsa understand that those kids are scorpions."

"What do you mean, Will?"

"Hold on a pinch, I got a story for ya," she said, continuing, "One day, Mr. Scorpion asked Mr. Frog to carry him across the river. Mr. Frog told him, 'I'd like to help you, but I'm afraid that if I do, you'll sting me.' 'Oh, trust me,' says Mr. Scorpion, 'I would never do that. Why, I'd be so grateful to you that I would never hurt you.' Old Mr. Frog was worried but still he told the scorpion, 'Okay, I'll trust you just this once, but only this one time. Hop on my back.' Then Mr. Frog started swimming across the river. And just as he got to the edge of the bank, Mr. Scorpion stung him and jumped off. Now, Mr. Frog can barely speak because he is slowly becoming paralyzed from Mr. Scorpion's poison but, still, he asks him in his weak little voice, 'Why would you kill me after I showed you the kindness of carrying you across the river?' Mr. Scorpion smiles and says, 'I couldn't help myself, Mr. Frog, it's in my nature.'"

I looked at her, wide eyed, trying to understand.

"You see child," Willie sang, "You are a frog and those ragamuffins ain't nothin' but a couple of scorpions. It's in their nature to be cruel, and no matter how much kindness you show 'em, they'll turn on you every time. The smartest thing you can learn is to stay away from 'em."

Though it took years for me to fully grasp the true wisdom in Willie's story, her words turned out to be one of the wisest things anyone ever taught me.

Willie

Harvey and Paulina with Jerry's kittens

AFTER THE FLAG incident, Harvey and I decided to spend a few days in the swamp, digging cypress knees. Bonnie and Jeff never went there and we figured we could make some movie money at the same time as avoiding the two of them.

When I went into the house to tell Willie that Harv and I were going for a walk, she was polishing the dining room table with sweet lemony oil, singing, "Go tell it on the mountain that Jesus Christ is born."

It made me happy to see Willie smiling. I skipped out to the garage to get a bucket for the knees and some spades to dig 'em up with. I couldn't find the spades right off, so while waiting for me Harvey made a deal with Willie to go buy her some cigarettes and took off on his bike. By the time I walked back into the kitchen,

Harvey had been gone about twenty-five minutes and Willie was clearly agitated.

"What's takin' your brother so long?" asked Wilhelmina, pacing around the kitchen.

"Heck if I know. I'm waiting on him myself."

I'd packed us a sack of toasted Kaiser rolls and American cheese slices to take with us, and wondered why he wasn't already back.

At age ten, Harvey, who competed with me over damn near everything, had recently started wheeling and dealing with Willie. This day, the two of them made a deal that he would ride to the Winn-Dixie and get her some cigarettes in exchange for her frying him up some salami.

Willie had a way of frying salami with lots of butter that made the edges turned crispy white while the insides got puffy and chewy. Just delicious. It was as good a trade as any, if I had anything to say about it. No sooner than Willie asked about him, the screen door opened with its creak, bang, and Harvey bounced in.

He looked at me. "Gab, you're not gonna' believe what I just got!"

Then he grabbed my arm and pulled me outside. Just out the back door was the largest cardboard box I'd ever seen.

"We'll have some fun with that!" I said, smiling and remembering the only other time we'd been lucky enough to get a refrigerator box.

We made a house out of it, first, by cutting windows out and a door. Then, after the walls began to collapse from the neighborhood kids and us four running in and out, we turned the box on its side, climbed in, and took turns rolling each other all around the yard. Once the box 'tube' got really torn up, we took the biggest piece of cardboard, laid it at the top of the front steps, and put a smaller piece under our butts so we could ride down. I think the whole adventure lasted about three days, if memory serves, and three days was a whole lot of fun to be had.

"How'd ya get it?" I asked.

"You know how on the way to Winn-Dixie there's Anderson's appliance store? I peddled around back to see if there was anything worth grabbin' and spotted it. I had to climb over the cyclone fence to get it."

I pointed to a rip in his pants and asked: "Got that hole, huh?"

"Anyway," he goes on without missing a beat, "I had to hold onto my handlebar with one hand and the box with the other all the way home, dragging the dang thing behind me."

"Well, it was worth it," I said, and headed back into the house, which was certainly cooler than outside. Harvey followed.

Willie cleared her throat, "Where are my cigarettes, Mista Harvey?"

"Uh, well, uh, I guess I got so excited when I saw the box. I, uh, wanted to get it before anyone else," he stuttered nervously.

Giving him a look of total disgust, Willie, usually the picture of patience, walked back to the stove, calm as a cucumber, picked up the iron skillet and flung the salami through the air, hitting the wall directly above Harvey's head. We stood there in horror as the buttery salami rounds slid down the wall, landing in a greasy little pile.

Stunned, I backed into the wall thinking, *I'll be damned, Willie's havin' a real nicotine fit.*

Harvey took one look at her and bolted out the back door, jumped on his Rollfast bike and peddled back to Winn-Dixie.

I had never seen sweet, humble Willie get angry. Though the Supreme Court had declared segregation illegal on public buses, here in Northern Florida, just half an hour from Georgia, the Negroes were afraid to sit anywhere except the back of the bus. They were just plumb too scared to do or say anything that might smack of them not knowing their place, which they were taught to do from infancy. I remembered back to several times when my parents had asked Willie to join us at the dinner table. She always politely said, "No, thank you, Miz Mack," and ate her helping outside.

Willie had been our nanny for four years. She was black as the ace of spades and joyful as the day is long. She was a bona fide holy rollin', filled-with-the-spirit, Southern Negro. She could make the bed with one hand while toting my two-year-old brother on her hip all the while singing, "Why don't you rock my soul in the bosom of Abraham? Oh, rock my soul."

Willie made very little money working for us, but she was too proud to accept welfare. Funny thing was that Mom made only a bit more as a clothing sales clerk but preferred to work outside the house rather than ride herd on her four rambunctious kids.

Mom referred to Willie as "her girl," which always seemed a curiosity to me since she was a mother like herself, not a girl like me and my sister.

At first glance, Willie looked skinny, and it certainly was true that she didn't have an extra ounce on her. Upon closer observation, however, her body was lean and muscular like a long-distance runner. Despite the fact that she often drank something called Wate-On, she just couldn't seem to gain a pound.

Her skinny, shiny self always wore a faded cotton dress that was a hand-me-down from my mother. In this way, she was lucky. Mom was a clotheshorse and they wore about the same size dress, but Willie was skinnier, so she tied her apron around her waist twice and knotted it in the front. She was not so lucky in the shoe department—Willie wore a size nine-and-a-half shoe and Mom wore a seven—but that didn't stop her. When Mom gave Willie a pair of shoes, her ritual was to cut the toes out, soak them in vinegar for a couple days, then squeeze her feet into them and wear them till they dried. She swore that this stretched them out but there was always a toe or two hanging out of the hole over the edge.

Her hair was something to behold—it was short and stuck out every which way. She told us once that it'd caught fire when she was a little girl and just hadn't grown back quite right since.

We believed her.

Despite her application of enormous amounts of Sweet Georgia Brown Pomade, her hair simply would not lie down flat. Once a year, though, to celebrate New Year's Eve, it was her tradition to get her hair "processed," as she called it. She told me they greased it up and plugged some hot rollers in to get her hair to behave. After she got her hair done, she'd head home and put a pot of hog jowls and black-eyed peas on the stove to cook, read Raymond and Marvin a bedtime story, then dress up in her finest clothing, sit herself down in her rocking chair, and wait for Mr. New Year to arrive.

When she arrived to work the day after, her hair would be in neat little tubular rolls that looked like Vienna sausages, covering all sides of her head. It'd only take a day or so before they weren't curls at all but what looked like half-finished birds' nests gone crazy on the top of her head.

Every hour or so, Willie'd sneak out to her little bathroom on the corner of the garage to grab a cigarette. She'd take a couple of puffs, smash the remaining part on the wall, put the butt in her apron pocket and come back into the house. The cement wall was covered with black streaks. Between the cigarettes and the pomade, she had a smoky, sweet smell about her.

Willie let us get away with murder until she knew it was just about time for Dad to get home from work, then she'd warn us, "Straighten up, yo' Daddy'll be home soon," and we'd run around and put away whatever household things we had strewn all over the yard and get to doing our homework.

We were the only house in our neighborhood with colored help. Having what my father described as "crackers" for neighbors was challenge enough, but some were definitely more ignorant than others. The particular type of ignorance that surrounded us provoked fear among me and my siblings, and Mr. Sherman was at the top of that list.

Phil Sherman was retired military and lived next door. He was a dyed-in-the-wool Ku Klux Klan member and mean as a rabid dog—and was, of course, home the day that Willie had her "spiritual experience," as she referred to it after the fact.

Willie was going about her usual routine cleaning the kitchen when, according to her, "The Holy Spirit done come down from the heavens and wrapped its lovin' arms around me."

That day, her usual praises to God were amplified beyond anything we had ever seen before. It started off innocently enough with her singing her favorite gospel songs, but soon she got louder and louder. Harvey and I ran into the kitchen just in time to watch her fall into the wall, knocking the bulletin board onto the floor. Next thing we knew, Willie was rolling around on the floor singing, then screaming, "Yes, Lord, oh God, I hear ya' now. Yes, I'm listening Lord. Thank you. Thank you, Jeeeessuus!"

Bang, bang, bang. Suddenly, a loud knock at the back door.

Mr. Sherman, and several neighbors who he'd rounded up, asked if we were "having problems with our nigger?" and "Should they call the police?"

I told him, "Don't worry sir, everything is just fine," knowing it was my job to protect Willie.

Once Willie realized neighbors were at the door, she managed to pull herself out of her trancelike state and get up off the floor.

Still, the damage was done. A rumor quickly grew throughout our neighborhood that she was a witch and that the devil himself had taken up residency inside her sweet, skinny, smoky self.

My biggest worry was that Mom and Dad would find out what happened and ask Willie to stop working for us. Lucky for us, that never happened, because they didn't talk to the neighbors other than a quick, "How do?"

Prior to Willie's episode, a couple of neighbors had refused to let their children play at our house when Willie's kids were over—which was most of the summer. But after that incident, not a single neighbor kid could step foot in our yard when Willie was there.

Mr. Sherman continued to badger Willie. After the episode, he took to pacing around the bus stop where she waited, repeatedly calling her the "N" word. So, I started waiting with her. Once he saw me with her each day, he seemed to lose interest in harassing her and, while that gave us some breathing room, I continued to feel concerned. I knew from my Sunday school lessons that it was people like Sherman who had persecuted the Jews throughout history. So, I continued to keep a close watch on him.

Between Bonnie and Jeff and Mr. Sherman and the neighbors, I'd learned the hard lesson that evil never took much of a break. *Sure enough,* I told myself, *he'll come up with another plan to frighten Willie and us.* And it wasn't long before he did just that.

QYI

Me, Harvey, and Paulina with Mr. Sherman's radio shack behind us

"QYI, QYI, ARE you there? Do you copy me? QYI, am I coming in?" Phil Sherman's short-wave radio prattle came right through the speakers on our TV, damn near obliterating the voice of Paw Cartwright.

"What an idiot," said Mom as she slumped into the couch, "Your father will deal with this when he gets home."

It wasn't the first time that Sherman's asininity had turned the auditory portion of our TV show into a soundtrack from a war zone. Once his snarly Georgia drawl began ripping holes in Pa Cartwright's dialogue, I knew *Bonanza* was over for the night— there'd be at least another couple of hours of the screaming meemies coming through our set. Even if Dad succeeded in getting Sherman to turn off his radio, it'd surely be past our bedtimes.

"Hey, y'all wanna play go fish?" I asked, in an attempt to distract my siblings from their disappointment.

They followed me with their little hangdog heads, mumbling assorted angry expletives.

"I hate that guy. Maybe Dad can do something when he gets home," piped Harvey.

I was sure there was no way Dad was going to knock on the door of our ex-military neighbor for fear of him pulling out a firearm. Still, I kept quiet so's not to stir up more animosity toward Mr. S.

Dad worked a lot and rarely watched the TV, which he often referred to as "the one-eyed monster."

"If you watch too much television," he'd say, "it will make it impossible for you to absorb your schoolwork."

I heard this more times than I could count. He was convinced that the "monster" would suck our brains clean out of our heads.

This night, Mom met Dad at the kitchen door and led him into the living room to offer him one more hassle that he wouldn't want to deal with.

"He's doing it again, Max," she told him, "Just listen."

Dad stared blankly at the flickering set bleating its staccato cacophony.

"I feel like spitting nails. He's trying to reach some other shmuck on the other side of town. Hear this?" she urged, again.

She recited, disgustedly, "QYI, QYI, stick your finger in your eye," rolling her eyes. "And, just listen to the monkey and that damn bird."

Not only did Sherman spend his evenings in his little ramshackle hut in the backyard messing with his shortwave radio set—he also had a spider monkey. The monkey must have hated the noise as much as we did because he constantly squealed as though competing with it. And then the monkey's antics set Sherman's Amazon parrot to screeching. But the bird only knew two words, "shed" and "up." So he squawked it over and over, "shedup, shedup."

Dad gave a little chuckle at Mom's feeble chant. "I'll call Silverman in the morning," he said, referring to an attorney he knew.

We had some quirky neighbors, but Mr. Sherman took the cake. Sherman hated us and we knew it. He made no secret of the fact that he was a member of the Ku Klux Klan and was a true Georgia cracker. He was boxy, and bow-legged with a potbelly, ruddy complexion, and a flat top. He had two kids, a daughter who was away at college, and a boy named Richard, which he pronounced, "Re-Ah-Chard."

Oddly, he had a beautiful olive-skinned wife whom he called "Blackie." Considering his disdain for "colored" folks, I was puzzled as to why he'd chosen this nickname for her, but I noticed that he said it in an affectionate manner.

Nobody in our family felt at ease with him next door. We were well aware that if Sherman wasn't hassling us, he was likely planning something to convey his hatred toward us, who he referred to as "the nigger-loving Jews next door."

Even without Sherman's shortwave-through-the-television debacle, Dad had been pretty sour lately. It no doubt had to do with Harvey, age ten, getting caught shoplifting a giant Hershey bar from Easterling's Pharmacy.

A few days after Harvey's crime, Dad came home from work to find us kids sitting in front of the mahogany console absorbed in *The Mickey Mouse Club*. We each glanced at him and gave a quick, "Hi," which sent him into a rage. He grabbed his toolbox, pulled out an x-acto knife, then ran around the back of the TV, and cut off the plug.

All four of us went into a silent, crazy spin on the spot. He knew it.

I stormed out to my room, the little kids in tow.

"I don't get why he does this crap," Harv said.

If you hadn't swiped the candy from Easterlings he might not have been so on edge, I thought, but didn't say aloud.

The little kids sat on the bed looking at me with question marks on their faces, as though I somehow had the answer.

Mom heard what was happening from the kitchen but had long since given up trying to reason with Dad when he was like this. And I'd given up attempting to solicit her help because she always said the same thing: "Your father feels very frustrated at work. When he comes home he needs to feel like he is King of the castle. I can't do a damn thing about it."

Mom's acceptance of Dad's craziness made me feel intense anger toward her. At age twelve, I couldn't buy the reasoning that it was okay for him to act like an ass toward the people he was supposed to love most in this world just because he didn't like his job. It plumb made no sense to me. And now, because he got such a dramatic response from his children, the television was a new weapon in his arsenal.

If it was attention Dad wanted, by surgically removing the one-eyed monster from his children, he certainly got it. Nobody spoke a word at dinner that night. I pushed the food around my plate thinking that eating my spaghetti and salad seemed beside the point.

On a Wednesday, after a few weeks of doing without television, Mom said, "You know, your father told me that he sure missed watching the Lawrence Welk show. I don't think he'll mind if I rent a TV for the weekend."

This was big-doings—Mom rarely went against Dad's dictates.

On Friday, I arrived home from school to find a small portable television atop our dead console. *Papa Bear, Baby Bear, hmm.* I wondered how welcome that little set was going to feel once Dad got home.

It turned out that Baby Bear was welcome that weekend, which surprised all of us kids.

Eventually Dad re-attached the cord to the original set. But then cut it off another couple of times during various temper tantrums. He started using the television as a way to punish us if our grades dropped. If one of us got a "C" on our report card, he'd pull out his favorite weapon and ban us all from watching the tube for the next six-week grading period. Before long the cord was too dang short to reach the electrical outlet on the wall behind it.

Paulina, who'd never seen the likes of a "C" in her life, was particularly irked.

The problem was, we had watched just enough TV to know what we were missing. With the TV antics, Dad had robbed us of our respite from the ongoing pandemonium in our house.

Harvey and I tried to figure out a way to reason with him but couldn't come up with anything we thought would work. It felt like everything we kids asked permission for was met with an immediate "no." This sent Harvey and me into fits of our own developing rage. Every argument ended with Dad slamming his big open palm on the dining room table declaring, "I'm the Father and I'll decide what goes on under my roof! N-O."

Then he'd add drama to his declaration by pushing his huge, reddened, open hand uncomfortably close to my face—a gesture that signified, "And, if you're smart you'll get the hell out of my sight." I experienced such anger toward him that at times it felt like the top of my head would open up and steam would fill the room.

It took a few months for the shortwave radio debacle to get settled—

and only when Mom and Dad hired a lawyer to represent them and take Sherman to court. The judge banned him from operating his ham radio anytime except between the hours of 11 p.m. and 8 a.m.

And while my parents looked on their victory over Sherman as a triumph, I thought, *what did it really accomplish given that Dad only allows us to watch TV sporadically, anyway?*

The cycle was pretty much always the same. Whatever small bit of relief my parents felt from Sherman, and us regaining our uninterrupted nightly viewing, was quickly followed by a sense of impending doom. Mom and Dad wondered aloud to one another "What do you think Sherman will do next?"

And I wondered, *what will Dad do next?*

We knew all too well that the philosophy of the KKK was to administer hatred—this was the creed that people like Sherman lived by. And dispensing it on the Negroes and the Jews was their number one priority. Knowing this, we understood that our family and Willie would continue to be his favorite targets, so we held our collective breath and waited.

Retaliation

Harvey and Benny boxing

W E DIDN'T HAVE to wait long to find out. Within a week after Mr. Sherman was told he couldn't play with his radio during half the hours of the day, he strategically strung a thin wire across the corner of his front yard— the exact route where Harvey took a shortcut each day after school.

Luckily, Dad was home early from work the day Harvey's face was sliced open from the sharp wire Sherman had installed. I thought Dad was going to have a heart attack as he scooped Harvey up and carried him to the car, blood spurting out of the gash above his left eye, to drive him to the hospital.

Dad called the police from the hospital but by the time he returned home and the patrol car arrived, the wire had been removed. This left Mom, Dad, and Harvey feeling victimized once more and set us to worrying about what would be next on

Sherman's hit parade of nasty tricks. We remained on guard, but it was impossible to know where to look for what would inevitably happen next.

A few weeks later, during a typical stormy summer day, the newest manifestation of his wrath caught us off-guard.

With one look at the darkening sky, we knew we were about to face another thunderstorm—they usually came after lunch between noon and two. Willie decided that she'd better catch the bus home a bit early to avoid getting soaked. She popped on the little newspaper sailboat hat she'd fashioned for herself and headed out the door.

"You girls are gonna have to bring in the wash, okay?" she told me and Paulina, "I gots to skedaddle before I get caught in this downpour." And off she went, leaving the four full lines of laundry twisting in the breeze.

Mom was at her bowling league and Dad still at work. As the wind kicked up and the pine needles fell in ribbons—Paulina and I ran around the yard trying to catch them before they hit the ground.

"Got one," I yelled. "Hey, Lina," my nickname for her, "Come help me."

I struggled against the wind to take the twisting and turning clothes from the line while still trying to catch an occasional pine needle flashing by. Rain started coming down. I got ahold of a sheet and immediately noticed that something didn't seem quite right—but ignored it in favor of grabbing Dad's jockstrap with a clothespin. I planned to fling it at Paulina but the sideways rain was planting large splotches on our laundry and the wind made it difficult to hold onto the sheet. As the rumbling thunder increased, I decided I'd better wait until we got inside to taunt her—but I couldn't resist. When she bent over and placed a pair of pants in the basket, I threw the jockstrap and hit her in the head.

"Yuck!" she squealed, picking it up with a clothespin and flung it back at me. We both hated the thing and played this game whenever we were stuck removing it from the line. I was going for the jockstrap a second time when I heard the first crack of lightning, my cue to head inside, knowing more was sure to follow. I threw the unmentionable on top of the other clothes and yelled for Paulina to follow. We wound our way down the sidewalk to the back door and into the kitchen.

I was genuinely afraid of lightning. In Florida, whenever there was a lightning storm most folks unplugged their irons, televisions, radios, or any other item that they thought might serve as a conduit to pull the destructive force into their homes. It was common for the electricity to go out, and every time I heard a loud crack and the house went dark, my mind rubber-banded back to scenes from every horror film I'd ever seen.

In the name of keeping us safe, our over-protective father was always showing up at dinner with one horrific newspaper article after another about something gone wrong—a kid blowing off a finger from a homemade firecracker or losing an eye from a BB gun, drowning, or getting struck by lightning. We were too young to know much about Dad's early life or what drove his extreme fear, so in these moments it seemed like his intensity was designed for one reason: to keep us from having fun.

Harvey and I joked that if some kid drowned in China, Dad would bring a newspaper article about it to dinner. Still, nothing could have prepared us for our worst experience involving lightning— and it didn't derive from one of Dad's newspaper clippings.

That was the terrible day one of Harvey's closest friends got struck by lightning and killed while fishing for mullet on a summer afternoon on the dock behind his house, at the edge of Cedar

Creek. Michael Roberson, age ten, was just standing there holding his cane pole with his best friend, Jimmy Morton, sitting nearby when he was struck dead on the dock of his very own home. The way Jimmy told the story was that the lightning bolt paralyzed Michael and he fell like a log into the creek and drowned. This story, repeated many times over, sent shock waves pulsing through our neighborhood.

I had the kind of mind that did not easily relinquish images like that of a stunned Michael falling into the creek, and with every crack of lightning I was reminded of the horror of it. I told myself, *Breathe...at this moment we are inside, safe and sound*—so as to appear calm to the younger kids.

Not quite ready to begin folding the laundry, I yelled, "Let's play 'hit the deck!'" to Paulina, Harvey, and Benny. They knew that meant grab your pillow off your bed and head to the screened porch.

I sang, "It's raining its pouring, the old man is snoring."

The little kids echoed back, "He went to bed and bumped his head and he couldn't wake up in the morning."

Each time we heard a crack of lightning everyone yelled, "Hit the deck!" then threw themselves on the cement floor and dove onto their pillows. When the thunder subsided, we got up and began running around like banshees again until we heard another blast of thunder or crack of lightning. Then somebody would invariably say, "Here comes the headless horseman,'" or "Oh my God, I think I see Ichabod Crane."

An occasional bit of rain or lightning would flash through the screens, causing a feeling of exhilaration and vulnerability at once.

"God must be re-arranging his furniture again," little Benny would pipe, as though he'd thought of the phrase himself.

This day, Paulina and I decided to take a break and go to the kitchen to make everybody a snack to eat on the porch. As she reached into the refrigerator to get a few slices of American cheese, I flung the jockstrap at her, sending her running. The thunder momentarily stopped, and it looked like the rain was slowing down, so it seemed like a good time to haul the laundry basket out.

"C'mon Lina, let's fold before Mom gets home."

She looked at me suspiciously.

"No more jockstrap for today—pinkie swear," I promised, reaching out my hand.

I set the basket out of reach on the tippy-top of the jalousie window and grabbed hold of a bed sheet.

"What the heck?" I exclaimed. "Hey Harv, look at this," I yelled, calling him over to us.

The sheet and a pair of shorts were streaked with orange and yellow goo. Next, I grabbed a blouse, then a pair of underwear, and saw green streaks mingled with more orange. Our entire load of laundry was splotched with this strange substance.

"I knew he was going to do something," said Harv.

"What do you mean?"

"Remember when I picked one of his peppers?"

Of course I did. Just the week before, Harvey had picked one of the bright red peppers that Mr. Sherman planted along our shared property line. I reflected—I'm sure he planted them knowing that the colorful peppers would be irresistible to us kids.

Our four clotheslines ran parallel to his fence at the edge of our lot line. Harvey, being the curious kid he was, had picked a pepper, taken a bite, then run in the house screaming to Willie that the thing was going to burn his tongue clean off and he needed water. When the water only served to increase the heat in his mouth, she gave him some ice cream which managed to take the heat out a bit. Unbeknownst to us, this alleged garden Mr. Sherman cultivated served a double purpose. Partly it was meant to burn our mouths, but he also intended to use the habanero peppers as an excuse to plot his revenge on our laundry.

"Do you think this could be insecticide, Harv? Mom is going to be furious."

As soon as she drove up the driveway in her little baby blue Rambler, I ran out to the car, grabbed her hand and pulled her out to the porch to show her the damage. I thought she was going to faint—or maybe even cry. Instead, she walked over, took one look, and collapsed onto the rattan couch.

"That S.O.B., look at this, just look at it," said Mom pulling one piece of stained clothing after the other out of the basket, covered in streaks of murky green and orange poison. "He ruined my best slacks and your pedal pushers, Benny's blue shirt, and Harvey's baseball jersey," she rattled on, inventorying every piece.

Mom loved clothes. There was nothing in the world that could have gotten her goat more than having our neighborhood maniac ruin them. As her anger and frustration gave way to exhaustion, she stretched out on the couch and closed her eyes. In that moment she seemed to shrink, looking tiny and defeated.

Once she gathered her wits about her, Mom called the Homeowner's Insurance Company and was told, "I'm sorry Mrs. Mack, but unless you can provide the original receipts for the clothing, I'm afraid there is nothing we can do."

It took many months to replace about half of the clothing we lost, the rest we learned to live without.

When she went shopping for replacements, Mom took me along. I wondered if having me in tow made the task a little easier. Though she never said, I could tell that the usual enjoyment she got out of picking out clothes for us wasn't there. She walked robotically around the store, and, every time she placed an item in her cart, I could see by the deepened scowl line between her eyes and her slumped shoulders that Mom had developed the stunned look of a person who had, as we said in the South, been "slapped upside the head."

Leave the Dishes in the Sink

We kids at Elinor Village

HARVEY, THE LITTLE kids, and I were plopped on the floor, watching *The Huckleberry Hound Show*, a Saturday morning favorite, when we heard Dad crooning an old Spike Jones song from the other room. We scrambled to the kitchen and watched him dance while he sang.

"Leave the dishes in the sink, Ma..."

He grabbed a towel, pulled Mom's hands out of the sink water, dabbed them dry and then two-stepped her around the room—certainly not the first time Dad had spontaneously swept her off her feet. He'd just returned from delivering a newspaper ad to the plumbing company, and his dynamic presence was energizing our lazy Labor Day weekend. I couldn't remember a Labor Day when we weren't already in the swimming pool at Elinor Village in Ormond Beach by Saturday.

It was clear Mom didn't want to be distracted. Still, she gave in to his swinging her around the kitchen to keep the peace. After completing a spot turn in the narrow space, he bowed.

"So, what's up, Max?" She asked, looking at him through her crooked glasses.

"Pack your bags, Ruth. We're going to Daytona!" He replied, grinning.

"You can't be serious—there's no way in hell we'll find a place to stay last minute like this."

"Have you forgotten you're with Big Max? Stick with me, Ruthie, we'll find a place. We don't want to miss out on the fireworks, do we?"

He turned to us kids and said, "Right, Redheads?"

"Right!" we screamed.

Mom knew it was futile to argue with him when he got stuck on an impulsive idea—even though it annoyed her to no end. So our tiny, flustered mother rolled her eyes, exhaled, hung up her apron, and proceeded to run around the house screeching out orders.

We kids were accustomed to Mom's New York slang even at our young ages, which ranged from eleven to three. In her world, a bathing suit was a 'suit,' a chicken was 'the bird,' and so on. In rapid fire she yelled, "Haaa-veee, pack two pair of shorts, yah deck pants, and yah suit. Paulina pack the yellow seeh-suckah outfit I just bought you, yah suit, and yah thongs."

"And, don't forget your suit, Gabrielle—you'd forget your head if it wasn't screwed on."

Harv and I threw our clothes, along with Paulina's and Benny's, onto our beds and awaited our parents' last swoop through the house to consolidate our belongings into two old suitcases.

But as soon as she packed the first shirt, Mom's doubts burst forth again.

"Max!" she yelled across the house, "it's La-bbah Day weekend. We got no rez-ah-vations. Wadda-ya crazy?"

Dad didn't respond.

"Dammit, are you listening to me?" She asked again.

Dad stepped into the living room looking like a bona fide tourist.

"Don't. Worry. Ruth," he said with a brief pause between words, "Just. Get. The. Kids. In. The. Car. See."

As his sentence unfurled in slow motion, I surveyed his faded Hawaiian shirt and khaki shorts. The few strands of brown and grey hair he had left were combed across the top of his balding head and freckled brow. His brown leather sandals with black nylon socks looked silly to me. Even at my young age, I knew this was not a good look.

His words, like a lasso, brought Mom under his control.

This was their dance: the louder and more frantic she became, the slower he responded.

Though his costume heightened his enthusiasm, for me it was not enough to hide the tired, old, balding man Dad had become by the age of forty-two. Even with his great physique, the years of tragedies in his life had taken their toll. Still, Dad was nothing if not an indomitable spirit. Despite every manner of obstacle, his unwillingness to give in to a lesser life, along with his desire to expose his charges to new experiences, kept him going.

When Dad got a wild urge to do something, nothing slowed him down—neither a car that barely functioned nor any amount of argument to the contrary. He repeated this motto, "If you don't take a vacation once in a while, you'll end up too sick or exhausted to enjoy one when you finally get one, see?"

Harvey, Paulina, and I climbed into the back seat. It was the best location in the car to avoid the occasional gigantic forearm and clenched fist that dad wielded blindly as the day got hotter and his temper flared. Benny, the youngest kid, got the worst of it—he rode sandwiched between Mom and Dad on the bench seat in the stifling car. Benny suffered the flatulence coming from Dad's car seat, steam rising from his hairy underarm, and Mom's stiff, lacquered bouffant poking him as he inhaled dirt that flew up from the hole in the rusted floorboard under Mom's feet.

Packed in like a can of sweaty kosher dill pickles, we headed south on Highway A1A.

This day, I was feeling equal parts excitement and trepidation because it was the first time we'd ever left home without Elinor Village waiting for us on the other side. The Village offered a four-day, three-night package for $29.95. It was only a tiny cottage, but it had three amenities we kids adored: air conditioning, a swimming pool, and Magic Fingers beds. Best of all, the management always cranked up the air-conditioning prior to our arrival.

The first thing we kids would do once we reached our destination was run in and lay down on the white muslin sheets in a row and wait for the magic fingers bed to sputter giggle it's welcome.

Mom would go into the kitchenette, unpack the groceries, and complain.

"You think this is a vacation for me? Cooking for six people?"

As soon as we heard her it was our cue to pull on our bathing suits and make a beeline for the pool.

Dad didn't believe in buying things on credit. So, when one of his jalopies died, he made a beeline for another fifty-dollar car from Max Crystal's Cars and Parts. They all had challenges. Some were cosmetic, like metal dings and peeling paint. Some were internal, like bad alternators or faulty wiring problems that would only reveal themselves once the car was on the road. So naturally, Dino, our 1953 Buick, had a few quirks. Instead of a horn, Max had jerry-rigged a doorbell to the dashboard to honk. Whenever he pressed the button, we kids would yell, "Ding-Dong, Avon calling, get out of my way!"

To pass the time, we had two primary activities: making faces and shooting the bird at surrounding cars, and singing. We figured if we could annoy our parents while also making each other laugh with our ridiculous antics, well, that was an added benefit.

I began with a chorus of "Row, Row, Row Your Boat."

Paulina and Harvey joined me.

And Little Benny sat up front singing, "Skidamarink, a dink a dink."

By the time the twenty-fifth boat had rowed merrily down the stream, we were all bored.

Then Harvey had an idea.

"OK, I know what to sing. 'Dayenu,'" he offered. "Dad'll like it—heck, he's paying a lot of money for us to go to Sunday school."

The song has fifteen verses that chronicle the miracles God orchestrated to take our people out of Egypt and into the Promised Land. The word, *dayenu*, roughly translated, means "it would have been enough." That is—it would have been enough if God had only performed one holy act, but behold, he performed fifteen.

Harv and I blustered and choked with laughter. I agreed with Harv that Dad would be happy about this song since it really meant, 'shuckey-darns what a great God we have.'

None of us knew all the verses, in Hebrew, by heart. But we did know the chorus. And we loved the tradition of singing faster and faster with each new verse. So we began, "Dai, dayenu, dai, dayenu, dai, dayenu, dayenu dayenu, dayenu," over and over, louder, louder, faster, faster, laughing ourselves into a frantic state, occasionally breaking from the rhythm to shoot the bird at a car behind us.

The faster we sang the less we cared that we were hot, tired, and hungry. It even seemed funny when dad's fist swung out over our heads, causing us to bob and weave and dive for the floorboards. Dad didn't seem to care that the song had a religious theme. It was annoying the hell out of him, and I could see in the rear-view mirror that his face was red and his neck veins were swollen. We'd reached our goal—cracking ourselves up and getting a rise out of Dad.

But I could tell he was about to blow, so I stopped singing and motioned to Paulina and Harvey, putting my finger over my lips in an attempt to shush them before Dad morphed into the Creature from the Black Lagoon.

Just then, a huge cloud of steam billowed out from the front of the car.

"Look," I pointed, thankful for the distraction and relieved that Dad hadn't pulled over to spank us with his belt.

Dad saw it, hit the brakes, and pulled off the highway onto the gravel shoulder while the family sat spellbound watching while plumes of smoke rose into the air.

"Ruth, the damn thing is ova-heatin'. Must need a new radiatah. We gotta' wait for it to cool down before we can pour water in."

He lifted his huge arm and pointed across the street, "Run in the 7-Eleven and get a bottle a watah," he directed.

"Max, I told you we shouldn't go to Daytona without rez-ah-vations," Mom screeched as she headed across the street.

We kids jumped out and lined up outside the car on the side of the road, baking in the brutal afternoon sun.

Mom returned with waters for us.

Harvey elbowed me in the ribs, and I frog-punched him in his shoulder muscle. Benny looked scared. Paulina wove her little fingers into my hand and held tight.

"Mom," I asked, "what are we going to do?"

"The hell if I know. Why don't you ask your father?" she said, looking toward him with cutting eyes.

I glanced at Dad. Like a boxer preparing for a fight, he'd stripped off his shirt down to his white, sweat-soaked, undershirt, reminding me of Paul Newman in *Cat on a Hot Tin Roof.*

There wasn't any shade—the store looked like the only place out of the sun. "Mom, okay if we go to the store?"

"What the hell for?" She snapped.

"To get some Life Savers and a couple of Cokes."

Mom handed me a few dimes out of resignation.

"C'mon, kids, let's go inside," I ordered. They scurried behind me.

By the time we returned, most of the smoke had dissipated—which I guessed meant that the car was cooling down a bit. We watched Dad grab a towel out of a suitcase and slowly turn the radiator cap, jumping back as each burst of steam blew out. Little by little he worked the cap loose while Mom looked on woefully.

"We should leave the car here and take a Greyhound back to Jacksonville, Max," Mom offered.

Dad looked furious. I could see by his widened stare and bulging eyes that a dissenting voice was the last thing he wanted to hear. Provoked by Mom's Greyhound comment, he leapt away from the steaming radiator cap, grabbed Mom by the forearms with his blackened hands and looked her dead in the eyes.

"Ruth, we're going to stay here as long as it takes for this piece of a car to cool down, see? If it takes all night we'll get to Daytona. Not another word about it."

Mom was shaking nervously, staring at the pavement. "Yes, Max," she mumbled.

Dad stomped back to the front of the car. Mom joined us on the sawgrass side of the road.

It was at this moment that all four of us kids entered what I would later refer to as the *Twilight Zone* phase of our experience that day. In an instant, we collectively moved from fear into hilarity—an emotional response I'm sure was magnified by the unforgiving heat. All it took for my siblings to begin laughing uproariously was me uttering the words, "Gawd, we must really look like a bunch of Bozos to the people driving by."

It was as though the adrenaline keeping the emotions of fear and panic at bay had evaporated, leaving us nothing to do but laugh. And laugh some more. Which felt great—but I worried our laughter was going to send Dad ballistic.

Mom must have had the same concern, so she started giving me "the claw"—digging her thumb and third finger into the tender skin above my elbow—something she did often, that hurt like hell.

"Stop it, make them stop it," she commanded me, her long nails digging into my arm. The pain got my attention at just at the moment Dad started yelling.

"Shut up! Shut up! Shut up!" he hollered over and over, getting louder with each repetition. He looked like he was going to come apart at the seams.

Mom digging her nails into my arm and Dad's big bad wolf routine only made it harder for me to quiet down the little kids—because it added to their hilarity.

I could feel in my bones that Dad was about to do something really crazy, so I herded the kids away from the car. We made it only a few steps toward the store, when I saw Dad slam the hood of the car closed, then plow his big fist into it. Then he took his bloody, swelling hand and started sliding his belt out of the loops of his shorts.

"The little kids have to pee," I said, grabbing Benny and Paulina by their hands and pulling them back toward the 7-Eleven. Harvey stumbled behind us. We lingered in the bathroom, then stayed in the air-conditioned store until I could sense that Hurricane Dad had blown over.

Finally, I said, "I think the coast is clear, kids."

We cautiously slunk out of the store, walked slowly toward the car, and waited to see what would happen next.

"Maybe we should turn around and head back home, Max," Mom urged, gently.

"Just get in the damn car," commanded Dad.

I turned to Paulina and Harv and whispered, "Shh."

Once the radiator cooled, and we were back on the road near Ormond Beach, I noticed, but wasn't about to mention, that every place we passed seemed to have a "No Vacancy" sign lit up. *But,* I thought wishfully, *surely, with all of the hotels on the strip, at least one will have a room.*

When Dad asked if anyone was hungry, I was relieved. We'd sort of reached our destination, and now that Dad was preoccupied with finding his favorite restaurant, a sense of momentary calm settled over the six of us.

The car limped into the parking lot of the Kon-Tiki Chinese Restaurant and expelled a large puff of steam as we piled out. Somehow, the reality that we were driving a less than reliable car didn't seem quite as important now that we had made it this far. Thoughts of chow mein, egg rolls, and won-ton soup happily danced in my head.

When the waiter took our order and asked little Benny what he would like, he said, "lasagna"—an adorable response that provided Mom and Dad a much-needed bit of comedic relief.

An hour later, with full bellies, we resumed our quest in earnest.

Now, Dad's modus operandi was to start at the southernmost end of the city and backtrack north, stopping along the coastal route to ask if each successive hotel had a vacancy.

"Just because the neon sign says 'No Vacancy' doesn't mean

someone hasn't cancelled their reservation at the last minute. The sign may be mistakenly lit, see?" he told Mom.

It didn't quell her doubt.

The cool ocean breeze caressing the car engine and a belly full of Chinese food put Dad into better spirits. "Maybe," he said, "we'll luck out and get a really great deal."

Thus began the next stage of our journey.

Dad pulled the car in front of each, successive, hotel lobby and instructed Mom to hop out, run in, and ask if they had a vacancy. Then Dad would reiterate his instructions by yelling at Mom's back in his typical, slow, measured manner, "Ruth. Check. The. Rates."

At each new motel, Mom enthusiastically bounced out of the car and hurried into each lobby only to return to the car with slumped shoulders and upraised hands. With a clenched jaw and her flaming bouffant getting sticky and limp from the ocean air I could see that she was trying her best not to repeat, "How the hell did you expect us to get a place to stay on Labb-ah Day weekend without a rez-ah-vation, Max?"

They replayed this scenario at The Cove, The Seabreeze, The Flamingo, The Robin Hood and, finally, The Ormond Beach Hotel. No luck. We barreled out of the Ormond Beach city limits and headed north. Nobody said a word as we drove for miles. I worried that we would soon pass through St. Augustine Beach and, before long, wind up back in our own too-hot house. Soon, there were no hotel signs at all, just long expanses of white sand.

Dad pulled off the coastal road and got onto the freeway.

"Maybe I can find a vacancy on the inland highway," he muttered, mostly to himself. Even the freeway motels had "No Vacancy" signs lit. We were a mere twenty minutes from home, now—if nobody had to get out of the car to use the bathroom and the car didn't overheat again. I sat tensely, hoping our entire trip wouldn't be a waste.

Paulina, Harvey, and I leaned into one another. We were completely exhausted and had long given-up when Dad said, "Ruth, I think I see one!" and quickly swerved to the right. He followed the long winding driveway through a lush green golf course. At the end of the road I saw it: the most beautiful hotel I'd ever seen rising up before us like a dream.

Mom ducked into the office and came rushing out a few minutes later screeching, "Max, I can't believe it! They have one room left! A suite with two king sized beds, and—interestingly enough—no kitchenette!"

Dad pulled in front of the room, and Harv, Paulina, and I jumped out, dragging our luggage behind us. Benny stumbled along sleepily. We popped the bags in our room, and the four of us zipped out the door to explore the property.

Harvey, the consummate athlete, loved to play miniature golf, so he fantasized about playing a game of real golf the next day. There was a fancy restaurant where we would eat breakfast, but far and away the most impressive feature was the huge cloverleaf-shaped swimming pool. We stood there for a moment looking at the blue lights under the water stream up at us, the surface reflecting the stars above. Then with a snicker, looked at one another and busted up laughing.

"I can't believe we're spending the night in this fancy place!" I said.

The next morning, my siblings and I got up with the birds and jumped into the gorgeous heated swimming pool. Harv and I swam until we couldn't move another muscle, and then we went into the restaurant to join our folks for a breakfast of pancakes, sausages, and freshly squeezed Florida orange juice.

"I feel like a rich kid," Paulina said,

Sunburned Harvey, playing the big shot, leaned back in the middle of the circular Naugahyde booth hands clasped behind his head, sighed and said, "There's nothing like the taste of a good meal after a swim."

"You can say that again, Br'er Harv," I echoed.

Dad chuckled.

The fancy hotel only had a one-night vacancy, so at noon the car was packed, and we pulled out of the parking lot. I knew that Dad wouldn't have been able to afford for us to stay the entire weekend, even if they had been able to accommodate us.

On the drive home Dad was quiet. He had a secret little smile on his face and a kind of calm about him, a look that said he no longer felt defeated. That he'd accomplished his goal. Despite all the challenges along the way, he had given us a new experience and made a memory. The Ponce de Leon Motor Court and Golf Resort was the nicest place our family ever stayed throughout our childhood. And although it was only one night and part of a day, thanks to Dad's tenacity, we never forgot that Labor Day weekend.

The Great Pastrami Heist

Family Passover before the feud

AD WAS STRUGGLING to make ends meet. He was between jobs, which always spelled trouble, and was burning the candle at both ends, balancing days between job seeking and picking up freelance work, and moonlighting at his drafting table in the garage at night. As always, we never knew exactly what was going to trigger his dark mood—or when it might happen.

This evening, he appeared at the back door wearing his I'm-mad-as-hell-and-I-ain't-gonna-take-it-no-more-face—looking like an anguished clown in paint-splattered baggy clothes and shoes. His sunburned scalp and red face reflected the misery of a day spent perched high in the air, painting billboards in the torturous sun. He'd picked up this grueling side job after losing his commercial art contract job due to downsizing. Truth was, the damn Florida heat exacerbated whatever woeful situation a person found themselves in.

Like most nights, I was in the kitchen setting the table. The younger kids had just begun seating themselves as Dad walked through the door.

I attempted a useless, "Hi, Dad."

He didn't reply.

We all understood that his bright-red face was a signal for us to sit and eat quietly. This was not a night for comedy acts.

Mom broke the silence, "What now, Max?"

He paced back and forth around the kitchen.

"I'm telling you, I'm making a new rule, Ruth. Never, and I mean never, step foot in Worman's Delicatessen again, see?"

God, he really does sound like either a gangster or Jackie Gleason in The Honeymooners, I thought.

"Do you hear me?" he asked.

"But, Max," said Mom in her nervous, high-pitched Yankee tone, "there's only one Jewish delicatessen in town—and that's Worman's!"

My siblings and I glanced at one another with the collective imaginings of four kids trying to grasp life without pastrami, corned beef, Jewish rye, the favorite challenge of cornering a kosher dill in the wooden pickle barrel, and halvah for dessert. Worst of all, no lox and bagels? It was impossible to imagine.

"But Dad," I pleaded.

His eyes shot daggers at me, as he continued his rant, "so listen to this, Ruth. So, I go into Worman's, see. And I ask, 'Saul, are the bagels fresh?' He says to me...he says, 'Waddaya think, Max? Of course, they're not fresh. You know I always save the stale ones just for you.' This makes my blood boil, see, so I walk around the store for a few more minutes and I think to myself, *Try talking to the S.O.B. one more time.*

"And then what?" asked Mom.

"So, Saul walks to the other end of the counter to help Mrs. Klein. That's what. Now I go back up to the counter and I say, 'Saul, I'm asking you again, see. Are the bagels fresh?' And he gives me this smart-ass reply, 'So Max, when was the last time I sold you a stale bagel?' I felt like wringing his skinny neck."

"Well, Max, has he ever sold you a stale bagel?" Mom asks.

Dad proceeded, "So I say to him. I say, 'Saul, this is the last time I'm going to ask you, are the blankity-blank-blank bagels fresh?' And you know what he does? He rolls his eyes and walks away, just walks away. Yeah. He doesn't even answer me, see. He just rolls his blankity-blank eyes at me, and walks to the other end of the counter, and starts folding paper bags. So I walk out of damn the store."

"I am telling you right now, Ruth, we will never again step foot inside Worman's, see. Do you hear me? Never again! You hear me?" Then he slammed his open hand on the table, raised it, and pushed his palm toward mom's face in a gesture that said "I don't wanna hear it."

Dad wolfed down his dinner and strode into the living room. Once we smelled cigar smoke and knew he was out of earshot, us kids began airing our discontent.

"Man, Harv, what a travesty," I said, using a word I'd recently learned. "This is really crazy. For one thing, Dad rarely even goes into Worman's—I'd bet he was just looking for someone to pick a fight with."

"Yeah, maybe," said my brother. "It does seem strange, 'cause Mom's usually the person who shops there."

I revisited the shop aisles in my mind.

"Just think of those thin slices of corned beef, smothered with Gulden's mustard on Jewish rye-bread, with a side of sauerkraut and pickled tomatoes. Geez, Louise, Harv," I continued, now salivating upon remembering the police lineup of kosher foods we both loved.

For years it had been our Sunday family tradition to spend lunchtime after Hebrew school sitting around the formal mahogany Duncan Phyfe dining room set eating deli. We all loved spinning the turquoise and green lazy Susan piled high with the aforementioned delicacies.

Paulina, six, pulled on my arm, "Does this mean we'll never, ever, be able to eat bagels again?"

Little Benny, three, turned to Paulina with a perplexed look on his face, "No bagels?"

"Dunno, hope not," was all I could answer.

While Harv and I washed and dried the dinner dishes, I wondered, *What about Passover? Worman's is the only place in town that sells matzoh.*

I glanced hopefully at Mom.

She met my eyes with the defeated look I'd seen more times than I wished to remember, and shrugged her shoulders.

A week later, Dad picked us up from Hebrew school with Mom in the car. Soon, we arrived at Morrison's Cafeteria downtown, a popular after-church destination.

We always got a kick out of the old Negro man who wore a three-piece tuxedo and a top hat as he walked back and forth on the sidewalk in front of the two-story restaurant, greeting each person as if they were long-lost family. His job was twofold, first to guide incoming foot traffic to the fastest seating area, and second, to greet folks as they arrived. So as we entered, low and behold, he was pivoting between, "Sho't line on the main flo'," and, "Hello sir, hello ma'am, wonderful to see you again, beautiful day we're havin', ain't that right?" only to go back to chanting, "Sho't line on the main flo'!"

He was a sweet, chocolate man with a warm and friendly way about him. Dad knew we kids loved Morrison's, partly because we could choose our own food as we meandered along the prep stations, and because it made us feel grown up. I was crazy about their fried eggplant and tapioca pudding.

Dad wasn't fooling me, though. I knew he was taking us there as a distraction from our missing corned beef and the like, which set me to wondering if we were going to eat at Morrison's every Sunday from here on out.

The next Sunday was Uncle Uly's turn to drive us and our cousin Julian to Hebrew school, so Dad could spend the day at work. He called back to Mom, "I'll see you about four."

While we were at Hebrew school, Mom, thinking she was the wiser, headed to Worman's. It was twelve-thirty when we arrived home—and Mom had surprised us by setting a beautiful table. The olive-green lazy Susan spilled over with our favorite kosher morsels. We were elated, laughing ourselves silly about how we'd pulled one over on Dad. Then, just as I sank my teeth into my beloved corned beef and rye sandwich, something rattled at the back door. I froze for a moment, then tore out of the dining room into the kitchen and almost smacked right into the dense bulk of my father.

He stood for an instant, smelled the kosher meats, and like a beast of prey flew into the dining room. It took him less than five seconds to see the food, whirl himself into the kitchen, grab the waxed paper bags from the countertop, and thunder back. He began hurling the deli into the bags as we sat frozen in disbelief. He lifted the Muenster cheese with his huge hands and slammed it into a sack. Then the corned beef. Then the pastrami.

We sat speechless as we watched him empty our precious lazy

Susan. He spoke not one word, until finally, "What did I tell you, Ruth? Didn't I forbid you from setting foot into Worman's?"

Mom, exasperated and utterly shocked, managed a weary, "Yes."

"What did you say, Ruth?" said Dad, slamming his open palm on the table.

"Yes," Mom repeated, a little more audibly.

"You mean 'Yes, sir,' don't you?" he urged.

Mom was silent.

"Yes what?" he repeated.

"Yes, sir."

This was not the first time Dad had belittled Mom in this way. Each time he did so, hot rage traveled up my spine to my shoulders and exploded into hateful thoughts that banged around inside my skull.

The military "Yes, sir" was only one of the many tactics he used to make Mom feel powerless.

"I'm going back to work, see?" he said as he tore through the back door.

We kids watched from the steps as he threw all our beautiful deli in the garbage can, jumped into the car, and slammed the door. As he sped down the drive, we walked to the backyard and collapsed onto the sturdy wooden seats of our swing set. I exhaled a long breath, pushed the little kids on the swings for a few minutes, then straggled back into the house. Benny and Paulina followed me into the living room and turned on the TV. I went to my bedroom and Harv disappeared down the street.

I threw myself onto my bed and began sobbing uncontrollably. I felt so bad for Mom—for all of us—and so utterly defeated. The phrase *it isn't fair* played over and over in my mind like a broken record. I felt helpless to stop the mushroom cloud of anger that started in my brain and filled every cell of my being.

Lying on my back, I raised my arm up and grasped at the air, searching for imaginary words that I hoped, by some miracle, would be floating there to help make sense of what had just happened. Maybe, I thought, if I could come up with the right concoction of syllables, I'd find something I could say to the little kids and Mom. But there were no imaginary words. And worse, the needle of the broken record in my mind had skipped from repeating *it's unfair* to *I hate you.*

A cacophony of angry thoughts ricocheted inside my mind. *Was there something, anything, I'd ever be able to do to protect us or make these hateful thoughts go away?*

As always, there was no one to ask about such things. I was the oldest. My grandparents were dead. A recent family feud had left me without my favorite aunt, Rudy, to seek out for advice. I was too ashamed to talk to Mrs. Kraus, Marsha's Mom, about Dad's temper tantrums. There was nobody. Just me alone with my anger.

The Gay Cock Inn

Aunt Rudy and Uncle Harry with Harv, me, and cousins

AFTER OUR LAST minute Daytona-Saint Augustine Labor Day vacation, Dad traded Dino in for another of Aaron Crystal's fifty-dollar cars, which this time, Mr. Crystal assured him, he could count on.

Shortly after, Dad also bought a print shop and was excited about making it a success. Some readymade clients came with the business, including a couple of attorneys and a clothing store that consistently ordered catalogues. Uncle Uly, now in charge of Mack Plumbing, offered to let Dad do their printed brochures—this way, Dad had a few customers to prime the pump of his new endeavor.

In an effort to learn the ropes of how to meet more people that he hoped would turn into clients, Dad enrolled in the Dale Carnegie Course, "How to Win Friends and Influence People." One of the requirements was to attend a regular Saturday afternoon luncheon of The Toastmaster's at the Waffle House, where each member gave a speech on a specific topic chosen the previous week. Sometimes he took me with him.

Dad amassed more books—all with titles like *How to Make Your First Million Dollars* and *Think and Grow Rich*.

One Saturday on the drive home from the Waffle House, he told me, "I'm learning to think like a successful person, daughta."

Mom was not impressed. "The people who are really making the money, Max," she whined, "are the ones selling the books."

And, though her observation had a ring of truth to it, I was glad Dad was doing something to try to improve his lot in life.

I took to riding the bus downtown after school to help him collate and staple the different colored documents together, praying to God that Dad's efforts would be rewarded. He was always happy to see me walk through the door, which felt good—he treated me like I was another soldier joining him in "fighting the good fight," as my Christian friends liked to say. And though he gave it his best effort, I could see worry screaming from his sweaty brow as I watched him work in the hot little shop. I was glad that I could help Dad feel like he had a pal, but I knew full well that for him the distance between worry and rage was a quick skip and a hop, so I treaded lightly.

As the weeks, then months, rolled on and the new business Dad hoped for didn't come in, his patience moved to the back seat and irritation jumped behind the wheel. I began fearing his temper and wanted to stop going there after school, but I thought, *How can I? He's counting on my help.* I could almost hear the explosives ticking in his head. I partly blamed myself: *I should have known better. Every time it looks like he's gonna be the "nice Dad," it never lasts.* I could feel the well-intentioned skillet I was standing on grow hotter.

The bad luck Dad experienced was magnified by the success

of his siblings—they and their families were reveling in the post-War economy. And, due to a rift between family members over the proceeds of the plumbing company, he found himself with no support other than the relationship with his one brother, Uly. As the story goes, Grandpa Ben intended for the plumbing company to be a business where each of the family members, the three brothers and one sister, Rudy, and her husband could share the success equally but, I overheard my parent's talking one night about the fact the oldest brother, my uncle Sid, who had a love for expensive things, had been embezzling money intended to be shared. According to my Dad, when the company was first opened, Grandpa Ben told my Aunt and Uncles that there was enough money for each of them to buy a car. Dad bought a non-air-conditioned station wagon. I don't remember what kind of cars Uncle Uly and Uncle Harry, Aunt Rudy's husband bought, but Uncle Sid bought a fancy, air-conditioned, Cadillac. When Mom asked Dad why he'd hadn't bought a nicer car Dad said, "If everyone takes a big piece of the pie pretty soon there will be no pie."

When it became known that Uncle Sid was stealing the family split in two. Aunt Rudy and Uncle Sid's family went one way and Uncle Uly and our family another.

Dad forbade Mom from seeing her favorite sisters-in-law, Rudy and Bertie, and we kids were banned from seeing our cousins, with the exception of Roxanna, who was much older and away at college, and Julian, my age, who was very shy and kept to himself.

I pined for the pre-feud "good ol' days" of summers past when we spent weekends at Aunt Rudy and Uncle Harry's lake house, The Gay Cock Inn, so named as an inside joke for their Jewish friends. I smiled, remembering the rooster sign mounted proudly at the end of the driveway to the lake house. Aunt Rudy got a kick out of the many Gentiles who'd knock on their cabin door, looking for lodging having no idea in that Gay Cock Inn loosely translated to the Yiddish *gay kocken offen yom*, which meant something akin to, "go poop in the ocean."

Uncle Harry was a boy scout leader and loved the great outdoors. In the city, they lived in a beautiful brick air-conditioned house in the same wonderful neighborhood where our other aunts, uncles, and cousins lived. To them, the rustic non-air-conditioned knotty pine cabin on Little Lake Brooklyn in Keystone Heights was roughing it. I'm sure they had no idea that we lived without air-conditioning every day of our lives.

Each of our cousins was assigned a job such as pulling the weeds along the shoreline during the winter and early spring, when the lake was low, so the shallow end would have a sandy bottom and be easier to walk on come summer. It was obvious, watching Uncle Harry's beaming face, that it brought him joy to see my cousins work together as a team while they washed, dried, and put away the dishes each night.

The cabin, out in the pucker brush of Keystone Heights, was about an hour's drive from Jacksonville. The best thing about it was Uncle Harry's boat tied to the long pier. Our cousins, Bruce, a year older than me, Leon, my age, and Michelle, the youngest, were all wonderful swimmers and water skiers. I was afraid of the water, having almost drowned in the fourth grade in the Day Camp pool when a counselor, seeing me sitting on the side, had thrown me in, yelling, "Sink or swim!" I immediately sank and would've drowned had an older cousin, a lifeguard at the camp, not pulled me out. Still, I liked to run along the shore where the minnows were, swish them into a clear drinking glass filled with lake water, and watch them awhile before gently placing them back into the lake.

Harvey, now nine, was a strong swimmer, and liked to swim out to the deep water at the end of the dock. Our cousin Michelle saw this as an invitation to dive off the dock stealthily, swim under water and sneak attack Harv by pulling his swim trunks down—something she did each time we visited. Poor infuriated Harvey ran to our parents and reported her behavior every time, but always got the same, unfulfilling, response from Dad: "Just ignore her."

Mom, on the other hand, responded with, "Smack her, that'll stop her."

This obvious difference in their parenting styles did little to give Harvey any clear direction, so he simply remained frustrated and tried to stay out of Michelle's way.

It always warmed my heart to see Aunt Rudy in her bathing suit, swimming. The polio epidemic had left her with one leg shorter than the other, that gave her a chronic limp. But in the water she swam like a mermaid. Aunt Rudy was a total character—she loved to laugh and tell dirty jokes. But behind her cheerful demeanor, she had the same melancholy eyes as my father. Both of them wore the look of those who had cheated death.

Harry and Rudy had a Norman Rockwell family. The kids water-skied three at a time, on double skis, and sometimes on a slalom—the stunt I liked best was when Leon and Bruce skied with Michelle standing one foot on each of their shoulders like a gymnast. They were fearless daredevils in the water. I envied their confidence.

The metal cooler was always nearby, filled with Nehi grape and orange soda pop, Hires root beer and, of course, Coca-Cola to wash down the boiled peanuts we snacked on. After our Saturday night dinner of barbecued ribs, potato salad, and watermelon or berry pie à la mode, we kids would walk down the country road to an overgrown field where wild boars lived and throw them our leftovers. It was impossible to get close to the primitive-looking creatures, with their flared nostrils and fiery eyes, without being scared. So the trick was to jump over the fence and throw down the food then scurry back over the fence before the boars could get us, which made for quite a thrill. They especially liked watermelon rinds, and we always had a bucket full.

On Sundays, we had a delicious brunch laden with Jewish kosher delicatessen: lox, bagels, matzobrei—crushed matzoh scrambled with eggs and onions—and pickled meats and cheeses.

Then one Sunday, seemingly out of the blue, Dad made an announcement.

"We are never. Going to the lake house. Again. See?"

I was devastated. The family feud had won.

Phantom Limb

Dad and me at Lake Brooklyn

When they were children, both our parents had the opportunity to enjoy nature in the summer. Dad spent summers with his extended family at Rockaway Beach, Long Island, where his relatives owned two large, rambling beach houses next door to one another. And, like many Jewish families, Dad also got to spend time at a family camp in the Catskills where he played drums in a band. Even as a foster kid, Mom spent a week at a summer camp in the mountains each year, through a program sponsored by the Children's Services Department of New York.

They both wanted Harvey and me to continue to have the experience of communing with nature, so Dad took to researching camps and discovered Camp Immokalee, a Seminole word meaning, "my home."

Ironically, the YMCA summer camp was located on Big Lake Brooklyn only a few miles from our aunt and uncle's place on Little Lake Brooklyn. The two lakes were divided only by a small bridge. For the next few summers, Dad drove down the exact same country roads as he used to when we went to the Gay Cock Inn. Only this time, at a particular fork in the road, he turned right to head to our camp on the big lake instead of left to the Gay Cock Inn.

The first summer he drove us, Harvey suggested we sing "Dayenu" to entertain ourselves on the long drive to Keystone Heights. No sooner than we left the Jacksonville City limits and Harvey started singing, Dad pulled over to the side of the road. Before we knew what was happening, Dad grabbed a shovel out of the trunk, opened the door and yanked Harvey out of the car, telling him, "Pull down yah pants."

Dad only smacked his bare behind once—but being hit with a shovel caused Harvey to come undone and he cried the rest of the drive to our camp. We never knew what was going to upset him. *Was it the singing? Or something to do with the too-familiar drive out to Keystone Heights?*

Around the same time, Dad and I were enjoying a brief period of peace. While at camp he wrote me postcards in a secret code, that only he and I knew how to transcribe. Each time I received one, which was often, I was elated. Finally, I was momentarily special in Dad's eyes.

LOVE,

Dad

I enjoyed camp, but I still felt much disappointment and emotion about being left out of the fun at the lake house. I was angry that suddenly, and without warning, relatives I loved had been snatched away from me and the younger kids. That Mom and Dad never explained what happened only stirred up more confusion and remorse.

The puzzle pieces from that sad time in life fell into place some five years later. While watching a war documentary on TV, they explained the phenomenon of the "phantom limb"—a term used to describe the lingering sensation of pain that a soldier sometimes continues to feel in their arm, leg, or other body part after it has been amputated. A lightbulb went on in my head, and I finally had a mental map for how to define the feeling of having being banned from seeing those I loved. I came to realize that the aunts, uncles, and cousins were my phantom limbs.

Betcha Goin' Fishin'

Harvey's big catch

I WAS STARTLED out of my dreams one Saturday morning by Dad's voice booming, "Hey daughtah, you wanna wet your hook?"

Harv was already jumping up and down in the hallway, silently exuding his excitement so he wouldn't awaken little Benny in the next room. I couldn't scramble out of bed fast enough.

We jumped into our matching plaid flannel shirts and jeans, ran past Willie's kids, Raymond and Marvin, Paulina and, now-awake, little Benny, sitting cross-legged on the living room floor, mesmerized by a Tom and Jerry cartoon. Willie worked a half day on Saturdays and always brought her kids. It was a special treat for little Benny, who joined in the fun by toddling around, playing with Ray, Marv, and Paulina.

Willie didn't have a TV set. I had a hunch that for Raymond

and Marvin, visiting us was probably the only time they'd ever been in a house with white folks.

We flew into the kitchen, passing our husky, balding, father in his many-pocketed fishing vest, on our way out the back door.

Willie was outside hanging laundry on the line.

"Where y'all goin' this fine mornin'?" she asked.

"Dad's takin' us fishin', Will. Why don't you send up one of your powerful prayers so we catch a slew of 'em, and can give you some, okay?"

"Sure, child," Willie said with a smile.

Harv and I ran to the car.

He yelled, "I've got shotgun,"

"No ya don't, it's my turn," I countered.

"Like hell it is!"

Back and forth we went until I finally gave in.

When it came to the siblings, I was usually the one to surrender in the name of keeping the peace. God only knows that I had bigger fish to fry—what with dealing with Dad's mood swings.

The day began, like most fishing days, with the two of us singing "Fishing Blues"—a popular Southern tune from the 1920s written by a freed slave, Henry "Ragtime" Thomas. It was a given that we'd sing our way to the ocean, because the car radio was always "on the blink," as Dad put it.

I started, "I'm a-goin' fishin' all of the time; baby's goin' fishin', too."

Harv joined in, "Bet your life, your sweet wife gonna catch more fish than you."

Suddenly, he stopped singing. "Oops, forgot my hat, be right back."

In a flash, Harv jumped out of the car and ran toward the house. Ever since he got his genuine Davy Crockett coonskin hat for his birthday, he hadn't taken it off his head except to sleep or play baseball. Back inside the car with the coonskin snugly on his head, we picked up where we'd left off.

"I went on to down my favorite fishin' hole; baby got me a pole an' line," I sang.

Dad always had the tackle, poles, a bucket and his toolbox packed in the car before he woke us up. We didn't have to watch to know he stood in the kitchen tossing Saltines, a jar of peanut butter, three bananas, and a package of Kraft American cheese slices into a paper sack while yelling to Mom, in the back of the house, "Hey Ruthie, we're heading out Heckscher Drive."

He said it that way because we never knew exactly where we'd end up. Plenty of times we'd driven out Heckscher and caught nothing but a sunburn because the fishing was so bad. Then, he'd take us to the gigantic white dunes, where we'd spend the day sliding down the steep sandy hills with cardboard under our behinds.

Even if they weren't biting, we never went home empty-handed. Those days, Dad stopped at the fish store at the south end of the drive and bought a big fish to bring home—and the three of us spent the hour drive making up a fish story to tell Mom about our great big catch.

Finally on the road, Harv and I sang in unison, "Caught a nine-pound catfish, on the bottom, yes I got him. And I brought him home to my mom about supper time."

Dad interrupted us, asking, "Did I ever tell you the story about Grandma Paulina and the mustache?"

"Don't recall it if you did," I answered.

We loved his stories—partly because they helped pass the time bumping down the road in our hot, dusty, station wagon more quickly.

"Well," he began, "when your Uncle Uly was about nineteen, he went to our parents and told Grandma Paulina he wanted to grow a mustache. You see, the movie stars of the time, like Errol Flynn and Clark Gable, were sporting them."

I interjected, "You mean like in *Gone with the Wind*?"

And Harv asked, "How 'bout Groucho Marx? He had a mustache."

Dad answered, "Well, yes, he had one, too, but I'm fairly certain your uncle wasn't trying to emulate the comedian. He was going for the look of the 'handsome leading man' in the movies. See, Uly wanted to look dashing because he wasn't married yet and was still living at home with Aunt Rudy and his parents—he hoped growing a mustache would attract the ladies and he would finally get married and move out. But, when he told Grandma Paulina, she said 'You are not growing a mustache under my roof!' She absolutely hated them."

"So, what happened next?" asked Harv.

"Well, to the consternation of his mother, your uncle started growing a mustache anyway. For the next few weeks, as the scraggly hair developed above his lip, Grandma didn't say a word to him about it—which Uly took as a good sign. He told me, 'I think she's forgotten about it, Max.' But forgetting is not a family trait, see. Your Grandma Paulina had a mind like an elephant. So, one day, just when he thought things had blown over, Uly came home tired from a long day at the plumbing company and went to bed early."

Dad paused.

"And?" I asked, on the literal edge of my bench seat.

"And—that very night your grandma snuck into his room. While Uly was in his deep sleep, she took out a razor and shaved off his left eyebrow and the right half of his mustache."

Dad let out a snicker with such force, he almost skidded across

TAP DANCING ON A HOT SKILLET

the white line of the highway, and laughed so hard he had to blow his nose into a kerchief. Then he slowed his speech, dramatically tiptoeing into the last part of his story.

"When...he...woke...up...the...next...morning...guess...what... happened?"

Dad took another break to wipe his runny nose, struggling to deliver the last few words of the story because he was laughing so hard he was damn near crying.

"C'mon Dad, what?" Harv and I urged.

"Well...it...looked...like....his...eyebrow..." he paused and inhaled then exhaled the last seven words fast, like he was spitting out watermelon seeds, "had fallen and landed on his lip!"

"Bahahahahahahahaha!" Harv was cracking up, holding his stomach—he'd bought Dad's story hook, line, and sinker.

But I was crafting a challenging question—saving my laughter until I knew for sure that this actually happened and wasn't another one of Dad's tall tales.

"Seriously, Dad, why didn't Uncle Uly wake up?" I asked.

"Well, ya see, deah, he was always a very deep sleeper."

"So, what did Uncle Uly do after?" I probed.

"In the end, he had no choice but to shave off the other half of his mustache. Worst of all, guess how long it took before his eyebrow grew back?"

"God, I don't know," I said.

Dad, still chuckling, "Well, it took over a month to start growing and another two months to become a full-fledged eyebrow again."

I spoke in favor of Grandma, "I guess he got his comeuppance."

Then, leaning forward, I tapped on Harv's shoulder. He turned his head and I whispered, "I'm pretty sure Dad is funnin' us, but it's still hilarious, huh?"

Out the window a mirage floated on the blacktop and seemed to be following us down the road.

Jeez, it's curious that the reflection of the sun on the road looks exactly like water, I thought.

Dad's curious story and mirage musings about both evaporated once the bridge at Brown's Fishing Camp came into view.

"You know what the name of this place makes me think of, Harv?" I asked.

Before he could guess, I started singing, "Fe-fe, fi-fi, fo-fo, fum..."

"Charlie Brown!" Harvey shouted

Dad stopped the car at the first bridge, turned around to shush us, then leaned out the window, supporting his head with a sunburned arm, and asked, "Are they biting?"

He always repeated the same line twice, slowly, so as to buy enough time to look into the pail of the fisherman—hoping to see something stir. Even though most of the guys shook their heads, Dad still damn near fell out of the car to grab a glance of fish flopping around in his bucket.

"Most of 'em lie because they don't want us fishing where they are, if they're biting good, see?" he said. "But I think this guy was telling the truth."

Fishing was part of the culture of living in Florida. As we pushed on another few miles to a second bridge just past the Clapboard Creek camp, I remembered another fishing excursion—the one and only time Dad brought me deep sea fishing.

My favorite cousin, Leon, my age, had come along with us that overcast day when the captain pulled up anchor on a boat named the Alibi III.

First thing we did before boarding was take our Dramamine pills for sea sickness. Still, we weren't five minutes from the dock when the choppy water left me feeling like I might lose my breakfast.

The boat thrust up and down, crossing waves that appeared to be growing higher by the second—I held tight to the side rail.

Seeing my frightened look, Dad walked over, put his arm around me and said, "Hold on, Sugar Plum, it'll only be about twenty minutes before we drop anchor."

His words gave little consolation.

I considered counting *one Mississippi, two Mississippi* to gauge the time, but couldn't focus on anything besides hanging on.

Meanwhile, at the front of the boat, each time we took a dip up or down Harv and Leon screamed, "Yee ha!" They were having a blast, whooping it up like there wasn't a fearful bone in their bodies.

Dad stood quietly next to me, gripping the railing, with a serious grimace as the boat continued to thrust itself this way and that. Then out of nowhere he shouted, "Hey kids! What are we gonna catch today on this rock-and-roll tub?"

I hollered, "Amberjack!"

Leon: "Barracuda!"

Harv: "Kingfish and yellowmouth!"

Dad's attempt at drawing our attention away from his increasing nausea didn't work—he suddenly started vomiting over the side of the boat. Once I saw it, there was no way I could hold back my own.

I tried to speak but only managed a desperate utterance of, "Dad, uh..." before I starting to hawking my guts out.

Dad's moaning was interrupted by Leon, from the bow of the boat, uttering, "Oh shit" and then, "Whoa," followed by his own barfing.

Harv was next.

I turned to the other side of the boat to catch sight of two other passengers, also throwing up. Just then, I had a momentary imagining. The entire scene like something from a cartoon, with background music provided by my family giving an orchestrated performance of gastronomic misery.

Smiling for a moment, I thought, *Yeah, it is pure orchestration, that's what it is,* until my musings were cut short by the dry heaves. My stomach, now empty, sent muscles clenching as they tried to expel what wasn't there. I choked and coughed, finally managing to spit out a long string of yellowy mucous.

Dad used a brief break from barfing to yell to the bow, "Hey guys, be careful."

Leon and Harv struggled to stop vomiting so they could focus on Dad's words.

He went on in his punctuated cadence, "I... have... something... really... important ...to say."

They guys squinted in concentration, hanging on every word.

Dad continued, "If you see something fly out of your mouth that looks like a brown silver dollar, be sure to grab it before it hits the water."

Harv yelled back, "What?! Why?"

"Because it's your asshole!" and he started cracking up. But Dad's attempt at levity lasted only a moment before he started dry heaving again.

I'd never heard Dad use such a word—none of us had, which made his warning even more hilarious.

Next it was Leon and Harvey's turn to begin their cycle of dry heaving.

We were a pitiful bunch. I felt like we were never going to get back on dry land.

Another half hour passed and, finally, the captain spoke. "Well, folks, it doesn't look like the ocean's gonna cooperate and calm down today. I think it's best to head back to shore."

If I hadn't been so sick, I would've shouted, "Hallelujah!"

Harv and Leon voiced their "aw shits" and "gosh dangs," then tried to appeal to the others aboard by saying they shouldn't chicken out just because of a little vomit. But most of the ten other folks on the boat looked relieved to be heading back. Dad and I were among them—the two of us had the same grateful look of drowning souls having been thrown a couple of life rings.

In the end, all we kids took away from our adventure were two things: Dad's "asshole story," which has been re-told many times, and an appreciation for the hard work of fisherman who put seafood on our tables.

The experience also accounted for why, from that day on, we mostly fished off of one of the many bridges along our old standby, Heckscher Drive, a twenty-mile road that crisscrossed over the snaking Intracoastal Waterway. This way, we had access to saltwater fish without having to wade into the salt marsh or bear the strong ocean winds at Mayport, where the road dead-ended at the Naval Base.

As we approached the second bridge, I was glad to be in the car, charging toward a bridge to fish, instead of heading out on the choppy water in a boat. Even fishing from the bridge was challenge enough, with my chronic fear of water and heights. It took every bit of courage I had not to look down as I climbed up the fishing bridges, with the wind squalling, to get to the deep part where we tossed in our hooks. Sometimes I imagined myself lifted into the air like the house in the *Wizard of Oz*, caught swirling in the center of the tornado.

My imagination already ran rampant—and we hadn't even decided yet where to fish.

To distract myself from what I knew would be a challenge once we got to our fishin' place—getting my frightened ass to the top of the yet-determined bridge—I engaged Harvey in conversation. The Charlie Brown song was still rolling through my mind.

"Hey Harv, remember the song that the cartoon character, Tennessee Frog sings?" I asked.

"Oh yeah, he's always dancing and singing with his top hat and cane when nobody is watching but, as soon as his owner tries to show him off he turns back into a squat little froggie who can't do anything but say, "rivet, rivet."

We both chucked, then I began to sing and he joined me.

"Hello ma Baby."

"Hello ma Honey."

"Hello ma Ragtime Gal."

We were interrupted by Dad asking, "Hey, buddy, are they biting?"

The answer the stranger gave determined where we'd spend the day. We crossed our fingers that Clapboard Bridge would not be our final destination. The fisherman showed Dad the contents of his pail, saying, "I got a few, but they're really small."

"I think we can do better," said Dad. "Thanks, just the same."

I held my arms above my head to stretch, then cracked my knuckles. Harv imitated me. We were both getting restless.

"I'm getting hungry, are you?" I asked.

"Yeah."

"Should be there soon, little brother."

We steadied ourselves for another several miles of bump-about driving.

Finally, the third bridge came into view. It was what we'd hoped for and so we shouted in unison: "Camp Overall!" Camp O, with its wind-beaten, half tumble-down glory, was our favorite. I felt happy as my eyes scanned the fishing poles leaning this way and that along with the tackle and bait signs outside.

Harv looked at me and exhaled a sigh of relief, "Whew."

Dad steered the car onto the crackling gravel of the parking area, while Harv and I held our door handles, competing to see who could jump out first, before the car came to a to a complete stop, something that unnerved Dad.

"Kids, slow down, dammit," he grunted.

We slowed our pace a bit in an attempt to quell our excitement and obey Dad. But once we noticed him step out of the car, turning his attention to something in the back, we picked up our pace to the shoreline to watch a handful of folks fishing for crab.

We stopped at the edge. I dug my tennis shoe into the gravel, twisting it back and forth, and watched as the man closest to me threw a chicken leg tied to a string into the shallow part of the bay, then walked backwards, ever so slowly, pulling the leg out of the water. Once he'd convinced the unsuspecting crab to take the bait, he swooped down on him with a net, threw the defenseless crab into an aluminum tub, and placed a heavy wooden lid with a rock on top to keep the crawly creature from pushing his way out. After two folks each got one, I was done—I always felt sorry for the poor critters and couldn't bear to see them tricked into losing their lives.

We never fished for crab—we were going for sport, yellowtail, or sheepshead, all the while hoping for whiting, croaker, or the occasional flounder—we could always buy crabs cheaply by the dozen if that was what we wanted.

As far as bridge-fishing bait went, most folks used night crawlers, a type of worm that could easily be caught in the evening in the back yard. But Dad liked to use frozen shrimp, which we brought from home.

I looked to see if Dad was heading from the car toward the wind-worn shanty—he was, so we ran to catch up with him. I knew the minute Dad walked through the squeaky door his next ploy would be to buy something, probably a couple of Cokes and potato chips, while he quizzed the man behind the counter as to how the fishing was. He taught us, "Never ask for a man's time without first buying something." Before asking directions at the filling station, he always bought a couple packs of Life Savers, usually butter rum.

He'd need more than Life Savers this time, though—because he planned to try to gain inside information as to which section of the bridge we should drop our lines. So, he scurried around gathering Cokes, bags of potato chips, and a couple of Baby Ruths, then put them on the counter asking, "How's the fishing been lately?"

This was our cue to scope out Overall's General Store from the vantage point of the soda fountain counter, which we did by climbing onto the round red Naugahyde seats and spinning ourselves around. I looked around at the battered old barn board on the walls and wondered aloud, "How long do you think this place has been here Harv, a hundred years?"

"Dunno."

The place never seemed to change—which accounted for half the reason I liked it so much. Living with a father who vacillated from loving to hostile in a New York minute left me feeling uneasy much of the time, so I sought out people and places that felt sure and steady.

Overall's was such a place.

Taking in the sheer simplicity of the little store, my eyes landed on the neon Pabst Blue Ribbon sign hanging above shelves lined with bar glasses. I'd always loved neon, and the reflection of the cobalt-blue logo dancing on the empty glasses struck me as utterly beautiful. To the same degree that I loved the reflecting, colored light, I was repulsed by the gallon jars of pickled eggs, dill pickles, and pickled pigs' feet at eye level on the countertop in front of me, impossible to ignore.

Seeing those pigs' feet floating in the nasty, foamy brine, reminded of a science assignment that Dad had once helped me with—we'd put tomato sauce in four small, clear custard dishes. In one, we put dirt we'd swept off the floor; in another, some snips of Tippy's dog hair; in a third, spit; and in the last, a tiny handful of crushed matzoh. Then we put them out on the screened porch and waited a few days to see what kind of bacterial mold would grow. The mold flourished; it worked like a charm.

"These pickled things look like science projects, Harv. Can you imagine yourself eating something that's been floating in formaldehyde since prehistoric times? Look at those pig feet!"

Harv, nine, responded by opening his mouth wide and sticking his finger inside to signifying gagging. "Heck no, I'd rather make myself vomit. On second thought," said Harv, "I might do it if you paid me a million bucks."

"Not me. If I had a million dollars, you know what I'd buy?"

"Nope."

"I'd buy a new butt...because the one I have has a crack in it."

I laughed at my own joke. Harv chuckled, "Good point, Sis."

"I know we wouldn't eat them, little brother, but I have to tell you, I've seen many an old fisherman sucking on those disgusting feet and washing em' down with beer at the end of a tough day on the bridge."

Harv interrupted my cogitating by tugging on me for help grabbing gear and heading up the bridge.

"We gotta go back to the car, Gab—Dad's already halfway up the bridge waiting for us."

"I'll carry our poles, if you carry the tackle box," I said.

I grabbed the poles and began singing—walking to the beat of the song, "Little fish bites if you gots good bait."

Harv joined in, "Here's a little tip I would like to relate."

"Big fish bites if you gots' good bait."

"I'm a-goin' fishin'. Momma's goin' fishin'."

"And the baby's goin' fishin', too."

When we reached the top, Dad held his old wooden-handled

scaling knife, with its deeply serrated blade, cutting shrimp into bait. Our poles had shiny chrome reels and double hooks—we grabbed a couple pieces and baited them.

"We'll need these in case we luck into a school of fish that are playing hooky," I touted, looking to the sharp, double prongs.

"Okay, fishermen, try not to cross your lines," said Dad, walking down the bridge toward his pole a few feet away.

I was willing to bait the hook but had long ago made a deal with Dad that it was his job to take the fish off it—I couldn't bear to see it get hurt.

Harvey and I dropped our lines, trying our best to keep from crossing them. A few times we'd snarled them up, which had turned out to be one hell of a mess and we'd lost valuable fishing time waiting for Dad to untangle them.

"Casting," I yelled.

"Me too," Harv echoed.

I watched as my reel emptied the line into the ocean. When it seemed like enough had gone out, I did what Dad taught me—pull up on the line then let it drop to see if I could feel the lead weight hitting the bottom. It had, and once I felt it, I threw the brake on my reel to stop it from unspooling.

"I'm in."

"Me too," said Harv.

Now, I wrapped the line around my third finger, pressed it to my thumb, and held tightly so I could tell even the tiniest nibble. If we got a strike, we knew what to do—wait a few seconds to determine if it was genuine or just a nibble and, if we felt that second bite, yank up on the line to snag the hook in the fish's mouth. If we caught him and could feel the fish struggle, we reeled in like there was no tomorrow.

With the sun in my face and wind whipping through my hair, I had a warm feeling that said, *this day we're not going home empty-*

handed. No sooner than I dropped my hook, a strong strike. I waited a few seconds, started reeling and yelled, "Hey Dad, I got a bite."

Dad ran over as I reeled in a decent-sized yellowtail. I set it down gently on the sidewalk of the bridge then heard Harvey yell, "I got one too!"

I watched as he reeled in like crazy.

Dad took out his pliers and carefully removed the hook from my fish. Then he eased the pointed needle of the stringer through its gill and threw him in the bucket, making it the first of the string of fish we hoped to catch.

I rebaited my hook and cast again.

Harv pulled his fish off the hook as Dad walked toward shore yelling, "I'm going to get some water for the bucket."

Dad liked to leave the fish breathing in the bucket until we got home. I thought this was kind, that he wanted to let them live an extra few hours before becoming dinner. What I didn't realize, until I got much older, was that the fish were slowly smothering to death as they competed for the tiny amount of water rapidly evaporating in the pail as the hours passed.

Even though I didn't fully understand what was happening, I sensed it. One time, we'd caught a beautiful croaker and as it flopped in the bucked behind my seat, I heard a haunting sound, exactly like the croaking of a frog. I loved frogs and had spent many a hot afternoon in the swamp playing with them. I told Harv I could've sworn that I heard that croaker pleading, "Help me. Help me"—his pitiful moan getting fainter and fainter as we drove closer to home.

I hated this part of fishing almost as much as I disliked taking a fish off the line. But, I reasoned, this was part of the deal, and I best get used to it.

Dad walked toward us with a second bucket of ocean water as Harvey yelled, "Hey, Dad, I got two!"

"Great," he yelled back. "Waddaya got, Harv?"

"Looks like a sheepshead and a yellowtail. Betcha four Archies I'll catch the most fish today," he bragged, looking at me.

"Deal," I replied.

We shook hands.

Then I reeled in two fish.

"Want to reconsider that bet, brother?" I asked.

Dad was so busy taking fish off hooks, cutting bait, running to Overall's to buy buckets to fill with salt water and hauling them back, that he had no time to fish that day. At first, I felt bad—but we just kept pulling them in one after another, and it made him so happy it didn't seem to matter. There were few times Dad was happier than when he was fishing. As a kid, his family went to Rockaway Beach in the summer and fished—he loved being close to nature.

As Dad threw the fish in the pail, then threaded them onto the line he hollered, "Five, seven, nine, eleven, rock bass, whiting, two more yellowtails!"

To spend the day with Dad when he was in a good mood was a rare treat for us. On those days, there was nobody kinder or more fun. In fact, I couldn't think of a single time that Dad had lost his temper on our fishing days. On these outings, he wanted us to experience winning, if only for a day, understanding that fishing was much like gambling, in that you never know if you are going to actually come home with anything—or at least anything edible.

To make fishing more fun—and to supplement the slow catching days—Dad created a reward system. The winner from each category received a round of applause and two silver dollars. Whoever caught: the most fish, first fish, biggest fish, smallest fish, or the most unusual fish, garnered an award—this pretty much covered the gamut. Invariably, one of us would snag a moray eel, skate, toadfish, or spiny blowfish—these counted in the "unusual" category. We could add them to our total, but we certainly weren't about to eat them, and Dad always threw them back. I watched tensely as he took these strange characters off the hook, especially the eels. Sometimes a little dribble of blood would show at the corner of their mouths where they'd been hooked. I always looked away and said a silent prayer as Dad tossed them back into the murky sea.

Taking the small fish off the hooks was also difficult. But he was careful as he plied the hooks out of the mouths of the odd fish and the babies. Then, as he was tossing the little guys back in the water, he'd bid the fish farewell in his best Kentucky Fried Chicken Colonel voice. "Now y'all come back and see me when you grow up, ya hear!" he'd shout, as they plopped into the sea below.

This day we only got two of the odd fish—pretty much everything else we caught was what we, in the South, call "good eatin.'"

"Dang, Harv, I can hardly believe this. Most of the time we figure on standing here at least an hour before they bite."

We each pulled up another two fish.

Dad unhooked mine and dropped them in the bucket, counting, "forty-eight, forty-nine."

"You know, nobody is gonna believe this," Harvey said.

"Willie will be thrilled," I chimed.

"Maybe it was a school holiday and the fish had the day off and were out swimming around for fun," offered Harvey, by way of a guess as to how we could have possibly done so well.

We'd broken a hundred and were still pulling them in.

I asked, "How many do you think we'll end up with, Harv?"

He was so busy taking fish off and baiting his hook that he didn't respond. It'd been four hours, and the fishing finally began slowing down—the flow had slowed from two at a time, to just one on the hook when we reeled.

I pulled in a flying fish which looked to me like a toadfish with wings. Dad hurried over and took it off my hook, so I could continue.

Another hour passed. Now we were casting and reeling up small fish—or pulling up empty hooks because we'd begun imagining bites we weren't actually getting.

The sun was starting to go down when Dad said, "C'mon kids, enough fishing for one day."

We reeled our lines in for the final time and took to counting our catch. We'd caught 140 fish that day, not counting the unusual ones or the babies.

A feeling of elated exhaustion swept over me as we carried the big buckets of fish down the bridge and set them gingerly in the back of the station wagon. Then, our exhilaration gave way to hunger.

"C'mon kids, let's eat!" Dad said, motioning to the shack at the edge of the water.

The three of us headed for the fishing shanty to warm ourselves and eat dinner.

"We finally have a fishing story of our own to tell these old locals, huh, Harv?"

"Sure do and a whopper at that," he replied.

We stuffed ourselves with grilled open-faced tuna and melted-cheese sandwiches and Campbell's cream of mushroom soup, punctuating each bite with giggles and grins as we basked in the day's success.

One old guy sauntered up, and Dad told him of our triumph. The man rebutted with his own story about a day when, according to him, he single-handedly pulled in one-hundred-twenty fish.

"Is that so..." Dad chimed, winking in our direction.

We didn't say that sounded like a fish story to us—Harv and I just kept chewing our food, looking down so as to be respectful.

As we walked back to the car, Dad announced, "He was lying."

"How can you tell?" I asked.

"I just can."

It was a grand ride home with the cool ocean breeze wafting through the car windows. We had a belly full of food and were completely and totally content—happy beyond anything in my near memory. It was as though what we experienced that day had transformed us into heroes, or movie stars. And since there were no words that could do justice to how good we felt, we rode silently home as the car wove its way south, shit-eating grins on all three of our faces.

As we turned off the highway a few minutes to home, I broke the silence, "You know, Dad, Mom's going to think we're telling her a fish stretcher."

"Yep, Sugar Plum, I'm sure that's exactly what she's going to think," he said, still grinning.

Then, there was nothing left to do but sing.

"Put him in the pot baby, put him in the pan. Mama, cook him till he's nice an' brown," I began.

"Get yourself a batch o' buttermilk whole cakes."

"Mama, put that sucker on the table and eat him on down."

"Any fish bite, if you've good bait."

"Well, here's a little something I would like to relate."

"Big fish bites if you gots good bait."

"I'm a-goin' fishin', Harvey's goin' fishin',"

"And, my Daddy's goin' fishin' too."

Money and the Lakeshore Theater

Dad in Cuba, 1958

I CAN'T REMEMBER a time I wasn't ashamed of my parents'
lack of money. There was no way to hide our horrible
furniture, so I avoided having friends over. I was sure if they
walked through the front door and saw our living room couch with
its exploding stuffing or the duct-tape-covered yellow Naugahyde
kitchen chairs and worn-down linoleum, they'd know just how
poor we were.

Whenever Dad gave me a ride, dressed in his paint splattered
clothes, perched behind the wheel of one of his fifty-dollar jalopies,
I asked to him to drop me off a block down the street. And though
I loved him fiercely, it was more than I could take. The conflicting
emotions of shame, anger, love, and guilt volleyed like a tennis
match inside my head and heart. Amidst all the feelings, I worked
to dull my emotions, knowing the only way to help the little kids

when Dad's moods switched from cucumber cool to fiery hot was to keep the emotional laces of my tap shoes tied in a double knot.

Work ethic was never Dad's problem but *mozel*, luck, was. Dad's full-time employment was on contract, so he always looked for a way to make an extra buck between assignments. For instance, when I was twelve, he went to night school to learn sign painting, then started a sign shop in the garage. The dribs and drabs of money he made from the signs helped, but he kept thinking there might a more lucrative way to bring in some extra cash.

One of the books Dad bought when he was taking the Dale Carnegie course suggested that the real estate business was one of the best ways to get rich quick—so he decided to check it out. At the end of the first day of his fact-finding mission, he blew through the back door yelling Mom's name, as if he was busting at the seams to share his exciting news. Mom emerged from the back of the house with the skeptical look of someone who'd been spun up one too many times.

"What is it, Max?" she asked, cautiously.

"Ruthie, listen to this! I went to the real estate school today and learned something incredible—once a person has their license, they can go to the title company and get a list of all the homeowners who are at least three months behind on their mortgage or property tax payments. Then, all they have to do is bring the payments current to take ownership of the house. Can you believe that? Buying a house for just three months back payments? Then we can rent 'em out—and the rents we collect make the payments to the bank. Real estate—that's where the real money is! I told you, Ruthie, if you stuck with Big Max, you'd be a millionaire one day."

Mom said not one word.

Dad often told us kids that he was already a millionaire.

"I have four million dollars," he'd say. "One for each of you, see?"

Dad was nothing without a goal, so he started painting signs during the day to free up his evenings to study for the real estate broker exam. Within six months, he passed the test. Then promptly took out a loan against our home which, he said, "had a lot of equity in it." This had something to do with the fact that he'd inherited it from Grandma and Grandpa, which made it "free and clear," a concept I didn't fully understand—but the words "equity" and "leverage" seemed to be the keys to Dad's imagined fortune.

Hmmmm, I thought, *it sure sounds like a brilliant plan*—but hearing Mom and Dad through their bedroom door, fighting every night, made me wonder. I had a feeling that the trajectory of dollar bills Dad envisioned dancing their way to our front door were light-years away. But at least Dad seemed happy, so maybe it was reason enough for him to pursue this dream.

"By the time we retire, the houses will be paid off. Then the rent money will be gravy, see? It's a foolproof plan," he told Mom, who feigned distraction.

He immediately acquired three rentals, after which his focus shifted to pushing Mom, who hated challenging herself, to get her real estate license. She dug her heels in like a mule, but after months of Dad's tutoring, and with a couple of failed tests under her belt, she finally succeeded in passing the test.

Though Dad had taken to referring to himself as 'Big Max,' Harvey and I knew that asking for money would provoke a grizzly, uncomfortable conversation. So we figured out ways to make our own cash, and to make it last. Whenever we rode the city bus, we got off before it crossed into a different zone, on the other side of the railroad tracks. By walking the rest of the way, we saved a dime. And, heck, a dime bought a whole bag of atomic fire balls, jaw breakers, wax lips and Bit-O-Honeys. If we saved up three of them, we could jump for half an hour at Trampoline World.

Sometimes, Dad paid us twenty-five cents an hour to work at his rentals, which we loved, because at the end of each workday he took us to a place that sold used comic books, two for a nickel. I was crazy about Archie and Little Lulu. Harvey liked Tom and Jerry and Chilly Willy. For us, our pay was equal to ten comic books an hour.

Generally speaking, boys could easily find ways to make money. They could bag groceries at the Winn-Dixie, have a paper route, or mow lawns. Not that it mattered—Harvey wouldn't benefit from working, because Mom and Dad vehemently disagreed about how he should spend his time. Mom thought a job would teach him responsibility, but Dad was convinced Harv should apply himself to his studies, so he refused to let him get one. Harvey, who excelled at sports, did not have a love affair with school. And though I knew Dad was barking up the wrong tree thinking Harv would one day be his highfalutin' doctor or lawyer, nothing or nobody could've told him otherwise. So, instead, Harvey and I spent a lot of our energy scheming and scamming to find ways to make money, mostly to escape the godforsaken heat at the movies.

One Thursday, knowing Saturday was closing in without movie money in our pockets, we were looking around for a scheme, when we snuck into Dad's art studio in the garage. No sooner than we stumbled in, we saw a case of adorable brown glass jars filled with rubber cement.

"Hmm," said Harv, "we could sell mucilage."

We busted up laughing. There was something about the sound of the word, along with the crazy idea of going door to door selling it, that was too silly to pass up. I ran into the house, grabbed a grocery sack and soon we were jangling down the street. We decided twenty-five cents each was a fair price. Then all we had to do was sell five and we'd have enough money for admission, popcorn, and a box of candy or a peppermint stick. Turns out, it was a snap—we managed to sell two that very day and another five on Friday.

I knew stealing from Dad for movie money was a sin, though I will confess that by the time I sank my ass into the padded leather seat at the Saturday matinee, whatever guilt I had magically vanished.

The next week we saved enough from our allowance to afford the movies. Then, the following week, we again found ourselves without movie money, so I did what had worked before—headed out to the garage. While scrounging around, I glimpsed a cardboard box in the corner behind Dad's drafting table, underneath a pile of newspapers. I reached in and felt something hard. I tried pulling it out with my right hand, but it took both hands to lift the heavy thing out of the box—a beautiful cherry-wood pedestal fruit bowl. *Why*, I wondered, *is this out here, and why is it thrown in the corner like a piece of trash?* I turned it over. It read: "To Mom and Dad, Love, Max and Martha, 1937."

Martha? Who the heck was that? I put it back in the box and threw the newspapers over the top of it. *I'll ask Dad about this later—for now, I'd better focus on finding something to sell.*

I took a deep breath and scanned the garage carefully until, "There you are," I said to out loud to no one but myself. "Behold! An unopened bag of fertilizer slumped against a wall—now, this is something I can work with."

Harv walked into the garage.

"Harvey, I've got it! Let's make some jars of rose food!"

"What?" He asked, perplexed.

"Hold on, I'm gonna run in and get some supplies—I'll make the labels and you fill the jars," I said, dashing into the house.

A few minutes later, I dropped a bag of jars, markers, tape, and paper labels on the garage floor, grabbed a nail and a hammer out of Dad's toolbox, placed the lids on an old tree stump, and began punching holes in a dozen lids. Next, I made "Rose Food" labels. Ta da! In less than an hour we had a new product to peddle. We sped down the street with a rattling burlap sack filled with what we would later dub "the funniest product we ever sold."

"Hide in the bushes and watch me—an award-winning actress—at work, Harv," I said, boastfully.

Convinced that people would love our new offering, I strolled up to the front door with all the panache of Mr. Toad in *Wind and the Willows* and knocked. A woman wearing an apron opened the door.

"Are you the lady of the house, Ma'am?" I asked.

Before she could respond, I continued, "Because if you are, I have in my hand this here product that will have your roses blooming beautifully within one week—or your money back. Only fifty-five cents per jar. How many would you like?"

By the time we arrived home for dinner, we'd managed to sell nine bottles for fifty-five cents each—movie money for the next few weeks.

"You know what Harv? I think we're damn geniuses," I said, still glowing.

Willie once told me that the pastor at her church gave a sermon on the dangers of being prideful. He warned the congregation to be careful not to get too puffed up because, he said, "Pride goeth before a fall."

Well, I was "puffed up" all right, but my of case having a big head over thinking up the rose-food product didn't last long. Nasty neighbor Bonnie Piehl found out about it and took to popping up in the strangest places on my walk to and from school chanting, "It's immature to sell manure."

At first it embarrassed me to no end—but I quickly figured out a secret survival tactic. Whenever she said it, I simply smiled and shrugged. I couldn't stop her from trying to get my goat, but I could take a quick trip in my mind to that glorious day in the movies. Each time she popped up looking to embarrass me, bink, zip, bang, I imagined sitting in the air conditioning, stuffing myself with Bit-O-Honeys and Dots, watching the irresistible scene in *G. I. Blues* where Elvis is riding in a gondola over Germany singing "Pocketful of Rainbows" with Juliet Prowse by his side. Then, I smiled wide like a chimpanzee and thought, *Harv and I had a great time that day, compliments of that manure. We weren't immature, we were damn, damn clever, yes we were.*

Lights Out, Empty Seats, and a Kiss in the Dark

JACKSONVILLE PACKED 'EM IN!

Saturday Matinee, Lakeshore Theatre

ONCE WE HAD money in our pockets, I'd ask Mom what movie was playing on Saturday just to hear her say, in her Yankee accent—"Lights out, empty seats, and a kiss in the dark! It's a double feature!"

Though she'd said it many times, it always gave me a chuckle. Then I'd say, "No, Mom, *really*."

She'd unfold the newspaper and tell Harvey and me what was showing. Not that it mattered—whatever the film, it was a given that we'd spend our day in the air-conditioned theatre.

Lakeshore Theatre was our salvation. When we first started going to Saturday matinees, admission cost twenty-five cents, then, a couple of years later, fifty. Candy was only five cents a box, popcorn ten. The best deals were peppermint sticks and Sugar Daddies—which were huge and lasted an entire movie. But Milk Duds were my favorite, except for one small problem—I couldn't keep from eating the chewy wonders all at once. Lik-M-Aid, Dots, Good & Plenty, and Black Crows were also regulars in our candy rotation.

On the rare Saturday when we only had a nickel to spend, we opted for Jujubes. This strange confection had the texture of broken glass, tasted like soapsuds, and looked like tiny colored baby teeth. It was damn near impossible to chew them well enough to soften into a consistency we could swallow, but when the giant leeches were sneaking up on the cowering humans, at least we'd have something to nervously gnaw. Those 'bees would outlast the movie, all right, which made them a steal, but every time we settled for them, I'd invariably tell Harv, "This is the last time we're buying those dang 'bees." But, then, once money was tight, we went right for the Jujubes anyway, only to regret it all over again.

Our weekly double feature provided a much-needed respite from boredom, family drama, and the never-ending heat. More than that, we discovered so much about ourselves from the movies. Harvey fell in love with instrumental music and convinced Dad to buy him the soundtrack from *Exodus*, which he played constantly. I fell in love with the power of song lyrics because of musicals like *The King and I, Annie Get Your Gun,* and the corny, but endearing, Doris Day films. *Pinocchio, Peter Pan* and, my favorite, *Lady and the Tramp*, taught us moral lessons. *Old Yeller* broke my heart and I was sure God looked just like Charlton Heston. Jules Verne films like *20,000 Leagues Under the Sea* showed us there was a much bigger universe than the one we were living in. I felt my first pubescent stirrings watching Elvis swivel around in *Jailhouse Rock* and later got felt up for the first time in the back row.

But it was the horror films that had the most profound impact on my psyche. *The Blob* was endlessly disturbing because the theatre in the film, where the slimy ooze careened down the aisles gobbling up the movie goers, looked exactly like the theatre we were sitting in. *The Fly* set my nerves on edge and invaded my nightmares, imagining a fly with a man's head caught in a web above my bed repeating, in a weak little voice, "Help me, help me."

But the two films that really scared the bejesus out of me were *The Creature from the Black Lagoon*—because it was filmed in Silver Springs, Florida, a place our family often visited—and *Revenge of the Creature*, which was filmed right there in our hometown of Jacksonville. The Gill Man, with his thick rubbery lips and webbed fingers, haunted me for years. Walking home on the day we saw *Revenge*, I insisted on staying in the exact center of the street and made Harvey walk next to the bushes we passed while hitting them with a stick to make certain there weren't any monsters hiding out.

The manager of our neighborhood movie theatre was Mr. Magnum. He was a short, dark man with a strange accent and perpetually angry scowl. It was rumored he had cameras hidden in the ceiling above the back rows where the teenagers sat to make out. Even so, when my friends and I were finally old enough to sit in those rows, the notion that Magnum might be spying did nothing to deter us from necking anyway.

Mr. M. spent the entire film berating us as he paced up and down the aisles with his huge metal flashlight, shining it from side to side into our faces. This was especially bothersome if you were making out in the back row. His incessant nagging consisted of either, "Feetdown, feetdown," or "Shedup, shedup, shedup." A minimum of three times per matinee, a kid would throw popcorn or a sticky candy bar toward the back of his head, occasionally hitting him.

Most weeks, Harv and I managed to pull enough money together for movie admission and candy. But one Saturday, after Sabbath services, on our walk to the bus stop in front of Willow Branch Library, we commiserated:

"How much money do you have?" I asked.

"A quarter. You?"

"Forty cents," I replied. "Dang, we don't have enough, Harv."

"Shit, I thought you had more."

"That makes two of us," I said, deflated.

I couldn't imagine missing our weekly escape. We agreed it was pointless to get off the bus before the railroad tracks that day because even if we saved two more dimes, we'd still be short money for admission. At least we wouldn't have to walk the two miles to our house.

"May as well pony up the extra dime and ride all the way, huh, Harv?"

"Guess so."

I leaned back on the bus seat and relaxed into the beautiful ride. The bus sailed along Lakeshore Blvd. following the St. John's River toward the end of the line, where it stopped at a place where the driver got off and called his office from the telephone mounted on a pole in front of a little store. This gave him a chance to stretch his legs, buy a snack, and use the bathroom.

We were the only passengers left on board when the driver pulled into the rest stop. He threw on the brakes, then turned to us and said, "I'll be right back kids."

"Okay sir," we said in unison.

My eyes followed as he hopped down the four metal steps and headed to the back of the store.

Then suddenly, like a seagull spotting a fish from the sky, my field of vision narrowed and zoomed toward the gleaming chrome coin dispenser clipped onto the ticket stand. I could've sworn the damn thing was glowing.

"Oh my God, Harv, that thing is loaded with cash—ya wanna get some?"

"Heck, yeah!" He sputtered, nearly jumping out of the seat.

I reached into my purse and pulled out the folded paper lunch sack I'd kept from earlier in the day, shook it open, and handed it to Harvey.

"You do the honors," I said. "And I'll keep watch."

Harv grabbed the sack and ran to the front of the bus. He started with the largest coins—I counted as he pumped out six fifty-cent pieces, six quarters, eight dimes, and a bunch of nickels. He was going back for more fifty-cent pieces when I yelped, "He's coming!"

Harv, red-faced and shaking, ran back to his seat next to me in the back of the bus.

I whispered, "Let's have him drop us off a couple of blocks before our house, just in case, okay?"

"Good idea."

We rode a few more stops, got off the bus, walked a few steps as the bus pulled away, then both exhaled a sigh of relief.

"Gawd, Gab, I can't believe we just did that."

"Me, either. But, hey, we better run home and change clothes, so we won't be late. I heard they're showing *Spooks Run Wild* and *Killers from Outer Space*."

We weren't proud of what we did that day, especially after Sabbath services, but thankfully we never got caught, and had the good sense never to try it again.

The Siam Sisters

Me and Harvey

ONE SATURDAY, MR. Magnum announced that the theatre was going to do something unusual the following Friday night and host live entertainment. Harv and I begged Dad to let us go. When he said yes, we couldn't believe it. We were the first people to arrive—and at ten and twelve, walking to the theatre in the dark, we felt very grown up.

"Aren't we lucky? We get to sit in the front row," I said to Harv.

He nodded, neck craning to look at the cavernous theater, before a real evening show.

We made our way up the aisle and plopped down in the first row, center stage, then stared anxiously at the thick velvet curtains. Over the next twenty minutes more people arrived. The sounds turned from rustling to settling, to calm—then a zing of excitement filled air as the curtains slowly opened to reveal Mr. Magnum standing center stage, in the middle of a blue spotlight, dapper in a three-piece suit. A sparkling crescent moon hung from the ceiling of the otherwise bare stage. I glanced at Harv, who had a dreamy look about him.

Then Magnum cleared his throat and announced: "Please give a warm Florida welcome to...the Siam Sisters!"

I scanned right and left then turned around and saw the audience had filled in only four rows behind us. As Mr. M exited stage left, the sound of ruffling, crisp crinolines and swishing chiffon filled the air.

"What?" I gasped, as a pair of tall, slim, female conjoined twins took tiny awkward steps, inching their way to the center of the stage.

Harv squeezed my hand.

Their lavender long-sleeved chiffon dresses, washed in the blue spotlight, gave them an other-worldly appearance. From where we sat, they appeared joined at the hip and shoulders with individual torsos, but sharing only two arms and legs. They stood for a moment, bowed, then started belting out "April Showers" and tap dancing.

"Those April showers they come in May..."

My heart pounded and my face was getting warm. Harvey and I both tried, desperately, to suppress our laughter—our typical nervous release. I was so uncomfortable, I wanted to dash, but didn't want to be rude and walk out during their first song—especially since we were sitting in the front row of a mostly-empty theatre.

Harv stirred nervously in his seat and kept elbowing me trying to get my attention. I stared straight ahead, knowing if I saw the expression on his face I'd make some kind of inappropriate sound. I tried to ignore him. He frog-punched me in my shoulder muscle. *Damn him*, I thought—but he kept elbowing me until I finally turned, looked at him and shrugged my shoulders with upturned palms gesturing, "I don't know—what do you expect me to do?" With my anxious heart pounding, I thought, *I'm having enough trouble trying not to have a conniption fit, myself!*

The Siam Sisters broke into their second song, "By the Light of the Silvery Moon." *This is perfect for them,* I thought. Harv and I both loved this song—it provoked fond memories of performing it with Dad on our vaudeville shower nights. Even so, by the time the number ended, my stomach was convulsing from holding back laughter and feeling sick at the sight of the twins' appearance. If I didn't get out of there soon, I was worried I might throw up. So as soon as the applause started, I crouched down low as I possibly could and duck-walked up the rows toward the exit door, Harv followed. Once outside we exhaled a joint, "Whew!" then rattled through a litany of emotions from shock and awe to hysterical laughter.

"Oh my God! Oh my gracious God!" Harv repeated over and over.

"I know, I know," I said, nodding my head.

We walked the eight blocks home in the dark, the "Good Gods," and "I knows" continuing until just around the corner from our house. Then I looped Harvey's arm in mine, then broke into song— and we walked in step, singing in harmony:

"By the light, (By the light, By the light),

"Of the silvery moon, (The silvery moon).

"I want to spoon, (Want to spoon, want to spoon)

"To my honey I'll croon love's tune."

At the end of the first verse, Harvey stopped and turned, grabbed me by both shoulders, looking directly into my eyes and said, "Gab, let's never go to another live show at the Lakeshore again—ever—okay?"

"Okay," I replied.

"Pinkie swear?"

"Yeah, pinkie swear."

We looped our fingers in a forever pact.

That night marked the first and last live-performance experience at our beloved Lakeshore Theatre, though the holy ritual of Saturday double-feature matinees continued the remainder of our childhood.

The Mystery Bowl

Grandma Paulina and Grandpa Ben at Rockaway Beach

THE MORNING AFTER the Siamese twins, I walked to the garage to grab my bike and found Dad sitting at his drawing table. It was a bright, calm morning and he seemed in a pleasant enough mood, so I decided to ask him about the wooden fruit bowl I'd found in the garage.

"Dad, who's Martha?" I asked, sidling up to his drafting table.

"I can't talk right now—I've got to get these paste-ups to the printer in an hour."

I knew better than to press him, so I shrugged and muttered, "Okay," figuring I'd ask Mom when she got home from the grocery store.

Now, having watched countless episodes of *Topper* on television, I was convinced we had ghosts living in our house. This fact surely accounted for Dad's moods changing so abruptly—he was dealing with people the rest of us couldn't see. Yes, that had to be it, *ghosts*. I was sure Grandma and Grandpa were hovering about—after all, like George and Marian Kerby in *Topper*, our family was living in the home our grandparents had built to live out the rest of their lives. Sometimes I sensed there were more—as to how many more, I couldn't be certain. I wondered if Martha was one of them.

They weren't only in our house, they seemed to show up anywhere. I was sure at least one was in the car when we drove to Daytona, and I was positive they were there when Dad showed off, walking on his hands down the beach at Ormond. And, sometimes, when Harvey, Dad, and me sat in front of the television set, playing poker and watching *Gillette Presents: The Fights*, I swore there was an apparition just outside my periphery.

Later that afternoon, I cornered Mom as she unpacked the groceries.

"Mom, who is Martha?" I asked.

"How the hell should I know? Come over here and help me make a salad."

As usual, Mom was no help at all.

Though Mom denied knowing who she was, I sensed something I'd never felt before—that Mom was lying. I was certain that whoever Martha was, she made Mom uncomfortable and was something she didn't want to think about. After dinner, I went to the garage to find the wooden bowl so I could show it to Mom. It was gone.

Mom, I began to realize, had a few go-to responses when I looked to her for answers or advice. When trying to pin her down on something she either didn't know the answer to, or didn't want to deal with, she either ignored it, walked away, made up an answer, or insulted me.

"You know what your problem is?" she'd say. "You got too much brains."

Because I wore my feelings on my sleeve, I assumed everyone else did too, especially my parents and my siblings—Dad certainly did. Hell, if I couldn't trust to get an honest answer from my family, there wasn't a heck of a lot that made sense in the world.

I was slow to realize Mom's responses were shaping something profound in my psyche—she was teaching me not to expect any kind of deep emotional involvement from her. It took many years to accept that fact. But once the reality of who she truly was began sinking in, I figured I'd best just reckon with it and learn to accept her less-than-helpful replies or continue to drive myself crazy.

So that day I plumb gave up and headed to my room to practice accordion—but the mystery bowl continued to torment my mind. I wished I could ask Aunt Rudy—she would surely know—but in light of the family feud, it was best to set my curiosity aside.

Music

Mr. Monroe's accordions

MUSIC HAD A big role in our family. In fact, in my first year of life I had a giant xylophone for a roommate. Dad liked to joke that when I was born Mom gave him an ultimatum, "Either get rid of the xylophone or the child."

"Well, I chose you," he'd say, "But I'm still not certain that was the right choice." Then he'd wink and flash me a wry smile.

Our first television was housed in a grand mahogany console with a ten-inch black and white screen on the right half, a built-in radio on the top left, and a pop-out turntable with storage under it—the whole shebang. Mom and Dad only owned a few records and they were all Big Band—the likes of the Benny Goodman, Count Basie, and Glen Miller proudly displayed in the wooden slots.

When Paulina was three, Dad invited her to stand atop his

big wingtip shoes while he soft-shoed around the living room. Thrilled, she danced and swayed along to the luscious rhythms of those treasured recordings.

One night, "In the Mood" blared from the record player. No sooner than the first few notes pumped out of the speakers, Dad reached out his big hand toward me.

"Come here, daughta, let's dance!"

He then taught me the moves to his go-to dance—hop on your right foot twice, left foot twice, then once on the right and back to the left—he called it the shag. I was certain he made it up. But later, at thirteen, when I became a jitterbug aficionado, I learned it was, in fact, a real dance called the Balboa—invented for the fast rhythms of Scott Joplin rags and the like—made popular in the roaring twenties by Scott and Zelda Fitzgerald.

Every day for my entire life, Dad got up with the birds, drove out to an orange grove and practiced his clarinet before starting work. The only thing he loved more than music was his children. To expand our knowledge of music, Mom and Dad collected classical music recordings, in part because Winn-Dixie offered a free album for every twenty-five dollars spent. The first one they brought home was by the Russian composer, Sergei Prokofiev. Dad loved it because it included the *Peter and the Wolf* composition, which was our first introduction to the many sections of the orchestra. Soon, our collection included Debussy, Stravinsky, Rimsky-Korsakov, and Mozart. When Walt Disney's movie *Fantasia* was released, Dad was ecstatic, seizing another opportunity to share his love for classical music with us.

Like most Jewish families, especially native New Yorkers, my parents adored live theatre—and despite the family's inconsistent cash flow, Mom and Dad always found a way to buy season tickets to our community Little Theatre. They took Harvey and me to most performances, so from a young age we were introduced to everything from murder mysteries like *Mousetrap* and thrillers like *Wait Until Dark*, to musicals—*Gypsy* was a resounding favorite. Dad determined all us kids must learn to read music and play a musical instrument, so one day he could have a family band.

There is an old Jewish joke that goes like this:

"Why are there so many Jewish violinists?"

"I don't know, why?"

"Because when the enemy (take your pick: Russians, Germans, Poles, Nazis) kicks you out of their country, you can always grab your instrument and run."

I wanted to learn to play the piano, but Dad bought me an accordion. Something portable. Turns out, we couldn't afford a piano—but that was never shared. Instead, Dad talked up the accordion's history of klezmer music, Yiddish theatre, and vaudeville. Even as a kid, I knew the accordion was a far cry from the sophistication of the piano, but hey, this was the fifties, and *The Lawrence Welk Show* was wildly popular. Every Saturday night, when our family gathered around to watch Mr. Welk on television, and he introduced the accordionist, Myron Floren whom he called, "The Happy Norwegian," I cringed.

In 1954 my six-year-old, red-haired, freckle-faced self struggled to carry a heavy squeezebox in its even heavier wooden case down the street, up the city bus steps and onto my seat for the five mile trek from Lakeshore to Five Points for my weekly accordion lesson. To this day, I still don't quite understand how Mom thought nothing of putting me on a cross-city bus alone at that young age.

Each week at lessons, I dutifully pulled out the Palmer Hughes Beginning Accordion Book and pumped out songs like "Yankee Doodle Dandy" and "She'll be Coming Around the Mountain," slowly graduating to "Drink to Me Only with Thine Eyes" and the "Merry Widow Waltz."

I practiced accordion in my room for half an hour each day—an eternity by kid standards. But I liked it—and was thrilled Dad enjoyed my music, especially the polkas, which he adored. When I could finally play "Hail, Hail, the Gang's All Here," Dad was thrilled. If he was home while I practiced, he'd dance around the room and sing, "No matter the weather, when we get together, we drink a toast for two!" Followed by many *da da da da da das*.

Now, this was the age where choruses were filled with *la la la las* and *da da da das*. And though no adult ever mentioned it, I was convinced the Jewish songs we sang in synagogue with their copious *la las* or *da das* were because sections of the songs were missing—because as the Jews were expelled from one country after another the nonsense words filled in the parts lost along the way.

When Harvey was seven, he started taking accordion lessons, too. And it would only be a few more years before he passed the accordion to Paulina. So off we kids went to Mr. Monroe's Accordion Studio Saturday mornings, learning our portable instruments—if it worked out the way Dad hoped, he'd be playing clarinet with us in no time.

Our accordion teacher, Mr. Monroe, was a grey-haired man with crooked yellow teeth, horrible breath, about seventy-five-years-old, or so we thought. It was hard to imagine what he might have looked like as a younger man. Mr. M. lived in a typical Florida bungalow—a cozy, single-level wood-frame house with a big screened porch across the front, that was crowded with furniture and junk as though he didn't throw anything out. One bedroom was his music studio, and, I assumed, the other was for sleeping. The studio, with its window air conditioner, was the only room that was cool. We waited our turn for our lesson outside on the steaming hot screened porch, on either a rattan couch or one of two chairs upholstered in bark cloth fabric with a palm frond design, all of them covered with cat hair.

Mr. M. had at least twenty cats. They meowed and pranced with tails in the air, rubbing their warm bodies against our hot legs, rolling around every which way on the floors and furniture. I loved animals, but the stench of cat urine, even more potent from the humidity, made the entire house stink to high heaven.

While I sat trying to ignore the stench with stinging nostrils, Dad, seemingly oblivious to it, sat reading the latest issue of *Monsters of Film Land.* Dad, always the dreamer, when not fixated on the family band, dreamed of building a miniature golf course full of huge, complex, sculptures—having recently figured out how to make the latest horror film creatures out of chicken wire, fiberglass, and cement. Knowing that the goal holes with mechanical moving parts were the most sought after, Dad was content to sit and sketch monsters from magazines. Meanwhile, Harvey and I tried to figure out ways to avoid throwing up as we inhaled the constant stream of cat fluff. We tried breathing only through our mouths or holding our breath until we reached the studio's clean air conditioning, but neither approach was a sure winner.

The studio was freezing cold and crammed full of accordions of different sizes, stacked on chairs and leaning against walls. Aside from the excess accordions, the only other things in the room were two straight-backed chairs and two metal music stands—which had sheet music clothes-pinned down to keep the air conditioning from blowing them onto the hardwoods.

The music Mr. Monroe assigned us was less than inspiring, but Dad supplemented it by buying us popular songs, like "Purple People Eater" and "Itsy Bitsy Teeny Weenie Yellow Polka Dot Bikini," which Harvey and I got a kick out of.

As if that wasn't enough, after our Saturday lessons, Dad rewarded us with ice cream at Howard Johnson's where we'd fill ourselves up with pistachio and mint chocolate chip. Harv, Dad, and I always had a delightful ride home—bellies full of ice cream, relieved we'd survived the day at Mr. Monroe's cat-pee house—so we'd make up harmonies to pop songs.

One day, on the drive home, Dad announced he'd written a poem in my honor. He began:
"Sweet little Gabrielle Rose
Was tired and sought some repose
She sat on a chair
But a tack was there
And
Sweet little Gabrielle rose."

After about a year, Harvey talked Dad into letting him quit; Paulina and I played for another few years. Ironically, Benny, the only kid who wasn't forced to play an instrument, became a musical prodigy anyway and learned to play bass, guitar, banjo, and mandolin.

As I turned the corner on my teenage years, hearing my first Peter, Paul and Mary song, I traded my accordion for a guitar, the most popular instrument of the folk and rock music era of the early 1960s. The red sparkly accordion sat locked in its wooden case, lost in the shuffle of growing up. But by then, music was alive inside us all, like a soundtrack playing against the backdrop of every scene of our lives.

Gillette Presents

Sugar Ray Robinson, 1947

THE FAMILY FEUD was going full steam, and since we were no longer spending weekends at the lake house, Dad looked for things he, Harvey and I could do together. It was 1959 and boxing was all the rage. On Friday nights, after the little kids were tucked into bed, the three of us took our places around the television for *Gillette Presents: The Fights.*

The night began by chatting with Dad about the boxers, weighing who might come out on top. At nine and eleven, Harv and I had no clue how to judge, but that didn't stop us pretending. Dad did his part by peppering in hints that, in most cases, helped us win our bets on the fight.

"Well, I don't know about you, but if I was wagering a bet, I'd put my money on Sugar Ray, Sonny, or Ortiz," Dad said, naming whichever boxer he though had the best chance of winning. "Why don't you two think on it for a minute while you change into your pajamas?"

We'd zip to our rooms, put on our PJs and meet back in the hall.

"Harv, let's bet on Sugar Ray, okay?" I said, leading the charge.

We shook on it, then decided how much of our allowance to bet on the fight. Dad reemerged in the living room, stripped down to his boxer shorts and undershirt, Harvey announced the bet, then we all sat down cross-legged in front of the TV.

While watching the fights, we played rounds of poker, using Necco wafers for chips. Harvey's job was to unwrap and arrange our "chips" in colored stacks—a job I assigned him after I caught Dad trying to eat them. Pink was worth twenty cents, lavender ten, and white, a nickel. Dad shuffled and dealt hands of five-card stud or draw with jokers and deuces wild. It was a grand time, sitting there watching the boxers on our little black and white TV, playing poker and cheering for "our man," immersed in our own happy reality.

One Friday, after a few months of watching boxing on television, Dad announced at dinner, "I want the two of you to get in the car. I have a surprise."

The sun slipped into the horizon as we pulled away from the house.

"Where are we going, Dad?"

"Out Beaver Street way," he told me.

I knew nothing about that side of town. Other than the fact that Mack Plumbing was located somewhere out there, it was a mystery to me. The longer we drove, the uglier it got. We passed boarded-up buildings and empty lots filled with broken pieces of concrete, piles of tree limbs and dry weeds. Harvey and I looked at each other and rolled our eyes, wondering how this could possibly be a "surprise."

When Dad finally pulled under the moorings of a bridge and

stopped, the two of us were wearing expressions that screamed "What the heck?" In front of us was a dismal cement building. With each uneasy step in its direction, I looked over my shoulder.

Dad stopped in front of a rumpled old man with a bristly face standing outside with a handful of tickets fanned out in his hand. They exchanged some cash for three tickets, then, wordlessly, the man gestured toward a heavy metal door. Dad pushed it open, then parted a thick velvet curtain and entered the dimly lit room. We bumbled after, hardly seeing where we stepped.

"Look," he said gleefully, ushering us to the hard, wooden seats with no backs, as though it was a stroke of good fortune there were seats close to the brightly lit center. I craned my neck toward the stage, straining to get a better look at what brought Dad such excitement.

"I'm pretty sure I'm the only girl in here," I whispered to Harv, scanning the room.

Two old men roamed up and down the aisles with crudely built wooden boxes tied to their waists yelling, "Peanuts, popcorn, cigars, cigarettes?"

Dad bought us bags of fresh roasted peanuts, which smelled delicious. Tiny footlights at the ends of the aisles and between the bleachers kept vendors from falling as they roamed up and down. It was nearly pitch-black inside, save for a lone spotlight streaming into the center of what I now understood to be a boxing ring. After about fifteen minutes of the spotlight swiveling from corner to corner, the boxers appeared, each in satin shorts and fancy robes.

A chill of anticipation pulsed through me. Harv and Dad beamed. The assistant gave each boxer some water and handed them something that looked like false teeth, which they popped in their mouths. Then the referee shouted from the middle of the ring, "In the right corner we have . . ."

I couldn't make out the boxer's name, so he became "Red Shorts"—the referee held up his gloved hand.

Next, he walked to the opposite corner and introduced his opponent—whom I dubbed "White Shorts."

"Hey Dad," I piped, "maybe they're going to set a new world record, huh?"

"We didn't wager a bet," Harv whispered, "That's strange, no?"

I shrugged my shoulders and he mimicked me.

"At least Dad is happy, Harv," I responded, looking toward Dad's glowing face.

A loud clang rang out and the two boxers slunk toward one another—and it began.

White Shorts threw his big gloved fist toward Red Shorts, then Red shorts ducked his blow, jumped back, then ran toward Whitey and planted his glove into Whitey's eye.

The crowd went wild—their thundering voices growing louder by the moment.

"C'mon, smack him, Joe!" "Yeah, get him, Reggie!" yelled the guys in the audience, each roaring out the name of their man.

I sat spellbound; my eyes transfixed on what looked like... could it be? The bright spotlights illuminated my worst fear—blood gushing from Whitey's face, flickering across the lights. Oh my God! I looked down as some drops of blood hit my arm. I wanted to dive under my seat. I wanted to run out of the place. The audience cheered—chanting the names of their man over and over, louder and louder. The names collided with one another as the crescendo rose along with the cigarette smoke. It was as though the entire place was filling with blood, screaming, and smoke, rising to consume all four corners of the building.

I grabbed Dad's forearm and squeaked out a feeble, "D-dad."

He looked at me and saw the absolute terror in my eyes, said, "C'mon kids let's go."

We wove our way through old men and cigar stench, arriving at the curtain that led to the metal door. Once outside I tried to get some clean air into my lungs but couldn't stop shaking. I swallowed, then exhaled hard in an attempt to try to blow away the fear and disgusting smell permeating my clothing and hair. I couldn't get the sound of roaring insanity out of my mind—of men cheering while other men were getting torn apart. None of it made any sense.

"Well, that was something, eh kids?" Dad asked, trying to lighten the mood.

"Yeah," said Harv, "that was really something, all right... something scary."

"I don't like real boxing," I said. "I think it's more fun on TV."

After a single night of experiencing the real thing, we went back to watching the fights on TV. I loved playing poker but couldn't look at the screen anymore. It didn't matter. Soon our Friday night ritual was replaced by another sport Dad couldn't wait to share—midget wrestling.

Giant and Midget Wrestling

Wrestlers Beauer and Tiny Tim in costume before a fight, 1957

I T WAS A balmy Florida evening when Harvey, Dad, and I
hurried down the sidewalk toward the Jacksonville Coliseum.
As soon as we took our seats in the cavernous building, which
was packed and freezing, I spotted the boxing ring in the center of
the floor, leaned over and asked Dad, "This isn't boxing again is
it?"

"No, Sugar Plum, I think you're gonna like this," he said with a
wry smile.

As the lights dimmed, I reached over and squeezed Harvey's
hand, then felt a wave of goosebumps as it went completely dark.
A spotlight flipped on, lighting up the ring. In the middle stood two
women, one in a leopard-print bikini, the other a fur toga. Next to
each woman stood a muscular midget in satin shorts. The crowd
screamed and clapped as each pair—woman and midget—went to

opposite corners. The referee rang a shiny gold gong, announcing the start of the fight.

In a flash, Midget #1 pulled his way up the ropes, sending himself flying through the air toward the Leopard Bikini Lady. He landed on her shoulders, grabbed her around the neck, and choked her with his legs while trying to gouge her eyes out. She struggled loose and he dropped to the floor, while kicking her in the knees. At the other end of the ring Midget #2 climbed the rubbery ropes and flung himself onto Furry Loincloth, grabbing her by her hair. She spun in circles trying to shake him off, as he hung by her mane, legs flinging around and around. Once Furry Loincloth managed to shake Midget #2 loose, she grabbed Leopard Bikini Lady and slammed her to the floor. Leopard Bikini Lady and Furry Loincloth pulled and pushed and wrestled each other while Midgets #1 and #2 crawled all over them, stepped on their hands, kicked wildly, and tried to strangle them.

I glanced at Harvey—his mouth hung open in disbelief.

Dad was laughing so hard tears streamed down his face.

The late 1950s and early '60s were the heyday of midget wrestling. Famous tiny wrestlers such as Sky Low Low, Little Beaver, Lord Littlebrook, and Fuzzy Cupid occasionally stopped in our hometown of Jacksonville.

Giant wrestling was also wildly popular. Our favorite was Haystacks Calhoun, billed as "the 640-pound Country Boy Colossus," who wore bib overalls and a real horseshoe necklace. The first time we saw Haystacks, Harvey was thrilled watching the barefoot giant pass right by him on the way down the aisle. That night he wrestled two German brothers at once—Kurt and Karl von Brauner. The brothers were decked out in a ridiculous get-up: matching black leather masks, tiny black bikini bathing suits and what appeared to be ballet shoes. Even with a match of two against one, they were no match for Haystacks.

These larger-than-life wrestling personas played to sold-out houses throughout the United States, Canada, and Mexico. Toward the end of the giant wrestling craze, the torch was passed to such wonders as Gorilla Monsoon and Andre the Giant, who stood at 7'4" and weighed 529 pounds. And real-life giants they were—victims of the genetic disease acromegaly, their bodies over-produced hormones that caused them to continue growing throughout their lives. For some, their stature brought incredible fame—Andre, at the peak of his career, wrestled three hundred times a year and had starring roles in several films.

For us, the fascination with weird wrestlers eventually wore off, and poker was replaced by Friday night swimming at the YMCA. The only remnant of our short-lived love affair with boxing and wrestling were the two photos that Dad kept hanging on the wall in his office. One, an autographed Haystacks Calhoun, barefoot and smiling in his signature bib overalls and, the other, a male Orangutan, above which was scrawled in all caps. "DON'T LET THIS HAPPEN TO YOU!"—a hilarious reminder for Dad, who adored food, to watch his weight.

Magical Thinking and the Gill Man

Mom and Dad dressed for their costume party

THE LION SLEEPS tonight...Harvey sang the melody while I yodeled the chorus, high as my voice could go. Whenever we looked after the younger kids, Harv and I whiled away our evenings singing along to the music on WAPE, (The Big Ape), our favorite radio station. When the parents were gone we had a grand time.

This week, Mom and Dad left for an event at their Jewish Social Club called *Ball and Chain*. This month it was a costume party, and the parents went all out—in drag. Mom was in a three-piece suit and fedora, while Dad climbed into a housedress with huge, fake bosoms and a flowery hair net over his mostly bald head. They were in stitches, laughing and giggling as they left the house—it was a welcome change, seeing them happy together.

Even so, I felt unsettled. We'd been at Lakeshore Theatre all afternoon, watching *The Blob* and *The Fly*, and though the evening began like any other babysitting night, my jangled nerves were still haunted by the slimy ooze traveling down the movie theater aisles, gobbling up the audience on its path of destruction.

"God, Gab, what if this happened to us in real life?" Harv asked.

"Aw, it was fake, little brother," I said, trying to calm myself as much as him.

Truth was, I hated horror movies, but jangled nerves in air conditioning was better than suffering through a stinkin' ass hot day at home.

Squeak...the sound of the front door creaking open, then slamming shut, interrupted our musings and made me jump from fright.

"C'mon!" I grabbed Benny and Paulina by their hands and flew out of the living room to the farthest spot in the house—our parent's bedroom.

Could it be the Blob? Or worse, the Gill Man—the Creature from the Black Lagoon? Or one of those damn ghosts I'd been seeing? This calls for Distraction Derby, I thought, recalling a method I'd mastered to help the kids focus on something other than Dad's crazy.

"C'mon kids, let's sing." I started, "Mock-yeah, ing-yeah..."

Harv harmonized, "Mock-yeah, ing-yeah, bird-yeah, mock-ing-bird."

Then me, "Everybody have you heard?"

Then another "Bang!" The sound of the heavy wooden front door slamming shut. Panicked, I turned the bedroom door lock. I was determined to keep my siblings safe while worrying what kind of hell I would catch from Dad if an intruder got into the house.

Lately, Dad was a walking keg of lighter fluid who'd taken to putting Harvey and me on restriction every time we turned around and spanking Benny and Paulina with the belt over the slightest provocation. Mom often re-iterated Dad's problem as, "He needs to feel like he's the king of his castle"—an answer that provoked a fiery white anger that traveled up my spine and took up permanent residency just under my every thought or feeling. Like vinegar with baking soda—Dad's pandemonium mixed with Mom's bitterness— the atmosphere in our house fizzled and popped, on the brink of catching fire, leaving me tap dancing on a hot skillet.

Damn, I thought, *I look forward to these nights when the parents are gone as a break from their hysteria. Now my peace is being disrupted by what sounds like an intruder in the house. The last thing I need is something to go haywire while I'm babysitting. Hmm...It's been twenty minutes since a sound. Maybe, I should take a look.*

I bolted into the kitchen, grabbed a flashlight, and opened the front door. Then I put one foot on the top step, took a quick look around the yard and ran back to the bedroom.

Just because I can't see anything, doesn't mean there isn't something there.

"Is the coast clear?" asked Benny and Harvey, peeking out of the bedroom door.

"I'm not sure," I said.

Panicked, adrenalin pumping, my imagination took over. In a flash, I stood with my siblings in the cool night air on the dock of the Lobster House, a restaurant we frequented. We were waiting for our parents to finish their meal when all of a sudden the Gill Man—a dark, six-foot-tall, scaly creature with huge lips—emerged from the water, grabbed my screaming brothers and sister, and dove back into the murky St. John's River. I ran back inside to tell my folks, who were still eating, wearing bibs covered with lobster guts. They looked dazed as though the crustaceans had cast a spell on them.

"Dad!" I screeched. He shook his head as if to wake himself, jumped up from the table, knocked the butter sauce onto the floor, and followed me outside to the dock.

"They're gone! He took 'em!" I shouted, distraught.

"Who?" asked Dad.

"The Creature from the Black Lagoon," I explained.

Mom started screaming at me, "Can't you do anything right?"

I blinked and was instantly back in the present, at home.

"Shh, wait a minute," I said, motioning to the kids to stay still, then putting one foot into the hall and craned my neck for a better look. The screen door was out of view from our vantage point, but it opened and banged shut again. Then, as the heavy inside door opened and thundered closed, I saw something that caused my entire body, fueled by blind fear, to shake like it had taken on a life of its own.

I shushed the little kids standing behind me, clutching my blouse, once more pulling the bedroom door closed and locking it. Then I took a long, deep breath, and cracked it open enough to peek through.

"Harv, look," I said, pointing to the edge of the door frame leading into the living room, where there stood a bare leg with a red sneaker on the foot below. I blinked and the leg disappeared. Then both doors slammed. *Did the intruder leave?* I wondered. For an hour, we took quick glances past the door but were afraid to come out of hiding.

After what felt like an eternity, the silence shattered—*ding dong*! The doorbell.

"Who's there?" I yelled

"Who do you think?" the voice echoed down the hall.

I tiptoed to the front door.

The fine line between reality and fantasy was stretched so thin, I half expected the Gill Man with his huge lips, scaly head, and fin fingers. But when I opened it, there stood Bonnie Piehl and her sinister brother Jeff, wearing a pair of red tennis shoes, laughing their fool heads off.

"I hate you," I screamed, slamming the door in their faces and turning the lock.

Then I remembered that just before Mom and Dad left, Bonnie came over to borrow a book. I'd retrieved it and asked, as she let herself out, to please lock the door. Instead, she left it ajar so she and Jeff could return and scare the pants off us.

"Harv," I said, "let this be a reminder for us to continue to stay as far away as we can from Bonnie and Jeff."

"Yeah, Sis," he agreed.

But, still, I thought to myself, *I really do want to be like Anne Frank and believe that people are basically good.*

Tippy and Fella

Harvey and Tippy

ONE BORING SUMMER day, some months after Harvey and I'd sworn Bonnie Piehl off with our pact, she strolled into our yard, offering up the suggestion that our family dogs, Tippy and Fella, should get married. Knowing Harvey and I were always scrounging for movie money, Bonnie sweetened the pot by suggesting we charge each neighbor kid a quarter to attend our furry friend's wedding. It got our attention. And we decided to give her another chance.

They will make a lovely pair, I thought. *Heck, they're both black and white.* Tippy was smooth coated like a Labrador retriever with a pointed head. Fella, part springer spaniel, was fluffier and had a square, boxy head.

Finally, Bonnie and I agreed on something, which I hoped, as an eternal optimist, might turn the tide of our friendship. That night, after playing a round of tree dodge, we hammered out the details of the wedding. I picked branches from the bridal veil bush in our backyard and wove them into a tiara, then attached part of an old white bedsheet so it would cascade down Tippy's neck and back. Bonnie stole a bowtie from her oldest brother David's room. We played "Here Comes the Bride"—me on the accordion and Bonnie on kazoo—while Harvey led the two black and white dogs down the sidewalk between the garage and back door, a path long enough to sing the chorus twice.

The next day, at sunset, a dozen neighborhood kids lined up on each side of the walkway to throw rice as we led the happy doggie couple toward our back door. When the ceremony ended, we yelled in unison, "You may now kiss the bride!"

I pushed Tippy's and Fella's heads together, so their noses touched—everybody clapped. Within minutes, the bride and groom transformed back into their doggy-selves—Tippy biting off her veil while Fella ran in circles trying to shake loose the bowtie from his neck. But the case of holy matrimony had been established, so we served the lemonade and cupcakes. Our plan went off without a hitch.

This was the singular time Harvey, Bonnie, Jeff and I worked together toward a common goal. We'd managed to distract ourselves from the ungodly heat of another summer afternoon and simultaneously create a holy union, so we thought ourselves clever and brilliant. When the hot sun set, and the neighbor kids said goodnight, they all wished the happy dog couple a long and beautiful life together.

Unfortunately, it wasn't to be.

Mr. Piehl liked to take Fella to work with him at the shipyard where he could spend all day following along his master's side, in the breeze off the river. But Mrs. Piehl was a true germaphobe—and banned Fella from riding in the car over her nervousness about the dog's hair, fleas, and what have you. Mr. and Mrs. P made a compromise that Fella was only allowed in the trunk as they traveled to and fro. One day, about six months after Tippy and Fella's wedding, Mr. P. loaded Fella into the trunk then let him out at the boatyard where Fella wiled away his hours of the ninety-five-degree day running alongside Mr. Piehl, exploring. For the return home, he loaded the faithful Fella back into the trunk and drove home. Once home, Mr. P. walked into the house, sat down to dinner and hours later, while watching the evening news, remembered he'd left the defenseless dog in the trunk. By the time he got to Fella, he was foaming at the mouth and convulsing. Poor Fella died a hideous death on the way to the veterinarian's office.

I was horrified. All of us kids were.

Tippy's husband was dead at the hands of an irresponsible grownup—I'd never felt so immensely helpless, angry, and sad all at once.

Poor Fella. The seething emotion of hatred bubbled inside me. I wanted to run next door and pound on the door and scream at Mr. Piehl and Mrs. Piehl. To think this smart and wonderful animal died at the hands of such ignorance—there was no outlet for my despair. And the event itself represented a culmination of all the nastiness Bonnie and Jeff had perpetuated since we met. From that day onward, I avoided Bonnie and Jeff in any way possible, and when passing their mother in the grocery store, I'd avert my gaze. It wasn't an easy task, but I managed to keep them out of my life. And I made God and myself a promise that when I became a grownup, I would do whatever I could to help animals.

The day after the sad story of Fella unfolded, Willie came to work to find me crying.

"Honey, those kids are scorpions, plain and simple," She said, echoing a reminder from years past. Something clicked, and I finally understood what the meaning of that familiar expression "the apple doesn't fall far from the tree" really meant.

The Belt

Harvey clowning around

DAD'S SPORADIC EMPLOYMENT magnified the chronic challenge of navigating the emotional chaos that plagued his every waking moment. Though I vaguely understood his "crazy" was due to the many unfortunate circumstances of his earlier life which occurred before I was born, the fact that he often took after us kids with a belt completely unnerved me. And even though he changed my punishment to being put on restriction when I got older, I continued to feel that I had to stop him from hitting the younger kids.

The day Dad arrived home pre-occupied with worry, having heard his Navy art department contract might be terminated, his anxiety grew teeth. I sensed that I should try to keep the little kids out of his way.

Dad was a ticking time bomb, impossible to ignore, and not

157

a man who suffered in silence. If he was going to be miserable, he'd make damn sure every one of us suffered right along with him. Whenever he was upset, a simmering undercurrent of sadistic irritability reverberated throughout our home.

Day after day he searched for ways to alleviate his stress by aggravating Harvey and me. Why he derived such sick pleasure out of frustrating us was beyond understanding. He started making us say, "Yes sir," after every command, badgering us with, "Louder. I can't hear you. What?" over and over until we were practically screaming. He was a dervish held captive in a whirlwind of his own making.

When he first started behaving like that, I searched to find a rationale for what I might have done to provoke him, hoping to avoid in the future whatever the heck it was I'd done to get him going. But I never seemed to find the answer and couldn't crack the code.

The tendency to protect my younger siblings didn't help, it just gave Dad a personal whipping boy. As the countdown closed in on the end of Dad's contract as an illustrator for the Navy, his disposition took a turn for the worse.

One evening, Paulina absent-mindedly set the one fan we owned, an old metal deal with no protective covering over the blades, on the floor to cool Harvey and her while they sat on Harvey's bottom bunk, playing a round of go fish. Paulina got up to use the bathroom and stumbled into the fan, nearly cutting off her baby toe on one of the spinning blades. Her hysterical screaming echoed down the hall—I went running into the boys' room to see what was the matter. Blood spurted out of her foot as she sat wailing. Thankfully, Dad was home—he rushed in and scooped her into his arms and ran out the door to the hospital.

Mom stumbled after, shrieking, "Haavee!"—what she said when

she was looking for someone to blame. I knew this meant there'd be hell to pay when they returned from the hospital.

Later that evening, Dad came through the door carrying an anesthetized Paulina, went down the hall and tucked her into bed. Mom followed, then trailed off to put Benny to bed.

A moment later, in his deep, angry voice, Dad shouted, "Haaavee, come heah," calling him into the living room.

Harvey nervously entered.

I followed.

"You will not leave this house for one month. For any reason, see." He hit the drum table for emphasis. "Is that clear?"

Harv's jaw went slack.

"B-But baseball, my team," Harvey whimpered.

Baseball practice season had just started—and Harvey lived for baseball.

"I don't give a damn about baseball. You should have thought about that before you hurt your sister. It's your job to look out for her, see."

Dad had a special kind of love for Paulina, his mother's namesake. And at age six, five years younger than Harvey, he viewed her as a precious, perfect, cherub doll.

Hearing the ruckus, Mom strode into the living room long enough to get the gist of the conversation, then mumbled a worthless, "Max," and exited the room, parking herself at the kitchen table.

I stood in the hall, spellbound, waiting to see what Dad was going do next.

He started again, in his deep, slow, gangster style voice, "Pull down your pants and bend over. And you betta not cry, or I'll give you something to cry about!" he chanted.

"But, Paulina..." Harvey begged, in a vain attempt to try and explain what happened—that she had brought the fan into his room.

But Dad was on a mission now and no explanation was going to change Harvey's fate. "Don't but me," he said, pulling his belt out of the loops of his pants.

Mom gave another feeble "Max" from the other room.

The next moment stretched out for a very long time and though I was an actor in it, I felt outside of myself, watching the scene unfold from the vantage point of someplace up high, almost to the ceiling, as if I had become a thin vapor that floated mid-air.

I walked into the dining room, looking for something heavy to grab. Peeking into the kitchen, I saw Mom had vanished. Then my eyes landed on the object and my right hand wrapped itself around the large vase that sat atop our mahogany buffet. A thought shot through my mind, so quickly it barely registered: this was Grandma Paulina's vase. And for a brief moment I took it in—it had a field of crackled cream glass decorated with tiny rosebuds. It was beautiful—and special. The sentimentality of the vase being Grandma's had me befuddled. I grappled with whether to put it back in its safe place on the buffet, but the part of me ready to smack Dad had taken over.

My dreamlike self squeezed the neck of the vase more tightly. It was now a projectile in my hand, no different than a lead bullet. I imagined it flying through the air and froze. There was nothing I could do to stop this. The trigger had been pulled.

"Stop! Just stop!" I yelled, snapping back into my body.

Dad suddenly came into focus, turned, and looked me straight in the eyes. I glared back at him and through him at once until, *what the hell? This enigma looked like my father, but no, like a mask of my father.* I didn't recognize the spirit of it/him. Whatever it was, it had the energy of a crazy demon-possessed person. More importantly, this creature was out to hurt my brother.

Now, pumped full of adrenalin, I had a singular focus—protecting Harvey.

For an eternal minute the three of us stood frozen, suspended in time. Dad blinked. I sensed a small part of him registering a blip on the Richter scale of his maniacal mind, and imagined it went something like this: "The angry teenager standing behind me, ready to smash a vase over my head, is my daughter."

"Put it down! Put down the belt! Now!" I screeched.

My clenched jaw caused the veins in my neck to swell and strain.

Dad's knuckles whitened as he tightened his grip on the belt.

Harv looked up at me, eyes glazed over with fear.

In that moment nothing else mattered but protecting my little brother.

There were no "what-ifs." No, "what if he grabs me? What if he heaves me through the air and throws me through the picture window?"—something he could easily have done with one hand tied behind his back. But I wasn't concerned. He was Godzilla and it was up to me to save my brother from the monster. My solitary thought: *This is going to stop now. Now. NOW.*

"Drop the belt, Dad! Drop it now," I screamed and again, "NOW!"

Mom walked back in the living room just long enough to realize she was in over her head. Dad raised the belt higher, hollering, "Ruth, get Gab out of here."

Mom slunk into the kitchen and did not return.

I looked into Dad's eyes again. They had changed to lakes of fire. Harvey stood frozen with his pants down, too afraid to flinch.

I was going to give Dad one last warning. Period.

"Dad. For the last and final time, drop the damn belt. If you don't, I swear to God I'm gonna break this over your head. Get up, Harv!"

Harvey wasn't about to move.

Dad looked whipped, like he was running out of energy to

continue this battle. He took a big step back, and exhaled. He folded the belt in half, set it on the coffee table, and stomped into his bedroom, slamming the door behind him.

Harvey pulled up his pants, grabbed my hand, and ran me to his bedroom. We locked the door and plopped ourselves down on the bottom bunk. Then he started to cry. Feeling that danger was still afoot, I said, "C'mon Harv. Let's go out to the garage."

So many emotions slammed around in my head, I couldn't sort and code them fast enough to define what I was feeling. For a while we sat cross-legged on the garage floor next to Tippy, leaning into the cement wall, mumbling incoherently to ourselves until we could form real words.

"I can't hardly believe it, Gab, the way you stood up to him. You're a warrior," Harvey finally said.

"We're too old to be whipped, Harv," I said, thinking of my eleven-year-old brother, pants around his ankles like that.

"No shit."

A few moments of silence passed and our minds wandered, then, pulling myself together I realized that we still had reason to be afraid.

"Ya know Harv, pretty soon they're gonna come looking for us. We'd be smart to go in, climb into our pajamas and pretend to be asleep."

"Yeah," said Harv. "Roger that."

We tiptoed inside.

Once in bed, I ruminated on the many "what ifs" and "if onlys" of the evening. I was pretty proud of myself for finally declaring that there needed to be a limit to Dad's lunacy. But the pride only lasted one long minute, then gave way to another kind of emotion—something like being a victim. *Why do I have to be the one to deal with him?* I asked—but quickly realized there was no simple answer. That night, I couldn't articulate the fact that as the oldest, the warrior, it was pre-destined for me to have this role. Over time I'd learn to accept the truth of my place in the order of things.

When sleep did finally come, I crashed hard. Something inside me had changed.

For years I had a recurring nightmare about the ghost of a man who haunted me almost every night, robbing me of sleep—he hid in the dogwood tree in the front yard, shined a flashlight on me, and watched my every move. In the days and weeks after my showdown with Dad, the ghost, who frightened me to my core, disappeared entirely.

Freedom Riders and Lee High

Lift ev'ry voice and sing
'Til earth and heaven ring
Ring with the harmonies of Liberty
Let our rejoicing rise
High as the list'ning skies
Let it resound loud as the rolling sea
Sing a song full of the faith that the dark past has taught us
Sing a song full of the hope that the present has brought us
Facing the rising sun of our new day begun
Let us march on 'til victory is won

*"Lift Every Voice and Sing," the Negro National Anthem written by
the Johnson Brothers from Jacksonville Florida*

A FTER YEARS OF being tricked and hassled by Bonnie and Jeff, I decided to make some new friends and now that I was in middle school, I felt the importance of them being people who were trustworthy and kind.

The first was Elaine. Her family was Syrian and Elaine, like her mother, had beautiful olive skin and thick black eyebrows. They lived in Riverside, the oldest neighborhood in Jacksonville, not far from our synagogue.

Throughout middle and high school, we spent most Friday nights at Elaine's house, which was always a-buzz with relatives coming and going. Her mom was a fantastic cook, even making her own cheeses. There were always a few cheese rounds hanging on the arms of wooden Adirondack chairs, drying on the front screened porch which meant cheese was the first thing a person would see, and smell, when approaching the house.

Every Thursday, Mrs. Massouh put a big pot of a chicken fricassee on the stove. By dinner on Friday the entire house—and half the neighborhood—smelled of her mouthwatering sauce. Elaine was the youngest, with an older brother and sister, and always had relatives popping in and out of the house. She called all her aunts simply "Aunt" and her uncles "Uncle," which I thought odd—but it looked like she had so many of them she didn't even bother with first names.

One of her very old uncles had a fishing shack built at the end of a rickety pier out Heckscher drive where they, like us, regularly went fishing. It had a small woodstove, a few chairs, a cot pushed against the wall, and a table with three chairs in the middle. We went twice, both were a swell time with windy days spent fishing off the end of the pier, going in only to grab a sandwich from the cooler or pour a cup of warm tea.

There was so much chaos in my family home, that getting away for a day of fishing was a much-needed respite, especially in light of the heart-wrenching events that were unfurling throughout the early sixties—racism, police clashes, and political upheaval.

One important day in May, I returned home late from school, passing through our yard where the grapefruit and pear trees were full of tiny spring fruit, and found Wilhelmina in the living room standing in front of the TV.

"What'cha watchin,' Willie?"

She looked startled for a moment and let out a quiet, "Oh, child."

Willie shook her head as if gathering herself—making the journey back from wherever it was her mind had been. She looked at me with her tired brown eyes, then at her calloused right hand holding a glass of tea. She gripped it tighter as though she'd forgotten she was holding it and didn't want the perspiration on the outside of the glass to cause it to slip out of her hand.

"Hey, Missy G, you're late ain't ya'?" Willie said next, trying to change the subject.

Her left hand searched her apron pocket to fiddle with the cigarette butt she always carried. Whenever she was nervous, she'd retrieve the butt and head out to her little bathroom to take a drag. This day, she acted like she'd been caught with her pants down, probably a knee-jerk response, worrying I'd think she was wasting time in front of the TV. But once she grasped the fact it was me, not one of my parents, she relaxed.

"What's up, Will?" I asked again, gently.

The wiggly lines across her forehead declared fear and worry.

"I'm checking on those Freedom Riders I told you about. I just heard they're tryin' to travel through the South for another whole week—tryin' to show the world we Negroes have the right to go anywhere we want. Just like white folks."

She took a long slug of her sweet tea.

Since 1946, there'd been a Federal law in place that declared segregated buses illegal for interstate travel, but this was the South, where old habits die hard, and the ruling was ignored by most of the Southern states. The Freedom Riders—both Black and white—took off, riding integrated buses across the country, bringing attention to their plight. The civil rights activists on the bus planned to travel across the South, eventually reaching New Orleans on May 17th, where a victory rally was waiting for them.

In the nine years Willie had been part of our family, I'd never seen her sit anywhere but the back of the bus. From the time we were babies, she'd taken us downtown and we always sat there, in the back, with her. We never gave it a second thought.

Over the next week, Willie spent a portion of her lunch hour glued to the news broadcasts. The moment I walked through the back door, she shared her worries with me.

"Ain't no way I'd do it. They're probably gonna get themselves killed," she said, shaking her head from side to side.

By the time the Riders were midway through their saga in May, unrest of another kind entered our home. Dad showed up late for dinner with an announcement, "Well, family, it doesn't look like I'll have a job past December."

As suspected a number of months earlier, the boat holding our family afloat was taking on water.

"Are you sure?" asked Mom.

"Yes, we had a meeting this morning and Smithee says there's not enough money in the budget to renew my contract."

I twisted the napkin in my hands, wanting to get up from the table. I'd seen this kind of thing before and knew Dad would only grow more agitated as the end of his contract drew closer. I could feel storm clouds gathering above our dinner table and knew that my getting up was all it'd take to light the match of Dad's incendiary mood. I didn't budge. Nobody spoke a word as Mom handed Dad his dinner.

Over the next weeks, Dad became sullen and distant and took to spending most of his time at home locked in his room. It would only be a matter of time before Hurricane Dad would make landfall. I had my own concerns and having Dad's discontent brewing in the background didn't help. As my ninth year of school was winding to a close, I'd received notice that I was one of the many in our graduating class earmarked to transfer to the new Forrest High School.

True to Southern fashion, the school was named in honor of Nathan Bedford Forrest, known for his extreme cruelty as a Confederate soldier, but best known as one of the founders, and Grand Wizard, of the first Ku Klux Klan. Our town of Jacksonville was home to one of the largest KKK enclaves in the country.

I was flabbergasted. I thought for sure I'd be going to Lee High with my closest friends. But the new school was completed ahead of schedule and all the kids in my neighborhood were re-assigned to Forrest. I'd spent the last year imagining myself sitting in the bleachers at historic Robert E. Lee, cheering for the best football team in Jacksonville.

Forrest High was built to absorb the burgeoning baby boomers entering high school. Across the Cedar Hills Bridge, a few miles away from our home, the school sat smack in the middle of a new subdivision filled with street after street of cheaply built, nondescript ranch-style houses, and the first shopping mall in our area. Developers were offering all sorts of incentives for folks to buy out there, which must've been hard to refuse, because my best friend Marsha's mom joined the mass exodus to the subdivision. Marsha's future had been decided.

The only benefit I could see to living in Cedar Hills was that it was close to Pritchett's Kitchens—a restaurant that offered all-you-can-eat fried shrimp, coleslaw, French fries or hush puppies, for ninety-nine cents once a week—and the grassy knoll above a dock where we sometimes went fishing.

Me, Harvey, and his friend Jimmy had a ritual we dubbed "Pritchett Tuesdays"—after eating our fill of shrimp, we'd run our bloated selves down the hill to a dock above Cedar Creek where we used bamboo poles to fish for mullet.

We generally caught at least two or three, and brought them

home to keep in the fridge for Willie to find the next day—she considered them a delicacy. Our parents, called them bottom fish. "According to Kosher Law," they said, "Jews aren't supposed eat scavengers or fish without scales, like catfish." But the Negroes loved them. And Mom and Dad, who couldn't seem to get enough shrimp, lobster, and crab, made me wonder why those crustaceans weren't also off limits.

Forrest High was also close to the newly opened Twin Hills Drive-In. Their grand opening special—a double feature for a dollar a carload—was a hit. After we cleared the gate and parked, we piled out of the trunk, and spent the evening on a blanket next to the car eating popcorn and swilling down Coca-Cola while trying to dodge the fumes from Bic mosquito spirals and cigarette smoke.

One Friday night, Harvey and three of his friends, all too young to borrow a car, made a scene when they showed up at the drive-in in a refrigerator box designed like a vehicle—windows and doors drawn on and all. They simply walked up to the ticket shack, paid their money, and sashayed in.

If I could figure out a way to go to Lee, I would do it in a heartbeat. I knew I'd miss Marsha, who would be at Forrest High, but figured we'd catch up on weekends at the Riverside Garden Club where we'd dance the night away to the two most popular Negro bands in town, The Jay-Notes and The Lemon Twisters who played a mix of soul, rhythm and blues, and rock and roll music. Theirs was music you couldn't sit still to, unless you had "no cut in your strut or glide in your slide," as Guy Williams the disc jockey at WOPB, "the Black spot on your dial," said.

Around the same time, Elvis was topping the charts with "Return to Sender" while the baby-faced Bobby Dee chimed "Take Good Care of My Baby." The soprano harmonies of the Four Seasons animated the dance floor with "Big Girl's Don't Cry," and dances like the Mashed Potato and the jitterbug, which we called "the bop," were all the rage. I loved to dance and once even managed to get on the television show *Top Ten Dance Party*—Jacksonville's version of Dick Clark's *American Bandstand*.

Robert E. Lee High, named after the Confederate general, was a stately brick building built in 1926. I searched my mind, desperate for a creative solution to ensure I could make Lee my high school, suddenly remembering one of Dad's stories of when he was a kid living with his family in Harlem in the 1920s. The schools in Harlem weren't very good at that time, so his family gave the fake address of an aunt in the Bronx as a way for him and his sister to attend a better school district. It worked like a charm. Armed with this story, I approached my parents with a similar proposal. Turns out it was surprisingly easy to convince them to let me give a fake address and then ride the city bus to Lee. Once securing their permission, I crossed my fingers the school would accept me—a decision that would come much later in the summer.

While holding my breath to discover my high school fate, Willie and I followed along as the Freedom Riders continued their journey across the South. The news reported that the first bus encountered very little resistance as they drove through the initial few states, but they felt the biggest challenge was yet to come in Alabama—a premonition that came true. Governor George Wallace, a diehard segregationist, had given Bull Connor, the Police Chief, an order to organize violence. Police Sergeant Tom Cook, an avid Ku Klux Klan member, along with Connor, planned a violent confrontation designed to show the Negroes once and for all that integration would never happen in their state.

On Mother's Day, May 14th, the first bus—with seven whites and six Blacks—entered the vicinity of Anniston, Alabama, a small town that boasted one of the most heinous Ku Klux Klan enclaves in the nation. The bus blew a tire and pulled into a service station several miles outside of town. Within minutes, an angry crowd of rabid racists surrounded the bus, screaming incendiary insults while attacking and firebombing it. The bus filled with smoke and flames. The frightened Riders franticly exited the bus, only to be beaten with baseball bats and chains, causing multiple injuries and serious burns. An investigation later revealed that Bull Connor told Sergeant Tom Cook he was allowed fifteen minutes with the bus before Wallace would make any attempt to stop the violence. One activist, who required fifty stitches in his head, was refused treatment at the closest hospital and many of the other injured were turned away or given almost no treatment.

When reports of the attack reached Attorney General Robert Kennedy, he asked President John F. Kennedy to issue a presidential order to send law enforcement to Anniston. The President's personal assistant, John Seigenthaler, was immediately sent to calm the frenzied crowd. Delta airlines also cooperated, getting Kennedy's assistant to Alabama overnight, and flying the Freedom Riders out of harm's way.

Willie, who rarely worked for us on Sunday, was at our house that fateful Mother's Day when the footage from Atlanta streamed in. The news showed the burned-out bus, then the injured Riders at the hospital. Willie and Dad stood together in front of the set, in utter horrorr.

"Oh, Mr. Mack when's this gonna end?" Willie pleaded, an exhausted look about her.

"I wish I could tell you, Wilhelmina. How 'bout you get dressed and I'll drive you home," Dad said, understanding Willie'd want to be with her people at a time like this.

I asked if I could come along.

I had only been to Willie's neck of the woods one other time.

She lived in something called "the projects." Block after block of grayish-green, swamp-colored, four-story apartment buildings filled the grounds. Even in the sunshine of late afternoon the place looked murky and dank, as though it was covered in a foggy mist. There were a couple of empty lots in the complex but no play areas or swing sets or monkey bars. Dad pulled up in front, got out and walked Willie to her door, then returned, locked the doors, and turned on the radio.

Before he pulled the car forward, I heard something odd.

"Wait a minute, Dad," I said, rolling down my window.

Then a sound I recognized: Willie squealing, "Oh my God, oh my God!" from her front door landing.

I jumped out of the car and raced up the steps. Dad followed.

"Willie!" I yelled, throwing open her creaky, beat-up screen door.

There was water everywhere. The couch damn near sagged to the floor weighted down by an indeterminable amount of water.

"It looks like somebody turned a hose on your place," Dad said, with a tone of fact mixed with disgust.

Willie's framed family photos were tossed about, underwater on the floor. The kitchen chairs were upturned in the lake that was her living room. The boys' mattresses, and hers, were sopping wet. Willie was hysterical. She kept repeating, "Why? Why? I didn't do nothin' to nobody."

"It isn't your fault, Willie," I said, forcing a tiny smile.

"It isn't your fault at all," Dad repeated. "We know it isn't anything you did," he said, patting her on the back.

Dad and I dragged the heavy mattresses onto the upstairs porch, where we managed to boost them over the handrails so they could drain more quickly. Thankfully, Raymond and Marvin were at a church outing and weren't yet home. We swept and mopped for a couple of hours, working to put the house back together and salvage what we could.

"Why don't you and the kids spend the night at our house tonight?" Dad offered.

But proud Willie shook her head. "I'll manage, Mr. Mack, thanks just the same."

"Are you sure you can't think of anyone who'd want to do this to you?" we asked, wanting to ensure her safety.

But Willie didn't have even an inkling of anyone who might be targeting her. These kinds of injustices happened often. There was such rampant hatred toward Negroes that most felt it was only a matter of time before something horrific would befall them.

As a Jew in the South, I felt a similar sense of impending doom that followed like the hot breath of a wolf. At school I tried to keep the fact that I was Jewish on the down-low, especially after the time my chai (symbol of eternal life) necklace was yanked off my throat on the playground by a cracker as he shouted, "You dirty Jew!" But the Negroes couldn't hide their difference—and this kind of cruelty was a regular part of being a Negro in the South, no matter how wrong it was.

Our well-meaning parents had taught us kids, "sticks and stones can break your bones, but words will never harm you." But they forgot that actions follow words, and now one of those ignorant crackers, like our racist neighbors, had hurt my beloved Willie. My heart ached inside.

James Meredith

Integrating Ole Miss

S FATE WOULD have it, my trick worked and I made
it to Lee High—I was ecstatic. Each day after school, I
returned home to Willie, who'd now been our nanny for
eleven years, pushing through the back door as she ordered, "Take
off your shoes! I don't want you puttin' nasty dirt on my clean
flo'"—the same thing she said every time she mopped.

Willie, unlike my parents who were caught in the net of their
own misery, asked me how I liked my new school while fixing me a
glass of her famous sweet tea. Our chat didn't last long. She seemed
to have something on her mind, and quickly excused herself to
run back into the living room to catch the remainder of the five
o'clock news. These days, Willie had taken to sneaking peeks at
the television on a regular basis. During the broadcast reports of
the Freedom Rides, she'd gotten a taste for the enormous difference

between viewing photojournalism on screen and the radio reports she'd known before. She was mesmerized.

"What'cha watchin', Willie?"

"I think he might just make it," she said.

"What? Who?"

"James Meredith—one of my people. He's trying to become the first Negro to attend Mississippi University."

I could see the sparkle of better times to come in Willie's eyes as the saga unfolded over two days and nights. All of us kids rooted for Meredith each time we caught Willie watching TV and, in the end, he prevailed. A Negro at Ole Miss. It was quite an accomplishment, but like all progress toward equal rights for Negroes in the South, the victory was hard won. A riot broke out to try to prevent Meredith from entering the University and within forty-eight hours three hundred people at the University were injured and two had died.

Cuba and Cruikshank

Ready for the beach

I'D BEEN TRYING to figure out a better way to decipher Dad's signals, to try to catch his crazy moods before they pummeled me and the rest of the family. I figured I'd better hold my cards close to my chest and not tell Dad anything about my personal life, but spend time observing him closely in an effort to learn to intuit his moods—a method I prayed might be the key to my sanity.

I shared my plan with Harvey. He rolled his eyes, which I took to mean, "You know there's only a snowball's chance in hell this will work."

I shrugged my shoulders, thinking, *At least I'm trying. Hell, I have to try something.*

I detested the job of being the one to stand up against Dad but, dammit, nobody else was going to do it. Mom tried to intervene in the beginning of Dad's "whipping with a belt phase," but she gave up after getting swatted by the leather strap a couple of times while attempting to stop him. Now, she just disappeared, leaving us to fend for ourselves.

One evening Harvey and I heard the song, "How Come You Do Me Like You Do," stream through my little transistor radio. I started singing and Harv joined me.

"How come you do me like you do do do?
How come you do me like you do?
Why do you try to make me feel so blue?
I've done nothing to you."

"Hey, Harv, I have an idea. How about we use this song as a signal when one of us notices a spell of "Crazy Dad" coming on, okay?"

The song gave us confirmation that we weren't the only teenagers having a hard time dealing with their parents.

Our early-warning system worked beautifully. Whenever Dad began to transform into a raging maniac, Harv and I started singing or humming, "How Come You Do Me Like You Do." The tune became a defense weapon—a way to let the other know when Dad was sitting on a powder keg. And, because we were sharing the sound of the warning together, we felt a little less anxious.

I adapted quickly to the new way of doing things in high school and made friends right away. I especially enjoyed those moments after the bell rung, changing classes in the hallway, where I used my "boydar" to scope out the cutest guys on the way to class. Yet at home I was tense to the point of physical illness, often having difficulty eating, wrought with stomach cramps.

And then the bad got worse.

On October 22nd, only a month and a half into my first year of high school, President Kennedy addressed the nation.

"Good evening my fellow citizens," he began.

Suddenly, our life at home, and the world at large, was teetering on the brink of destruction. My parents sat glued to the television screen, hanging on the President's every word, as he explained that the Soviet Union had sent nuclear missiles to Cuba and they were capable of traveling over 1,000 nautical miles within minutes. For our family sitting in Jacksonville, Florida, those missiles were too close for comfort. We listened as JFK described the situation in detail, the bombs, how they got there, the danger, and then the path forward—and though my knuckles were white with fear, it wasn't only about Cuba. It was that the world seemed tipped on its axis—the end of Dad's job on a collision course with the escalating Cuban Crisis.

As the days passed, Mom and Dad continued to spend their evening watching the national emergency play out on screen. *At least now they have something other than bickering to occupy their time*, coursed through my mind.

Many of our neighbors began stockpiling canned goods at the urging of President Kennedy and constructing bomb shelters in their backyards. Words like "Communists," "Third World War," "Fallout," and "Radiation" found their way into everyday speech.

One evening, I overheard Dad from the other room, "Did you hear that, Ruth? Cape Canaveral, that's Florida! In minutes, we could be blown to kingdom come!" The possibility sounded fantastical and impossible to grasp—nevertheless, it gave me chills.

Beginning in 1951, the US began massive testing of nuclear bombs. Entire small towns were built in the desert about one hundred miles from Las Vegas that simulated neighborhoods with average-sized houses occupied by human-sized mannequins to see how well they would fare in the event of a nuclear blast. In Nevada, the public was so naïve about the danger of the fallout from these tests that they held picnics outdoors to observe the sky lighting up from the bomb testings as though they were a carnival attraction. They even created special cocktails to swill down while they were watching the fireworks from their picnic blanket. The Atomic Cocktail, F Bomb, and Atmospheric River to name a few. Ass Juice became all the rage. Though the bartenders were not allowed to divulge what combination of alcohol was used, it got a lot of attention because it was served on the Las Vegas strip in shot glasses designed to look like small, white, porcelain toilets to keep as a souvenir.

We kids didn't really grasp the seriousness of the situation; the phenomenon of war in our country was, to us, incomprehensible. Still, the fear of impending peril was impossible to ignore. At school, it became mandatory for us to participate in duck-and-cover drills. Several times a day, whenever we heard the raspy, school loudspeakers eking out their obnoxious beeping, we were commanded to squat under our desks or dive on the floor next to a wall and clasp our hands tightly behind our heads, covering our eyes with our elbows. The exercises seemed more disruptive and ridiculous than frightening.

The school also showed us short films of what to do in case we heard the warning signifying that a nuclear blast was about to happen nearby. The most popular nuclear informational children's film featured a cartoon character called Bert the Turtle. Humble Bert is seen strolling along a lane when a monkey appears, hanging out of a tree with a lit stick of dynamite, and drops it on Bert. Bert, who happens to be wearing a helmet, ducks inside his shell. The words, "Don't forget to duck and cover" are heard, and we see that because Bert has popped his little head and feet inside the shell, he only experiences rocking from the blast.

One afternoon, I told Willie, "I'm more worried about Dad's temper escalating than the Cubans. You know, it's October, Will, and Dad's job with the Navy Exchange ends in December."

"I know, child," she replied, "and it's not just your Dad who's having a hard time right now. My people done spent their lives worrying about the crackers and the Klan and now they gots to worry about the Cubans, too."

We looked at each other and sighed.

Then, on November 2nd, after two months of sitting on the brink of catastrophe, our nation caught a break. At the eleventh hour, thanks to Robert Kennedy's supreme negotiating skills, he was able to convince the administration to move ahead on a complex plan that strategically blocked Cuba's next move. Instead of taking military action that could have led to nuclear war, he negotiated with the Soviet Union to have the weapons in Cuba removed. It was a remarkable diplomatic feat.

President Kennedy addressed the nation again. This time to assure America that the Soviet missiles were being dismantled and, through aerial surveillance, the U.S. Military would see that every one of them was destroyed or removed. Thankfully, this incident, at least the parts that were shared with the nation, only lasted for two months.

And, though this was a relatively short-lived crisis, it was the first time we were faced with the possibility that the threat of war from an outside invader could actually take place in our country—a reality that riveted the nation in a way that caused most Americans, including my parents, to feel we would never stand on solid ground again. This was especially true for those of us living in close proximity to Cuba.

Once the threat of Cuba had blown over, my parents breathed a momentary sigh of relief. At least we weren't going to be reduced to smithereens. I was relieved that the duck-and-cover drills had stopped so the imaginary boyfriends I had dancing in my head could resume their places in the front row seats of my hormonal theatre. My focus shifted to other important questions like what band would be playing at the Riverside Garden Club Hall on Saturday night.

But the luxury of youthful teenage thoughts wasn't entirely available to me as a place to get lost in because Dad grew more and more anxious as the last day of his job drew closer. I could see the mushroom cloud of his fear and anger brewing on the horizon and knew the fallout from it would soon rain havoc on our household—and I'd be first in line at the chopping block as he re-directed his focus by controlling my every move.

Then it happened.

Dad made it his mission to ruin anything I looked forward to. Any attempt to ask his permission, no matter the activity, was met with this:

"Dad?" I'd ask.

"Yes?" He'd reply.

"Can I—?"

"No!"

"But you didn't even hear what I was going to ask," I'd plead.

"The answer is no. Unequivocally. Irrefutably. Undeniably. Irrevocably. Indefatigably. Indisputably, N-O!"

Dad, who loved to discover new words (and had been taking the dictionary with him into the bathroom for years), seemed to especially like words that began with the letter 'I' or 'U' when telling me no.

At first, I tried to involve Mom: "You have to talk to him, pu-leeze, I want to go to the football game Friday night."

"But..."

"The answer is N-O!"

At the beginning of Dad's "NO" hysteria, Mom attempted to

181

help by going into the bedroom where Dad was spending most of his time, pleading with him to let me go. While I appreciated Mom's smattering of support, I knew she'd give up easily. She did.

Harvey got the same exasperating treatment, although he was better at wearing Dad down to get what he wanted. I chalked it up to his being a boy. In fact, one time Dad gave in with a laugh, then added, "You know son, you'd make a good lawyer." He never gave in to me.

The double standards and inequity only served to make me angrier. Then with the added escalation of his badgering Mom, I felt, for first time in my life, a feeling of true hatred toward him.

One evening, he demanded Mom repeat, "Yes, sir," to him, in response to some unimportant question he posed, which went something like this:

Dad: "You mean, 'yes, sir,' don't you?"

Mom: "Yes, sir."

Dad: "What? I can't hear you."

Mom: (louder) "Yes, sir."

Dad: "I didn't quite make that out."

Mom: (louder again) "Yes. Sir."

On and on again he bullied her, until finally, Mom grabbed my hand and said, "C'mon we're going to Easterlings," a nearby pharmacy.

Mom, a reluctant driver, gunned the engine as she sped out the driveway, leaving me shocked. My stomach hurt. I wanted to offer something consoling but couldn't grab hold of any words that would make sense to her—well, our—dilemma. Silence filled the void as she pulled the car over to the side of the road and let her head flop onto the steering wheel. Her anger permeated the air like hot steam. Finally, after what seemed like a long time, she raised her head and shook it slowly side to side, signifying defeat. I waited and waited. I didn't even know what I was waiting for—an opening, I guess.

Then, I said, "Mom, why don't you just leave?" shocking myself as I heard the words fly out of my mouth.

She didn't answer.

"But why?" I pressed.

She continued silently shaking her head, with her look of defeat. Finally, she raised her hands, and with a tone of exasperation said, "I can't, I have nowhere to go."

I'd hear this answer again and again during future dashes from the house. Until that first night, I'd never realized it before, but it was true—Mom really had nobody to turn to.

I took mental inventory of her situation: her father was a poor man with a thick Polish accent and very little formal education who sold Fuller Brush products door to door. Her only sibling, Jack, lived in an institution for the developmentally delayed, and they were both in New York. It had never been easy for Mom to make friends, in large part because she didn't think before she blurted out her opinions, which were usually judgmental. She had a house full of children. Jewish women didn't collect welfare. Her hands were tied.

After an hour, we returned to the house and Mom walked straight past Dad, standing in the kitchen, into their bedroom. She didn't utter a single word or look at him, for that matter. A few minutes later, he followed.

I listened outside their door but was met only with the sound of silence.

This man, my father, who I thought loved me had suddenly, for some reason I couldn't put my finger on, begun to despise me.

Why should I be surprised? I thought, *look at the way he treats his wife.*

The confusing part was that he wasn't always like this. So

even though "Dad the Horrible" seemed to be the main character animating his body of late, I found it impossible to forget the guy who used to tuck me in at night, play poker with Harvey and me, and take us fishing—the sweet Dad. I cogitated on the notion: *maybe it would be easier if he acted like a bastard all the time.*

There was another side to Dad's story, as there always is. But I was a teenager and all I wanted to do was be happy, accepted, and live in a peaceful home. And since I wasn't privy to the things in Dad's past that caused him to swing from one mood to another, my reality was limited to what I experienced on a daily basis.

If I had known about the two well-guarded family secrets packed away in my father's luggage, maybe it would have helped me understand the emotional fragility of this behemoth of a man. But I couldn't know the delicacy of his situation—that he spent his days navigating a tightrope with no safety net. Or that it took every ounce of strength and courage he had to, barely, keep his family together and show up for work.

If I'd known about his traumatic past, it might have been easier to grasp and understand that I represented yet another of the many things he'd been unable to control in his life. I was another young woman, like the ghost of a different one he'd lost along the way. If only I'd understood that somewhere deep inside of him he knew that if another damn thing knocked him for a loop he might unravel permanently.

But I didn't know. So I believed there must be something wrong with me that ignited his "crazy" as my mere presence seemed to. Lacking the essential pieces of the puzzle, all I could figure was that he simply hated me.

His flair for the dramatic, which in the past made him seem funny and eccentric, had now become my worst enemy. On the rare occasion I finally managed to get his permission to go out on the weekend, I'd be so physically and emotionally worn out from begging for a "yes" that I couldn't even enjoy myself. I dreaded being at home, was distracted at school and continued having a hard time digesting food. I was diagnosed with stomach ulcers.

Not yet fifteen years old, I was utterly and completely trapped and exhausted. A well of hatred toward him consumed me. Lying in bed on nights I couldn't sleep, the voice in my head repeated, "I hate you, I hate you," like a record off its groove.

One evening, after he forbade me a weekend dance, I listened outside my parents' door.

"You know," he said, "if we keep letting her go out with non-Jewish boys, one day she will end up marrying a Shaygets (Gentile)."

"Max," Mom tried to interrupt, but Dad ignored her.

"So, Ruth, we have a new rule in this house, see. If she wants to date, she can go out with a non-Jewish boy one weekend if she goes out with a Jewish boy the next."

"But, Max, there are no Jewish boys in her school," Mom reminded him.

"Well, there are plenty of Jewish boys in her Sunday school class," he scoffed, demonstrating his shrewdness.

"But—their parents won't drive them all the way over here to pick her up for a date..." Mom's voice faded away.

As Dad's combative behavior continued, I developed a new skill—I got faster in transitioning from anger to resolve. He was teaching me, I'd realize many years later, how to think on my feet, a skill that would save my ass many a time throughout my life.

Listening outside my parents' door that night, a shift occurred in how I thought about the problem and went from feeling mad as hell at him and sorry for myself, to a steely resolve. A conversation with myself followed that went something like this: *Yeah, so, this is how you want to play it, Br'er Fox (Dad)? You should know by now you're messin' with one smart rabbit (me). I'll figure something out, I just know I will. I'm fixin' to stupefy you, and when I do I will sashay outta this damn house whenever the hell I feel like it. Just you wait and see.*

This was not the first time I'd been forced to strategize how to get around Dad's angry mandates. In the past, his obsession with our grades resulted in banning all of us from watching television, which was unfair enough to get me started. But now that I was older, and he'd decided that he would put me on restriction from leaving the house for the next six-week grading period if I got anything less than a B, I knew I had to figure something out. His tactic worked the first time he tried it—the following term my grades went back to A's and B's. But they slipped again once I'd met the challenge, was bored with school and was spending weekends out with friends. It was a simple formula: restriction equals better grades, fun equals more restriction. It took only two of these cycles to determine the social schizophrenia was not going to prevail.

So, I hatched a plan.

The next time report cards came out I went to the Dean's office and told her I'd lost mine and needed a replacement to bring home for my parents to sign. I felt like one slippery salamander when, within minutes, the office issued me another.

Aha, I thought, *now I'll forge the real one and give it back to the school. Then I'll fill out the new one with A's and B's and have my parents sign that one. Brilliant, right?* I smiled, thinking, *this slick rabbit is hopping around the briar patch now.* I didn't even tell Harvey about the report card.

I was on the Honor Roll the entire year.

Dad definitely paved the road to hell with his good intentions that time. His overly strict rules taught me a lesson—that to survive in his household, I'd better learn how to sneak and lie. But within two weeks, my new philosophy would really be put to the test—a first attempt at bold-faced lying was about to unfold.

The next Friday night, I told Dad my date to the football game was with a Jewish guy, Ron Cruikshank, a guy in my class. In my naiveté, I figured because Ron's name sounded a little unusual, kind of like Rosenberg or Blumstein, I could pass him off to Dad as a Jew. I had no idea in hell that Cruikshank was a Scottish name.

Ron, who knew nothing of my scheme, sauntered up to the door and rang the bell.

I invited him in and introduced him to Dad, who immediately drew his face so close to Ron's that that their noses almost touched. Then, staring Ron straight in the eyes Dad asked, "Ron, who is your father?"

Ron just stood there stunned. I'd not prepared him for this attack. In fact, Ron didn't even know I was Jewish. I had no clue that Dad would know Ron wasn't Jewish the minute he heard his name, much less once laid eyes on him.

When Ron didn't respond, Dad pushed his finger into Ron's chest, saying, "What synagogue do you belong to?" Punctuating each word with a jab into Ron's chest.

A pause.

Then, Dad started again, "Who. Is. Your. Father?"

In the light of Dad's interrogation, my cheeks burned red. I was completely panicked, powerless, and embarrassed.

My stunned gentleman caller ran out our front door into the night.

I flew to my bedroom, slammed and locked the door, then collapsed into a crying heap.

Dad followed and knocked on the door, repeatedly shouting my name. I refused to answer. Finally, I yelled, "Go away!"

Stunned, Harvey watched from the hall as Dad opened the palm of his gigantic hand and smashed out the upper panel of my solid wood bedroom door, reached in and turned the lock.

Once inside he yelled at the top of his lungs, "This fiasco is over once and for all. I'll decide who you can date and who you can't. Good, see."

Then he pulled his big hand back like he was going to smack me in the face. I ducked. He turned and stomped away. I closed my door, then collapsed onto my bed in tears.

Sweet 16 in Ponte Vedra

The Love Machine

THE NIGHT DAD chased Ron out of the house, he succeeded in teaching me the lesson that boys weren't welcome in my life unless, that is, they were Jewish. *Hmm*, I thought, as I closed my eyes to go to sleep, *I'm the only Jewish kid in my high school. It looks like the only way I'll have a social life is to tell Dad I'm going out with a girlfriend or, better yet, spending the night with one.*

At four on the dot, Tommy's beat up Volkswagen Bug, "The Love Machine," squealed into the parking lot of Cedar Creek Bowl and slammed on the brakes in front of Marsha and me. Tommy leaned over and flung the passenger door open. Marsha reached inside and folded down the front seat so Oscar, a guy in my Algebra class I'd recently developed a crush on, and I could climb in the back, then plopped herself down next to Tommy. A crackling version of The Beach Boys' "Surfin' Safari" blasted from the radio.

In our school, students fell into one of three categories—the first two groups were the cool kids. The "preppies" from Ortega, a wealthy suburb across the river from my neighborhood. Most of the cheerleaders and football players in our school fell into this group. The "greasers" were usually the children of military folks—they were a rough bunch who rode motorcycles and drag-raced on Friday nights—they were usually the best dancers. The rest were nerdy kids nobody wanted to hang out with. I had friends in all three groups.

Baby-faced Oscar was a preppie. He looked snappy and wholesome in his Kelly green Izod golf shirt and Beatles mop top hair style.

Tommy, Marsha's date, was a greaser, who combed his hair in a D.A., or ducktail, like the singer Conway Twitty. He was ruggedly handsome in his denim shirt with the sleeves rolled up, but his pock-marked face told a story of a tough life.

Dad had been short-tempered and irrational the last few weeks. I knew he was still angry about catching me trying to pass off Ron Cruikshank as Jewish, so I had a slim chance of getting out of the house for the weekend. If I was gonna spring myself out, I'd have to dream up a whopper of a scam.

Sometimes desperation triggers creativity. It took only five minutes for the idea to arrive: I'd ask if I could spend the night with Marsha and she'd ask if she could stay at my house. Then we'd go out dancing and hang out on the beach until dawn and then head home. It was brilliant. Dad thought Marsha was a good influence. This I found hilarious, given she was the sneakiest hell-raiser I knew.

I bragged on myself to Marsha telling her, "It takes a genius to come up with a scam that's absolutely foolproof."

Tommy lowered the volume and turned around. "How ya' doin' girls?"

I flashed him my cheesy smile, then said, "Not as good as the Beach Boys but better'n you two."

"Surf's up!" Tommy yelled,

Oscar sang, "Surfin' safari..."

We oowee-ooed together as we bombed west on Beach Boulevard toward the Atlantic. With any luck, we'd reach Ponte Vedra before sunset—I couldn't wait to see the huge alabaster dunes.

Oscar reached in his rucksack and grabbed four Dixie cups, leaned his head against my shoulder, then stretched to reach the cooler squeezed between our legs and pulled out a bottle of Southern Comfort.

"Here hold 'em...steady now," he said, handing me two white cups.

"My drink ready?" Tommy asked, reaching his arm toward the back seat—then swerving to avoid a pothole, causing the car to sway back and forth for what seemed like a very long minute before finally righting itself.

"Jeez man, cool it," piped Oscar.

Ginger ale had spilled all over my thigh.

"Plop, plop, fizz, fizz, oh what a relief it is," sang Oscar, dropping a couple of ice cubes in my cup, stirring it with his pinky.

"Here ya go, big guy," he said, passing Tommy a drink. "And, madam," as he gave a little head nod, handing Marsha hers.

I gripped our drinks tightly, waiting for Oscar to slide the whiskey and ginger ale back in their rightful places. Then, as I handed him his cup, I let go of a long exhale as the smoky, smooth, liquid caressed my throat and flowed into my body. My muscles and mind began to unwind.

I reached over and squeezed his hand.

"Sure needed this break, Osky."

He broke into a wide grin, winked and squeezed my hand, then said, "We can always count on Wilma to show us a good time."

"Wilma" was the formal name of Tommy's VW dune buggy, named after Fred Flintstone's wife—though we mostly called her the Love Machine. The music changed to Little Eva belting "The Loco-Motion."

Marsha and I broke into song as the boys swilled down their drinks and we continued speeding toward the beach.

Once the car began to slow, I knew Tommy had spotted the access road. He pulled to a stop across the road from the dunes. Marsha jumped out first. I squeezed past her and threw the bag of pimento cheese slices from the cooler into her turquoise striped tote bag. Next came the saltines, Vienna sausages, and Lay's Potato Chips. I wrangled two blankets out of the trunk, rolling mine on the hood of the car and tossing one to Marsha. The boys grabbed the cooler handles, struggling to haul the bulky thing across the street.

"Whoa, slow down, this is heavy, man," said Oscar.

"Aw, stop your whining," chimed Tommy with a twinge of distain.

I winced. His sarcasm set me to wondering whether his father spoke that way to his mother. I felt bad for Osky, who was smaller as they stumbled against the wind, fighting the deep shifting sand in the moonlight.

A few feet behind them, Marsha and I wandered down the sand, busting up laughing about how silly the boys looked—and how hilarious it was that our parents had believed our story.

"Are we the coolest, or what?" I yelled, throwing my fist in the air in a victory salute.

"Yes, ma'am," Marsha hollered back.

"Hey, guys, we're gonna wade a few minutes—race ya, Marsh!" I flung my shoes to the sand, running toward the moonlit ocean.

The boys stopped and set down the cooler, but didn't follow.

"It's so beautiful...the full moon...reflecting off the waves like that," I said, mesmerized. *What a mystery the ocean is,* I thought, *the way it can be both so delicate and so powerful. There's nothing I love more than watching that big ol' body of water churn and dance.*

The moonlight reflected the ocean's cyclical journey back to the shoreline.

"Marsh, did you ever stop to think that the ocean here is the same ocean that's in New York—or even in England?"

"Let's just go par-tay, oh-kaay?" She replied, her focus elsewhere. Even in the dark, I could see she rolled her eyes.

"Gimme another few minutes."

I sat on the edge of the shoreline, imagining a lone fisherman waist-deep in the blue-black shallows, casting a net into the pulsating waves, then walking back and forth, coaxing it this way and that to gather his catch, finally pulling the net back toward him. The apparition faded into a mediation—I felt such peace by the sea.

"C'mon let's get over the dunes," Marsha yelled, disrupting my musings.

"Just another minute, Marsh—God worked really hard on this painting." *And,* I thought, *I'd like to spend a little more time with the fisherman.*

Reluctant to leave, I took in one last, deep, breath of salty air then stepped backward, slowly, so as to drink in the beauty of it all before heading up the dune.

After reaching my tennis shoes, I wiped the sand off my feet with a blanket, then carried on—glad Marsh was leading as we fought the wind—on our trek up the steep, shifting sand dune. I had to repeatedly stop to dump sand out of my low-tops, squinting to keep it out of my eyes. For a time I walked barefoot, but the broken twigs buried under the sand were treacherous.

Once finally at the top, I turned my back to the wind and arched, stretching my arms above me, like the girl in the famous Maxfield Parrish painting, throwing my head backward and shaking it to try to get the sand out of my hair, then unfurled my blanket.

"Each one take a corner," I yelled to the wind, crouching down to fight the gusts, working to get the blanket to stay flat. When it wouldn't cooperate, I threw myself in the middle, creating a human weight. Oscar joined me.

"C'mon guys, let's take a break. Come join Osky and me," I shouted to Tommy and Marsha. "Ready for hors d'oeuvres, fellow partiers?" I asked.

"If one of you'll make me a cocktail, I'll do the honors" said Marsha.

"Sure, I'll have me some whore's ovaries any old time of day," piped Tommy.

"Marsh, give me a hand," I said, wrestling with the Saltines package, until I bit a small opening along the waxed paper edge careful to keep them from flying onto the sand. "I'll put the cheese on if you'll cut up the Vienna sausage, Marsha."

Once each little snack was finished, I announced. "Well, sports fans, I'll be damned if they don't look like gen-u-ine appetizers," passing the plate around while Marsha handed each of us a napkin with a handful of potato chips in the middle.

"Too bad you didn't remember to bring pickles, Sherlock," teased Marsha.

"Hey guys, look—the wind has finally died down" said Oscar.

"Yeah, the pickles would've been a nice addition, Watson," I replied.

Oscar jumped up, stretching out his arms wide like he'd just conquered the tallest mountain, "Nothing like a great dinner and some ocean air to revive a chap, whew!" he said, patting himself on the chest. Then he exhaled, threw himself down on the blanket, flipped onto his side, leaned on his elbow, and propped his head up with his hand, "I could get used to this." He flashed me a wry smile.

Tommy monkeyed with his transistor radio, trying to pick up a signal. "Hey, shush y'all, I think I got WAPE."

We quieted and leaned in, waiting for the Tarzan yodel—the Big Ape's trademark—to verify whether he'd succeeded in dialing in our favorite station.

Once the crackly rock and roll began flowing out of the radio, Oscar jumped up and yelped, "Hey, Daddy-o, I think you done did it."

I joined him, singing along to "He's a Rebel" and pointing to Oscar on the "rebel" part.

The song changed and Chubby Checker started crooning about "The Twist"—everybody jumped to their feet.

"How low can you go?" chimed Tommy. Then again, "How low can you go?"

I twisted carefully on the uneven sand, trying to keep from getting my feet tangled in the blanket, while still twisting all the way down then back up again. I'd done it a hundred times, but this time I was trying not to spill the drink in my hand.

Marsha stopped me and said, "Hey, I gotta go visit my Chinese friend, Toi Let, come with me?"

Together, we sloshed through the sand toward the sawgrass on the downward side of our cream-colored mountain.

"Y'all come back now, ya hear?" called Oscar after us.

"Yes, sir, Colonel," I played back.

Once we were out of earshot Marsha whispered, "What do you think they're gonna try tonight?"

"Dunno, but only first base for me." It didn't occur to me that the boys were hoping to go all the way.

Marsha and I knew each other so well that we didn't have to discuss the details—that we were up for some necking, but we were both still virgins—and had no plans to lose our virginity that very night. But, gawd, we were having a great time getting drunk and laughing—well, until, that is, I stood to pull up my shorts.

"Whoa, Marsh. I feel like my head is spinning on my shoulders. Shit, something bit my foot," I said, and while reaching down to scratch it, almost fell over.

Marsha pointed, "Look!"

I had to scrunch my eyes to see them, but damn if we hadn't been squatting in the middle of a swarm of mosquitos and sand fleas.

We ran back to the boys.

"Jeezus, guys, we're being attacked," I said, gathering up the blankets. "We gotta go back to the car right this minute. C'mon."

"Calm down, girls," said Tommy. "We don't wanna leave—hell, we just got here."

"Yeah, man," echoed Oscar.

Neither of them were about to have their plans ruined by a few bugs, never mind a couple of screaming girls.

"Help me with this blanket, Osky," I said, ignoring their dismisses, and handed him a corner of the blanket, then ran out a few feet and shook the sand off of it.

Tommy walked over, reluctantly, to help Marsha. I was operating on pure insect adrenaline—I hated mosquitos, nothing was going to stop me. I grabbed Osky's corner of the blanket and rolled it fast like a crazy woman, then helped Marsha throw the leftover food into the cooler and beach bag. Then, again, experienced the sensation of the entire planet rotating around me.

"Dangit," I said as we zig-zagged our way down the steep sand.

I fell twice, pulled myself up, and continued hopping down the steep drop-off, which seemed a lot higher than on the way up.

Finally on the beach, we stumbled our drunk asses toward Wilma and climbed in.

We'd left the windows down to keep the car cool upon our return. But as soon as we sat down, we heard a concert of mosquitos buzzing around our heads.

"Quick roll the windows up!"

"Great, now we're trapped in a car full of buzzing blood suckers," I piped, then pondered aloud, "Do y'all think we brought them with us from the dunes or these are new ones?"

"I have an idea, guys," offered Tommy, "what if we roll all the windows down and drive north for a while. Maybe the wind will blow them skeeters outta the car." He backed up, turned the car around, and headed toward the highway.

I tapped Marsha on the shoulder, "Get this. Mom told me mosquitos particularly love redheads. She says our fair skin makes it easier for them to see our veins. Lucky you have olive-colored skin. The veins between my wrist and my elbow must look like a dang landing strip for the little buggers."

Nobody responded—my humor was the last thing anyone cared about. We rode in silence, waiting for the wind to work its magic.

The buzzing slowly subsided, though I didn't see them fly away. And for a minute I stopped itching, but realized it was a trick of the imagination.

"Think it worked, guys, let's pull over and park on the beach," said Tommy.

He drove Wilma off the highway onto a dirt road that led to the beach, slammed on the brakes, and turned around with, "Ta dah! All you little apes out there, I have an announcement." He did the Tarzan yodel like the Big Ape, the radio station mascot, then made his hands into a megaphone. "Intermission is officially over— the party has resumed."

A hush came over the car, as though we were all pondering the same thought: *Guess there's only one thing to do, try to forget about the itching and proceed with making out.*

In the backseat Oscar leaned over and started French kissing me, while struggling to undo my bra strap.

Marsha and Tommy twisted and gyrated, emitting assorted oohs and aahs. Marsha's seat was so far back it crushed my knees as she thrashed about. Then, suddenly, the car got quiet—but my itching had become unbearable—I was damn near tearing the skin off my legs, rendering whatever Oscar's hormones were trying to convey, pointless.

I tried to change the mood with a joke, "Hey, guys, you know why only the girl mosquitos bite? It's God's way of punishing the boys for leaving the toilet seat up."

Nobody laughed.

"Can you just pipe down?" pleaded Tommy, still trying to make out with Marsha.

"Is anybody else itchy?" I asked.

"Yeah, a little," said Oscar. "You know it might be sand fleas."

"Be quiet," Tommy urged, leaning back over toward Marsha.

"You're ruining the mood," Marsha added.

"Well, in case anyone is interested, I feel like my skin is on fire," I half-mumbled.

Our bug-infested terrarium was now a prison of our own making. And, as far as I was concerned, no amount of hormones or hard-ons could stop the sensation of being eaten alive. Now, at almost three o'clock in the morning, we had no choice but to ride it out. Sexy mood squelched, I said, "We may as well head into town, guys."

Marsha squirreled around to straighten out her clothes.

The boys voiced their various, "Aw shits, craps, and, damns," eventually giving way to a frustrated exhale from Tommy and, finally, a reticent "all right," from Oscar.

"Just take us back to the bowling alley," I directed.

I figured if we got dropped off there Marsha and I could figure out where to hang out until daybreak. Tommy put the radio on and the front of the car fell silent on the ride back to town.

"Whelp, sorry guys," I muttered, "that this night didn't turn out like we hoped."

Still, Oscar, not one to give up easily, tried to get his hand up my blouse while sucking on my neck.

"Stop—what do you think I am, a barbecued rib from Bonos?" I asked, referring to Lou Bono's, a favorite teen hangout.

I fought him off by pinching the tender part of his forearm, a stunt I'd learned from Mom. Finally, he subsided, and a funereal hush came over the last leg of the drive like the family dog had died or something. We were midway through our saga and I couldn't wait for it to be over.

Finally, we turned from Blanding Boulevard and to Lakeshore, and the car screeched to a halt in front of the bowling alley.

I'd already gathered my things, ready to jump out of the car the minute it stopped. Though the mood was tense, I felt I should say something, so I muttered an awkward, "Well, uh, goodnight."

After the boys drove off, I looked to Marsha and shrugged. She did the same.

"Not exactly the romantic night we were aiming for, huh?"

"Nope," she sighed.

Nope. With a single word, Marsha summed up the miserable night—and an entire week's worth of planning and scheming. Then she asked, with a dirty look, "What the hell are we gonna do for the next five hours, genius?"

I grimaced, held my chin, and thoughtfully bobbed my head up and down for a minute, "Hmm...Let me think, Watson. I know! Let's go over to Robin's, I bet her parents are gone."

Robin's mom was a nurse who worked the night shift and her father, an alcoholic, was often at a bar 'till the early hours.

"You stay in front and I'll go around back and tap on her window," I said once we got to the house.

"Fingers crossed."

It didn't take more than a couple of tiny taps for Robin to move her bedroom curtain aside.

"What? Gaby, what are you doing here?" Robin asked, half asleep.

"I need to come in. Are your parents' gone?"

I heard her feet hit the floor and pad her way toward the front door. "C'mon, hurry," she said, ushering us in, "Dad'll be home any minute. What the hell? The two of you look like warmed over shit."

"We were at the beach all night and got bitten to hell and back," I replied, confirming there was a reason we were such a mess.

She ran to the bathroom, returned with two bottles and some cotton. "Here, first rub some of this alcohol on your bites, then put on some calamine lotion," she said, nursing us.

Pretty sure calamine lotion is just pink food coloring mixed with flour and water. It didn't help when I had the chicken pox and it ain't helping now, I thought, but did as she told.

"Thanks, Robin," I said aloud, remembering my manners.

I told her all about our scheme and the horrible night. She suggested we try to get some shuteye. The three of us piled in her double bed and talked, laughed, and scratched until the sun came up.

Around 8:30 I walked with Marsha to the Cedar Creek Bridge, then headed for home.

There was dew on the grass and the morning birds were chirping as I tiptoed to the door, using the hidden key to let myself in. Quietly, I eased the door open so as not to wake Dad, then gently pulled out the bottom drawer of my dresser for some pajamas, careful not to awaken Paulina—and caught a glimpse of myself in the mirror.

"Jesus," I had to stop myself from squealing, "Oh my God."

My entire neck was covered in black and blue marks. Hickeys.

I grabbed a scarf, fumbling as I tried to fashion an ascot out of it, then hurried to my closet for a bathrobe, and realized I had to pee. Pulling the bathrobe tightly around me, I drew up the collar far as I could—hoping it would hold the ascot in place—and headed toward the bathroom.

After only a few steps, Dad's bedroom door creaked open. His big head leaned out. "What are you doing back so early?"

I sped up toward the bathroom and mumbled, "Marsha wanted to go to early Mass, so I asked her Mom if she'd drop me off on the way."

"Don't wake your sister," he ordered, turning back to his room.

I breathed a sigh of relief, then unwrapped the scarf and pulled off my robe to examine my neck more closely.

"Oh my God, passion marks," I said out loud, then caught myself, retreating to an inner dialogue. *Well, shit, Oscar must've done this when he was sucking on my neck. All I want is to take a shower and go to sleep. But, no, I can't shower now, I need to get in bed and think.*

I threw my robe back on, and grabbed the silky ascot, again attempting to cover the marks. *Now, if only I could get back to my bedroom.* The damn scarf kept slipping so I held it with one hand while scurrying down the hall. Just as I grabbed the door handle, breathing a sigh of relief, I saw Dad—standing in the hall, and dressed for the day—barreling toward me.

"What are your plans for the day, daughta?" he asked, in a rather jovial mood.

"Umm," I said looking at the floor, casually turning the door handle and trying to step forward into my bedroom, "I'm gonna sleep a little longer, I think."

"Wait," Dad said, as he came closer craning his neck, then lowered his glasses for a closer look.

His eyes looked like they were going to pop clean out of his head. "What the hell happened to your neck?" He demanded, a mix of angry and confused.

"Well, uh, Kip and I were wrestling last night and he grabbed my neck, pretending he was going to choke me...it doesn't hurt or anything, he was just kidding," I sputtered.

Kip was Marsha's older brother.

"Well, that is the stupidest damn thing I've ever heard. I'm going to call Mrs. Kraus right this minute."

He stormed down the hall to the kitchen, and picked up the wall phone.

I followed after him.

"What's her phone number?" He asked, pointing to the phone. Then, "Never mind, here, you dial it."

He handed me the receiver.

Scrambled Eggs and Civil Rights

Freedom Rider mugshots, 1961

ONE LATE AFTERNOON in 1962, I returned home from school to find Paulina and Benny, ages seven and five, lying on the hardwood floor in their underpants under the attic fan—waiting for it to work its magic. A couple of years earlier when Paulina damn near cut her toe off, Dad outlawed portables, so here we were again—trying to come up with creative means to endure the stinky-ass Florida heat. And stinky ass it was. So much so that little Benny invented new words to describe the prickly heat rash that made our behinds go from pink to purplish-red as they chaffed and stung. Nothing helped soothe it. Not even the copious amounts of Panthoderm cream we applied to our stinging behinds.

We kids widely adopted Benny's newly-coined word for the

initial, pink and annoying, stage—"the hoosh." Then Paulina named the later stage—the flaming-red baboon ass—"the squeem."

Over the past few days we were fighting bad cases of the hoosh and the squeem, so we took to standing in the cold shower—a rare moment of relief—until hair and bodies were soaked and shivering, then we'd lay down shoulder-to-shoulder on the hardwood beneath the attic fan, until the water droplets evaporated. We'd spend hours taking turns in and out of the shower stall on brutally hot afternoons like these. The little kids found momentary contentment, but eventually they'd give up on the shower-evaporation cycle and return to being hot and miserable.

As the oldest, I long ago appointed myself Chief of Cooling Operations—inclusive of both actually cooling, and scheduled distractions to mitigate awareness of the heat. Sensing the shower cycle was coming to a swift end, I turned on the TV in search something to capture their attention. While scrolling the channels looking for cartoons, the airwaves were interrupted by footage of riots that had just broken out in Mississippi. I paused a moment to listen, then kept scrolling, eventually landing on *Truth or Consequences*, and called for Benny and Paulina to come watch. After they were settled, I headed to my bedroom where Harvey and I took turns spraying each other with a plastic water bottle while dancing to Chubby Checker's "The Twist."

"It really is a miracle that a piece of plastic can make sounds, don't you think?" I pondered aloud, looking at the small black plastic 45 RPM record spinning away on the turntable.

Harv smiled and gave a quick nod, then resumed wiggle dancing to Chubby.

We were making good use of the light blue suitcase-style phonograph Mom bought me for my birthday with her S & H green stamps—one of the few times Dad didn't pick a fight with Mom for spending money on my present.

Motown sounds were alive and kicking, providing the soundtrack to our lives. Lately, if Harv and I weren't singing rhythm and blues or soul classics, we were practicing our falsettos—singing "Maria" from *West Side Story*, Harvey's favorite.

"Remember that time Mom tried to teach Dad how to do the twist?" asked Harvey, sputtering out a laugh.

"Gawd, Harv, didn't they look hilarious standing in front of each other, gyrating around?"

As Harv and I twisted away, we recounted—amidst laughter—the recent evening Mom overheard us play "The Twist," and ran to get Dad.

"Here, Max, grab this towel," she commanded, throwing him a bath towel—which he caught in midair. "Here's how you do it," she instructed. You stick your right toe out in front of you and twist it on the ground—like you're putting out a cigarette with your foot—while moving your tuchus like you're drying off with the towel."

Our parents' short-lived interest in learning to partner dance was ignited when they were offered a free class at Arthur Murray by a phone solicitor. In recent months, they'd spent most evenings practicing in the living room by following the guide of feet, numbers and arrows drawn on a plastic tarp. Most nights, they waited to practice until we kids were all in bed—but after they thought we were asleep, Harv and I snuck into the hall, trying to suppress our laughter, as we watched them pace through the cha-cha, rhumba, and foxtrot.

Our moment of reminiscing screeched to an abrupt halt as the sound of the heavy wooden front door slammed—so loud the record player needle jumped. Paulina, eight, ran into my room holding little Benny's hand, whispering loudly, "Come here, y'all! Hurry—you are not going to believe this."

We held hands, walking slowly to the edge of the hall, then peered into the living room where crazy Dad stood in a sweat-soaked white T-shirt and paint-stained khakis. Hearing his four kids scuffle nearby, Dad glanced our direction, and because I was closest to the doorway, his angry gaze met my eyes first. I fanned my hand behind me to signal the younger kids to hide. For a brief second Dad's and my eyes locked—fury was written all over his face. The veins in his jowly neck swelled, cheeks burned red, and brown eyes looked as if they were fixing to bulge clean out of his head. Little Benny shivered behind me, crying, Paulina laughed nervously, Harvey was stunned.

Horrified, I tried to speak, but only managed two words, "D-Dad, what," before looking down to the end of his muscular left arm, where he held a cardboard egg carton, then the eggs clutched in his right hand.

"So," he said in his deep, slow-motion voice, pacing back and forth. Then he exhaled, heaving an egg at the defenseless front door.

He continued, "One of the guys at work told me that the best stress reliever he knows is to break something."

He paused. Then threw another two eggs. "I figured eggs were as a good candidate as any, see?" he said, as if in a meditation.

He heaved a fourth egg at the door.

With a quick smack-crunch, the gooey yellow and transparent membranes mingled with pieces of eggshell and slid down the wooden door. Frozen with shock, the four of us kids looked on from the safety of the hall as our father—the one-man egg smasher— emptied the entire carton. Once out of eggs, he drew a deep breath, paused, and released a long exhale. Then he cocked his head, stepped back, wiping his hands on his pants, crossed his arms and admired his handiwork as though gazing upon a fine work of art.

My heart raced, fueled by the familiar surge of Dad-related adrenaline. Not knowing what might happen next, I pulled Benny and Paulina to the relative safety of my bedroom—Harvey was already there waiting for us.

I say relative because the upper panel of my bedroom door was only duct-tape strong—since earlier when Dad busted it—and after this display atop the other outbursts, I feared what he might do next. For all the good it would do, I went ahead and locked the door anyway. We piled onto my bed where I tried to dispel Benny's and Paulina's fear by distracting them with a task—proposing we watch for Mom's baby blue two-door Nash Rambler out the picture window. It worked.

"Well this is sure a new one, huh, Harv?"

He shook his head while making a circular motion with his finger around his ear, signifying, "He's cuckoo for Cocoa Puffs." Then said, "I sure hope Mom gets home soon."

The fifteen minutes it took for Mom's car to pull around the corner into the driveway felt like an eternity. Mom wasn't terribly successful in dealing with Dad, but at least with her home we had another adult nearby.

The sound of the screen door creaked open and Mom's spiked high heels tapped across the linoleum floor into the living room, lending a momentary feeling of relief. Now, a bit less frightened, we resumed our post in the hallway, waiting for Mom to discover Dad's mess. Upon entering the living room, she found Dad lying on our faded pink couch with protruding stuffing, looking like Emmett Kelly, the sad clown.

"Waddaya doin', Max? Where are the kids?" She inquired with a twinge of concern. Then lowered her glasses, craning her neck so as to glance out onto the screened porch, looking for us. Seeing the living room door in her periphery she stopped, squinted, and walked toward it, finally turning to Dad, asking, "What the hell is this?" as she squatted, surveying the pile of eggshells and crumpled egg carton on the floor. As she stood, raising her gaze, the raw yellow yoke splatters came into view.

"Max! What the hell happened?" she shouted, exasperated.

Dad tried to conjure a reply but couldn't find a sensible excuse for destroying a dozen eggs. Finally, he said quietly and defeated, "I, uh, was trying to release some anger and frustration I've been feeling lately, Ruth."

"So, as tight as money is, you waste a dozen eggs? Waddaya, crazy? We needed those for breakfast tomorrow."

Deadpan. No emotion. Just facts.

This was Mom's way of responding to most any crisis—made more annoying by the brashness of her Yankee accent. She reverted to the lowest common denominator, relying on the only weaponry she possessed—wise-ass New York retorts. Early on, I learned that complaining to her was simply not worth the effort. Her three go-to responses to any problem Harv or I voiced were:

"So, waddaya' want me to do about it?"

"Waddaya want, an egg in your beer?"

"The problem is, you're too sensitive."

Mom came into her marriage with the skills needed for challenges no more complicated than writing checks for bills, keeping kids dressed in the latest fashions, and handling the day-to-day running of the house, which, in many respects, fell on Willie. Now that Dad's finances were in a downward spiral, Mom's lack of problem-solving abilities became even more magnified as she found herself, in what we teenagers in the South described as, "up to her eyeballs in alligator shit."

The life Mom imagined when she boarded the train from New York to Florida—the Promised Land, the Sunshine State—was a foggy, distant, memory. Her fairy-tale prince had metamorphosed into a guy whose anger was triggered by even the most inane detail—and Mom's skills lacked the tools needed to tighten Dad's screws or extinguish his fire. So she did what came naturally, pulled out her arsenal of wisecracks.

In a manner of speaking, her verbal defense was effective in that it served two purposes. First, succeeding in distracting Dad long enough to slow him, giving him time to gather himself. Second, acting as a release valve for her own anger while helping her feel she had some small amount of control so she could make headway toward something practical, like getting dinner on the table.

Now, after observing Mom's anger toward Dad over the eggs, it seemed prudent for us to wait out the remaining storm of Hurricane Dad in my bedroom. I figured it wouldn't be long before He went into his room, signaling the demon of madness had retreated. So I waited for the sounds to know it was safe to climb out of our foxhole.

This day, it only took about five minutes. Once his door clunked closed, the four of us bee-lined to the living room, sitting in wait, cross-legged on the hardwoods, for the TV to work its magic. I couldn't wait for the perfect reality of *Leave it to Beaver* to lighten the mood, but no sooner than breathing a sigh of relief, Mom screeched my name, calling to help make a salad. Ensuring a regular nightly dinner routine was one of the few touchstones helping Mom make sense of our wacky life.

"Haavey, come in heah and set the table," she called into the living room.

Although the question hung on our tongues, we knew better than to ask what had pissed Dad off this time.

There was an unwritten rule disallowing voicing anything that smacked of disrespect to our parents. Dad could yell insults at Mom, and she could argue, make unpleasant faces, and whine sarcastically to him, but we kids couldn't say a damn thing about either of them to the other.

I watched as Mom used her fingers to grab, and abruptly pile, sliced corned beef and cabbage on our plates—a sight that disgusted me. The disdain she displayed toward the simple act of serving a meal did little to inspire an appetite.

Dad's eggy angst was a new variation of his rage—this one even stranger than cutting off the plug on the television monster.

By the time he slunk into the kitchen for dinner, we all pretended the egg debacle had never even happened. We knew if we spoke, we'd likely set off another angry outburst. So we sat in complete silence, inhaling the humid, dread-filled, air.

"How come you do me like you do" played on a loop in my head.

By the age of fourteen, I'd seen so many of Dad's hysterical episodes that I knew today's antics foretold only the tip of the iceberg. These were the kinds of evenings when a simple mispronunciation from Harv or me could provoke him to reaching across the table and smacking us in the mouth. So we ate silently, all the time anxiously searching for a signal for when we could safely be excused, knowing when it finally came, disappearing to our bedrooms would be the order of the evening.

My suspicion turned out to be correct, that Dad's ability to maintain control would continue to deteriorate. Within months, we'd discover that his eggy theatrics were but a preview of coming attractions to a movie none of us wanted to see, a film of six people drifting out to sea in a lifeboat taking on water.

Miss Sue in Saint Augustine

Black college students sit in protest at a whites-only lunch counter

Miss Sue, Miss Sue,
Miss Sue from Alabama.
Sitting in her rocker,
Eating Betty Crocker,
Watching the clock go
Tick-tock, tick-tock banana rock
Tick-tock, tick-tock banana rock.
A B C D E F G
Wash those spots right off of me.
OOsha mama, oosha mama,
Oosha mama, FREEZE!

HARV AND I were down to our last "oosha mama, oosha mama." "Miss Sue," a jump rope rhyme from the turn of the 20th century, has an interesting history. It was allegedly about a Black prostitute that lured white men to bed then manipulated them into doing favors for the Black men on the plantation. As usual we sang our way home from the movies walking to the rhythm of the beat, when we pushed open the back door. The stiff, humid air hit me straight on. Summer had just begun and my primary goal was to survive the three months without getting put on restriction.

Hearing us enter, Willie scurried into the kitchen, appearing rattled, a sure sign she'd been watching TV. She relaxed when she realized it was just Harv and me.

"What movie did y'all see?" she asked.

"Oh, a film called *Dr. No*, Will, about a British spy. I loved it."

"Me too," echoed Harv.

It was the first in the long series of James Bond films I followed throughout my life.

"Can I fix you some sweet tea?" she asked, pulling down glasses from the shelf.

"Sure," we replied.

While Willie fixed the tea, Harvey and I migrated to the living room television, watching as twenty college-age Negro protestors were led out of Woolworths in Saint Augustine for attempting to eat at the food counter—their protest a response to the death threats the Ku Klux Klan were leveling against the local activists. The civil rights movement had been gaining steam under the leadership of a black dentist named Dr. Hayling, who publicly declared that if the KKK didn't back off, his group would defend themselves with firearms. On this perspective, Hayling was at odds with Martin Luther King—who didn't believe in using weapons in the fight for social justice. The poor kids at Woolworths eventually ended up in reform school for a term of six months.

Willie handed us the tea while directing our attention to President Kennedy, speaking on the news. But she was so busy screeching, "Hallelujah!" we could hardly hear the President's words.

"Thank the good Lord that president's gonna' show the world once and for all they can't stop our people from attending any college we want," she hollered, carrying on.

"It has been over a hundred years since President Lincoln freed the slaves, yet they are not fully free," Kennedy began.

She gave an enthusiastic, "Amen!"

Our handsome young president's speech was music to Willie's ears.

"The time has come for this nation to fulfill its promise," he continued.

Another "Amen!" from Willie.

President Kennedy went on to say he was working on a bill called The Civil Rights Act, in which he would call on all Americans to finally end discrimination against Negros.

"Will, do you think he wrote this speech because of having to send the National Guard to Alabama to protect those two kids trying to enroll in the university?"

"Maybe it was the final straw, child," responded Willie.

The president continued, "This moral issue is as old as the Scriptures and as clear as the American Constitution."

"You tell it, President. Hallelujah! I say, Hallelujah! Can I get an amen?" Willie shouted, shaking her torso and raising palms to the air.

Together Harvey and I yelled, "Amen!"

Then Willie danced around the living room.

"It's about damn time, Willie," I said,

"Sure is," chimed Harv.

I smiled wide and looked to our nanny, caregiver, friend... family with so much love I thought my heart might just explode right that minute. I loved seeing Willie so full of hope.

But it wouldn't last for long. The very next morning Willie showed up for work wearing a sad face.

"I'm sorry, Will," I said, putting my arm around her shoulder.

We both knew without speaking that several hours after the President's speech, Medgar Evers, the Secretary of the NAACP who'd been working to overturn segregation at the University of Mississippi, was shot to death at his home in Decatur, Georgia.

I watched the horror on television. She'd heard it on the radio.

"You can kill a man, but you can't kill an idea," Medgar Evers said—a quote that would resonate long into the future fight for the civil rights that lay ahead.

The world seemed like it was going crazy—and it was. Life was imitating art, and the Mack Family of Jacksonville, Florida was not immune.

One weekend in the early 1960s, before the racial protests grew in their frequency and intensity, our family took an afternoon ride to St. Augustine. Dad loved the historical merit of the place, especially Castillo de San Marcos, the elaborate four-pointed Spanish fort built in 1672 on Matanzas Bay. He explained that the fort was made of something called coquina rock—a mixture of crushed seashells and sand.

"If you look closely, you can see the tiny shells peeking out of the cement," he instructed, leaning in toward the rock wall.

The drawbridge over the moat leading to the fort was my favorite part, and on this day a baby shark swam in the water below, a special treat. Once inside, we were led to tiny cave-like rooms with heavy iron chains mounted into the thick walls, where prisoners had been kept. Then we climbed to the roof, fortified by cannons posted every five feet.

"The fort's construction took the Spanish twenty-three years," Dad explained, "And they used it to imprison all kinds of Indians— the most famous was the Seminole Chief, Osceola."

There was only one door in and out of the entire fort, making it particularly eerie.

Next, Dad, who never missed an opportunity to share a historically significant event with us, walked us over to the "slave market" in the middle of the town square. The iron shackles that bound the slaves waiting to be sold to a new master was a grim reminder of how cruel humankind could be.

"And this is where slaves were sold like livestock." He motioned with his muscular arm, grimacing. "They hurt and killed people and even separated families—it was an abomination," Dad expounded, with one of his fifty-dollar words.

The sheer notion of it sent chills down my spine. It was a gut-wrenching sight. I imagined ships pulling into the nearby bay, unloading the poor people who'd been kidnapped from their homes in Africa and made prisoners, then auctioned off as slaves.

Our third stop was "the oldest wooden schoolhouse," my favorite place. Each time we visited, my parents bought me a little brown clay baby with jointed arms and legs, wearing a diaper, to add to my collection. They called the little dolly a "Pickaninny," a word that took years for me to fully understand.

The first slaves brought to America arrived in Saint Augustine in 1565, so it seemed fitting that St. Augustine had become a pivotal site the Civil Rights Movement's success.

As I pondered the image of the poor slaves being sold in the town square, I thought about Willie.

The days of slavery were over, but everywhere I looked I still saw injustice toward anybody who wasn't a white-skinned Christian.

No less than a month after our trip to St. Augustine, the Klan staged a rally of over three hundred Klansmen on the outskirts of town, seizing Dr. Robert Hayling and three other NAACP activists, beating them with fists, chains, and clubs. The four Black men were rescued by Florida Highway Patrol officers. The four white men were arrested for the beating, but blamed the four unarmed Blacks for starting the fight. Eventually, all the charges against the Klansmen were dismissed, while Dr. Hayling was convicted of "criminal assault" against the KKK mob.

The outcome of the trial only escalated tensions, and within a month a carload of KKK night riders raced through the black neighborhood of Lincolnville, randomly shooting into homes. A firefight broke out, leaving one Klansman dead. The racial tension and violence continued unchecked for another year.

One Saturday, Harvey and I rode the bus downtown, stumbling into a huge parade of Klansmen marching in the middle of the street. We guessed there were at least four hundred people dressed in white sheets and pointed hoods—it was a shocking sight. But once we saw, in detail, the costumes of men in front of the pack, we couldn't help laughing. The Grand Dragon donned a green satin cape with matching hood, and the Imperial Wizard a white satin cape with red lining—but we dubbed the award winner for the "most ridiculous getup" to the Exalted Cyclops, sporting a peach cape and huge pointed dunce cap with an enormous eye filling out the center.

"Remember that movie?" asked Harv, elbowing me in the ribs.

"Of course, how could I forget that horrible image."

A couple years earlier Dad had taken us to see *The Seventh Voyage of Sinbad*, and the cyclops roasting a sailor on a pit over an open fire was something neither of us could forget.

And much like the lingering memory of that terrible movie scene, Saint Augustine would continue to be a hotbed of civil unrest throughout the 1960s, leaving a painful memory seared in many minds into the future.

The Dallas Thomas Debacle

Dad being silly

THE FLORIDA TOURISM industry promoted the place as a warm, lazy piece of earth where a person could pick an orange off a tree then nap under a palm while sipping mint juleps all day—but there was a dark underpinning to our state.

Most folks had no way of knowing that in the first half of the century, Florida led the nation with the highest number of lynchings per capita. And that hatred didn't disappear when the lynchings stopped. It went underground—and was alive and well in North Florida. It was no secret that the Klan hated Jews almost as much as Blacks.

While I sympathized with Willie and her people, I was still struggling with severe digestive problems—and Dad's contract with the Navy Exchange had expired. He'd been unemployed for months and had taken to spending huge amounts of time in his room, which I recognized as a definite sign of trouble. A dark storm loomed on the horizon just beyond the rising sun of each new day.

For Dad, idle hands were, in fact, the devil's workshop. So when his brother Uly—a friend of City Commissioner Dallas Thomas—told Dad he could pull strings to get him a draftsman job at City Hall if he learned the skill, Dad figured he'd better force himself to sign up for a drafting class. Once enrolled, he approached it with all the enthusiasm of a prisoner facing a long, hot day on the chain gang.

Each morning as Dad left the house he said, "Get out the whip, Ruth, and send me back to the salt mines!" as he hunched over and walked slowly out the door with a grimace across his face.

Dad hated the idea of "drawing lines all day," something, he exclaimed, "a well-trained monkey could do." That he was a fine commercial artist and illustrator plain didn't seem to matter if he couldn't pay the bills. It would be a tedious and unfulfilling job—this he knew—but we were in desperate times.

"My unemployment checks aren't going to last forever—guess I have no choice but to try and learn to be an obedient monkey."

At least he'll be out of the house all day, I thought.

A quick study, Dad learned enough about drafting within the first few months that he could complete the daily tasks required at City Hall.

"The pay isn't great," he admitted, "but at least this way I'll have health insurance for the entire family and a steady paycheck," he reasoned.

Dad strived to take the high road by accepting the position, but over time the anguish of giving in to something so mundane—and so far beneath his skillset—eventually took its toll.

He started gaining weight, something he tried to fight by replacing his lunch calories with a can of Metrical each day—a chalky canned meal replacement that was all the rage in the early sixties. It came in fourteen different flavors, including the two newest—tuna and chicken noodle. Even those overwhelming flavor profiles did little to make the drink palatable. Many of his co-workers took to lacing their contents with liquor to make it tolerable enough to swallow.

He even took his photo of the giant orangutan standing next to Haystacks Calhoun, the 640-pound wrestler, and plastered it on the wall near his drafting table—trying to lighten the mood.

His first drafting assignment was to design and create more natural environments for the animals at our local zoo. Dad relished the notion that the settings that he designed might help the animals feel more at home than the current ones, which exhibited a strong sense of being held captive in the God-forsaken humidity. He loved animals and was passionate about doing something that had some lasting good.

While the project brought him a sense of purpose, one afternoon I overheard him say to Mom, "You know it's funny, Ruth, I'm really the animal in the cage in all of this. Honestly, every morning when I sit down at my drafting table I pray, 'God, please help me make it through this day,' then I watch the clock that barely seems to move."

Mom, who loved quoting old adages, reminded him, "A watched pot never boils."

I could tell from the look on Dad's face that Mom's words weren't the sympathetic, healing balm he was hoping for. Still, he needed a job and that was that.

The tediousness of the job was rewarded by one perk: free family passes to the zoo. The little kids and I were elated. Now, we could visit the animals any time we wanted—and go on the carnival rides for free. Each weekend after Sunday school, Dad walked us proudly around the zoo grounds, checking on the building progress of his new designs.

But, as the Hebrew saying goes, "Man plans, and God laughs."

After all Dad's hootin' and hollerin' about how he hated his job and didn't want to be a draftsman, he finally began to surrender to the idea that he was, indeed, a draftsman, accepting that the job wasn't all bad and admitting it still offered some creative opportunity. No sooner than he moved to this place of acceptance, bordering on contentment, he was to be ferreted out as collateral damage during the city's upcoming administrative purge.

This is how it shook out. There was an investigation centered around the massive building campaigns organized during the commissioner's time in office. The result of an independent investigation determined that City Commissioner Thomas had skimmed money off the top of the projects by padding building material invoices for the new municipal buildings. In the end, Dallas Thomas was found guilty of fifty counts of grand larceny.

The group of employees blacklisted and set to be fired included everyone who was hired during commissioner Thomas's administration. Dad's job was one of many on the chopping block. Uncle Uly, who helped Dad get the job and currently owned the family plumbing business, had supplied some of Thomas's projects with plumbing materials. He was called into court, where he testified against the commissioner, protecting himself against any charges that might be brought against him.

But Dad didn't get so lucky—his fledgling career as a draftsman disappeared like so many things in his life had before—suddenly and without warning.

This signified a new low.

Most of Dad's rental homes had been vacated and Dad had not been able to find new renters for them. The money he'd borrowed against our house as a second mortgage was almost gone. Each day when I returned home from school, he was either working at the drafting table in the garage or painting signs. He looked so incredibly tired for a man of only forty-four. Most of his hair had fallen out, and he wore thick trifocals. Sometimes, after dinner, he'd head into his room, asking Mom to wake him up in fifteen minutes so he could take a tiny nap in hopes it would give him enough energy to return to the hot garage and finish whatever thankless side job he was working on.

As I observed my parents' financial world collapsing, I could tell Willie wondered how long she was going to have her job. She took to listening closely to whispered conversations, trying to suss out if her world might soon fall apart, too. All the adults in my life seemed to have fear in their eyes. Tension electrified the atmosphere both inside and outside our home.

On June 11, 1963, in a televised speech, President Kennedy finally showed himself as a proponent of the Civil Rights Movement. He asserted that the pursuit of racial equality was a just cause. And, while the address signified a shift in his administration's policy toward stronger support of the movement, many Blacks felt that he waited far too long to speak out and, as his time in office ensued, they became increasingly impatient with the lack of social progress amidst escalating racial tensions.

In light of the threat of new civil rights policies proclaimed in the president's speech, the KKK stepped up their hate-filled campaigns. Just four months later four innocent young Black girls, aged eleven to fourteen, lost their lives in the devastation of a Baptist church bombing in Birmingham.

That Monday morning in September, the day after the bombing, I worried Willie might faint dead away as she stood in front of the TV, her brown eyes spilling over with tears.

Though the main part of the 16th Street Baptist church was solid brick, the wood-frame Sunday school addition was reduced to rubble. It was later discovered that four members of the Klan placed at least fifteen sticks of dynamite and a timer under the wooden structure the night before Sunday church services, with the full intent of detonating the explosives just as soon as church services were underway. In addition to the four young girls murdered, another twenty-two people were injured.

The gruesome nature of this event, having children killed while at church, managed to garner enough public attention to propel awareness of the importance of civil rights throughout much of the United States. Still, the fact that there had been another twenty-one separate explosions in the previous eight years leading up to the 16th Street Church bombing was a sad commentary on how long it took for even small movements against hatred to progress.

The Day Time Stopped

John F. Kennedy & Jacqueline Kennedy Onassis

THERE ARE ONLY a few events in one's life where time seems to stop, when a person can tell you exactly where they were and what they were doing the moment they learned the news. For me, President John Fitzgerald Kennedy's assassination is such an event.

I was a junior in high school and had just finished physical education class—where we wore shapeless white cotton one-piece jumpsuits with a snap closure. I'd just opened my locker to change into regular school clothes and head to my last class of the day when Elaine ran toward me.

"Oh my God, Gabrielle, did you hear the news?" She asked, near panting in exasperation.

"Uh, no, what?" I replied, perplexed.

"President Kennedy's been shot!"

I have no recollection of the moments that followed: of changing my clothes, of whether Elaine waited, or how I got outside to the football field—finally coming to on the grass lawn surrounded by hundreds of dazed students. Some stood stone still. Others paced nervously. Then a megaphone voice asked, "Students, may I have your attention?" And then, "I am so sorry to have to announce that our President, John F. Kennedy, has died. School is dismissed."

I must have made my way to the bus stop because, my next memory is walking through the back door of our house, throwing my arms around Willie, and the two of us standing in the kitchen bawling our eyes out. All the while the vague cycling of a repeated thought, *This must be a stunt, this can't really be happening. Nobody kills the president.*

I turned on the television.

One by one, the little kids and Harvey arrived home from school and joined me around the television set, which repeated the same sad story about the president and first lady riding in a motorcade in Dallas when suddenly he was gunned down.

When Mom and Dad got home from work, they too watched the news broadcast until Mom walked into the kitchen and warmed up a mishmash of leftovers for dinner. If there was dinner table conversation of some kind that night, I sure don't remember it.

The days that followed felt robotic. I, like most Americans, went on automatic pilot. Our communal grief left us to go through the motions of what was necessary to push life forward. Until, slowly, things returned to normal—whatever "normal" was—it had shifted into something no one, not kids or adults, could seem to define.

In the weeks that followed, I heard Dad tell Mom that they might have to sell our house. Now, after the killing of President Kennedy, and the possibility of our home being ripped away, I felt I was standing smack dab in the middle of an earthquake. In the preceding months Dad had built up a casual narrative about "How great it would be to live on the Southside where the Jewish people were," something he had never expressed before.

Still, the fact that we weren't allowed to spend time with our relatives who lived in that part of town, paired with the fact all my friends were in our current neighborhood, made the notion feel somehow distant and impossible to imagine—like President Kennedy's assassination—a thing that could never actually happen.

Truth was, I was so busy trying to survive the litany of shocking events that it never crossed my mind to try and make sense of any of them. Instead, the survival mechanism of denial kicked in. I told myself, *Whatever is going to happen isn't going to happen today. What I really need is to think about something entirely different for now. I'll ask Harvey if he wants to go to the movies.*

The film we saw the Saturday after President Kennedy's assassination was *It's a Mad, Mad, Mad, Mad, World* and, like so many other recent happenings, another strange experience. The name alone reflected the insanity of the world around us. Stanley Kramer, the director, was known for films that conveyed a strong sense of morality. This time he made *Mad World* on a dare—to prove he was capable of directing a comedy. Our nation was in desperate need of a laugh, and Kramer's slapstick story, thinly veiled as a poignant statement on greed was, in fact, a worthy parody for the times.

It seemed to me, the film's main purpose was to employ nearly every living comedian—starting with Jimmy Durante as Smiler Grogan, a suspect in a tuna factory robbery some fifteen years earlier and a fugitive from the police. In one scene, Smiler recklessly passes a number of vehicles on a twisting mountain road in Southern California's Mojave Desert before careening his car off a cliff, crashing below. Five motorists passing the wreckage stop to assist: a dentist, Melville Crump, played by Sid Caesar; a furniture mover, Lennie Pike, played by Jonathan Winters. "Dingy" Bell, (Mickey Rooney), and Benjy, played by Buddy Hackett, two friends on their way to Las Vegas. Finally, Entrepreneur J. Russell Finch, (Milton Berle), stops as well. Right before his untimely death, Smiler told the men about $350,000 in cash buried "under a big 'W'" in Santa Rosita State Park—thus begins the race to the Park to dig up the cash.

Jack Benny, the Three Stooges, Buster Keaton, Carl Reiner, and Don Knotts are a few other comedians making an appearance as part of the 110 actors who performed in the ridiculous romp.

Walking home from the movie that day, neither Harvey nor I were sure what the hell we'd just experienced. I told Harv, "Maybe after all the bad news lately, people really needed a laugh."

We certainly did, but laughter didn't come easily that day—we were still in a state of shock.

Squeaky Cutshaw Got My Cherry

Glamour girl

SOMETIMES IN LIFE it's not until I'm on the other side of a whole mess of trouble that I realize a special moment has come and gone in a way that's the exact opposite of what I'd have chosen if only I'd had more sense at the time.

It seems to me God gives us each a handful of puzzle pieces and our job is to spend the rest of our lives tracking down the others needed to complete the picture. Some folks are lucky. They get a big sack of parts early in life. I got a small pile at birth and not a whole lot more growing up. Without enough pieces of the jigsaw, I spent a lot of time making crapshoot choices based on partial information. And, though my desire was to act intelligently—so that in the end it wouldn't look like a fool had lived my life—much of the time my roll of the dice didn't produce a win.

At sixteen, I realized a little too late that five years earlier

Mom failed in adding enough puzzle pieces for me to successfully navigate the obstacle course of puberty. In her rush to get through an uncomfortable conversation with her eleven-year-old daughter, she plumb left me without a map.

It was a summer day in 1959. I was eleven going on twelve. I was standing next to the stove, waiting for the broiler to brown the top of a Kaiser roll smothered in oleomargarine, thinking, *I'm gonna wrap this and bring it with me to the swamp—it is one stinkin'-ass hot day.* I grabbed the roll from the cookie sheet, wrapped it in wax paper and made for the back door, yelling, "Going for a walk, Mom."

Before I could turn the doorknob, Mom scurried up, grabbed the back of my arm above my elbow, and dug her long nails into the tender skin and muscle—giving me "the claw"—a painful way of getting our attention when rounding up her brood, kinda like a Border Collie nipping at the legs of their herd of sheep. Only I'm convinced Mom's method hurts more.

"Come heah," she commanded.

The shrill sound of her Yankee voice jarred my nerves. A prickly rush of fear raced up my spine. As I followed her to the bedroom, I wondered what the heck I'd done this time. She and Willie had spent the morning painting the walls pink. Fumes stung my nostrils, causing my eyes to tear up.

Mom closed the door and looked at me cockeyed through her thick lenses, asking, "Have you ever heard a girl say, 'She fell off the roof?'"

"Uh, no—why?" I replied, confused.

"Well, because one day you might find some blood in your panties a...n...d...when you do, you'll know that you've started men-ooh-straight-ing."

I looked at her, dumbfounded.

She continued, "When it happens, tell me, so I can buy you a sanitary belt and some sanitary pads."

Then she turned her back to me, dipped her paintbrush into the can, and continued painting. This, I surmised, was my clue that the conversation had ended.

"Okay well, uh, see ya later, Mom."

I closed the door and hurried into her bedroom, grabbed two Salem cigarettes out of her purse, and ran out the back door. I felt the need to keep running, but decided walking fast would suffice. I wondered what Mom meant about blood in my panties. I felt stunned, like a foggy mist was filling the inside of my head. Once I reached my watery refuge, I kicked off my flip flops, lit the cigarette, stepped into the creek bed, and headed toward the darkest part of the swampy patch of Cypress trees. The squishy mud squeezing between my toes felt lovely. I inhaled a long drag of menthol and held my breath, Mom's words pinging inside my head. *A girl fell off the roof?* I struggled to make sense of the conversation I'd just escaped from. *How could she tell me one day I'll find blood in my underpants as easily as asking if I wanted a sandwich?* What I really wanted to do was to throw her words to the ground, dig a hole in the mud, and bury them.

A month later, the telltale blood appeared. I was barely twelve. Mom neglected to convey the most important detail—that once I started having periods, I'd be capable of getting pregnant. As I aged, I would come to realize there was another part missing from Mom's talk—one which my Catholic girlfriends were told—that having sex before wedlock was a sin.

"It's a known fact. If a girl does it with a boy, that sinful act will guarantee her a one-way ticket to hell, where she'll burn for eternity," Marsha told me.

The Southern Baptists further embellished their "talk" by telling their daughters the reason women bled each month was punishment on account of Eve disobeying God by eating the apple offered by Satan in the form of a snake.

At sixteen, a week before the end of junior year, Don "Squeaky" Cutshaw, a senior, sidled up to me in the hall on my way to Phys. Ed. He was a year older and was fixing to graduate. I'd run into him at a couple of football games and drag races, but didn't know him well.

"Hey, Gaby, stop. Next weekend I'll get my diploma—wanna celebrate with me? The Jay Notes are playing Saturday night."

I was crazy about that soulful R&B band. He didn't have to ask me twice.

Squeaky was skinny, and had leathery skin, even at his young age, he was attractive in a "rode hard, put away wet" sort of way. His brown denim jeans and faded button-down cowboy shirt, a size too small, spoke to the fact his people were mill workers who, I'd wager a bet, had never caught a break. I wasn't certain what he was going to do after high school, but was pretty sure college wasn't in his plans.

Because I'd grown up as a kid who thought it was my job to cheer up Mom and the siblings as we zig-zagged our way through the family mine field, the fact Don had the wrinkled brow of a confused guy didn't discourage me. In fact, I figured he was cogitating on some important philosophical questions. He seemed moody, all right, but in my naiveté I thought I was up for the challenge. And, when he became the joyful person I just knew was alive inside him, he'd find a white horse and show up at our house, where he'd toss me up and we'd gallop away toward sunset. And, since my very presence in his life would make him a joyful person, he'd cherish and adore me the rest of my born days.

Truly, I'd been watching too many Elvis movies.

I liked hanging out with Squeaky because I enjoyed his friends. Two were football players with cheerleader girlfriends—and his closest, Lenny and Peaches, were engaged, planning to marry after high school and move to the beach where Lenny had a lifeguard job lined up. I learned why this was the plan later on—Peaches had "gotten in trouble" and ballooned up a week after graduating.

Not wanting to get into a hassle with Dad by asking permission for a date with a Gentile boy, I instead inquired if I could take the bus to the dance with my friend Elaine.

"Elaine's dad will drive us home," I added, giving him one less reason to say no.

Dad looked spent. He was worn out from job hunting and probably didn't have the wherewithal to fight me if he'd wanted to—a fact that was sad for Dad, but lucky for me.

At school on Friday I told Squeak I'd meet him at the dance.

Anticipation tends to slow down time, so getting to Saturday seemed to take forever. When it finally arrived, I dressed in my new yellow and white seersucker sundress so as not to get too hot on the dance floor. Elaine and I'd spent the past few days excitedly planning to dance the night away. After a long walk from the bus stop at Willow Branch Park, we stepped onto the landscaped grounds of the Riverside Garden Club, where I came to an abrupt stop.

"Hey, Elaine," I said, "take a whiff of these gardenias, isn't that scent divine?"

It was a beautiful, balmy May evening with a lovely breeze. As we approached the stately Georgian Colonial building, I spotted Squeaky waiting for me at the door.

"Well, hello, beautiful," he proclaimed, then grabbed my hand and paid for both of us. Elaine slid in next to me so she wouldn't look like she arrived alone. I headed toward a table for four.

"Wanna dance?" Squeaky asked.

"I'd prefer to wait a little while so Elaine can find a dance partner first—so she isn't stuck sitting here alone."

Really, I was enjoying basking in the air conditioning after our long walk from the bus stop.

Ten minutes later, Elaine's brother, Raymond, arrived and asked if she wanted to dance.

I turned to Squeaky, "Still wanna cut a rug?"

He sprang out of his chair, grabbed my hand, and together we made our way to the dance floor. The band played "Rock Around the Clock," a number that had everyone on their feet. We danced a simple jitterbug. Squeaky had rhythm, but didn't know all the fancy turns like I did.

"Watch this," I said, taking a quick spin around him then stepping forward, grabbing both his hands, then I jumped back and hopped forward before returning to the basic step-step-rock-step of the bop. He flashed a smile. The next song was "Mashed Potato," to which he did a respectable job. After the third fast song, The Jay Notes broke into, "I Can't Stop Loving You," by Ray Charles. Every fourth song was a slow dance—this way, kids who didn't dance well could feel more comfortable joining in. Squeaky bowed, I curtsied, then he led me in a basic box step. We circumnavigated the dance floor twice, then he slowed his steps until we were not so much dancing as huddled in an embrace, swaying back and forth, barely moving our feet in a tight little circle.

With each step his warmth and the scent of Old Spice cologne seemed to spin a gossamer web wrapping the two of us into our own singular cocoon. Ray continued, "I can't stop loving you, it's useless to say..."

I glanced up at the colored lights on the ceiling, then laid my head on Squeaky's shoulder. It was as though we'd entered our very own magical universe and everyone else had vanished. That is, until the leader of the band announced to all of us Kool Kats and Hip Chicks they were going to take a quick break and, like a slap in the face, the fluorescent lights flashed and broke the spell.

“Come on, let’s get some fresh air,” said Squeak, giving my hand a forceful tug.

“Wait a minute, I’ve gotta tell Elaine.”

I ran toward our table to find Elaine and asked if she was okay with my going outside for a few minutes.

“Sure,” she said, and winked.

The cool breeze off the St John’s River tousled my hair and felt good against my damp skin. I walked slowly so as to perpetuate the dreamy state of mind I was in. But Squeak’s steps were hurried, and he pulled me along toward the parking lot.

“Where are we going?”

“I want to get a blanket out of my car so we can sit by the river,” he replied.

Once at his car, he opened the door and grabbed the blanket from the back seat.

"Okay, but I want to be back when the music starts," I said.

When we got to the railroad tracks on the bluff, above the expanse of lawn we had to cross to get down to the river, he stopped, threw the blanket down and plopped himself down cross-legged between the rails. Still holding tightly onto my hand, he pulled me onto his lap.

“This is crazy. Isn’t the railroad tie digging into your butt?” I asked.

He didn’t answer. Instead, he began kissing all over my face while simultaneously fumbling around until he found my dress arm hole, then slid his hand in, touching my breast. I liked the feel of his hand on my breast but was also overcome with a sensation of panic.

“C’mon, Squeak, let’s go back to the dance. I’m sure by now the band has returned.”

“No,” he said sternly.

He had me by the arm and refused to let go.

"I want to go all the way with you. I know you've already done it with Michael Johnson," he urged.

"What? I don't know how you heard such a thing! I'm a virgin."

As I processed the words he'd said, perplexed at such a blatant untruth, I felt him force his hand under my dress, trying to pull down my panties.

"I don't believe you," said Squeak.

"I want to go back," I demanded, struggling to get onto my feet.

Squeaky clenched my arm tighter, yanking me back down, saying, "Everybody says you're not a virgin. If you're a virgin, prove it."

If I'd had a nickel's worth of sense, I'd have said, "I don't give a damn if you believe me or not," and kicked him in the balls and run the heck out of there. But my entire life had been an exercise in learning to accept irrational behavior.

Mom often said, "As bad as it is with your father, it'd be a hell of a lot worse without him." Because this was her truth, it also became mine. I'd spent so much of my life being badgered by Dad that I didn't recognize a fool when one was standing right in front of me. Instead, I became the fool. I didn't recognize the danger just inside the door of the cozy cocoon we'd been spinning for ourselves all evening. So when it finally arrived, I followed along like a sheep led to slaughter—like some kind of bizarre human sacrifice.

Finally, I said, "If this is the only way you'll believe me, get it over with."

He knelt in front of me and pulled down my underpants. Then climbed on top of me. The steel railroad tracks dug into my shoulder blades. He tried to push himself inside me, but it wasn't easy because I held my legs closed. When he finally succeeded, I screeched—it hurt like hell. He didn't say a damn word to console me, just did a few "Ooh, oohs," then, a long exhale, and that was that.

He hopped off me, pulled up his pants and zipped his zipper, then turned away from me, crossed his arms and stared out at the river. In a daze I struggled to stand. He offered no help. I felt like a floundering roach on its back. Thinking, *people talk about having sex for the first time as if it's something romantic? They must be crazy—it's painful and humiliating.*

Squeaky turned and looked at me with vacant eyes. Once able to stand, I pulled up my undies and patted the bottom of my dress into place in a feeble attempt to regain some sense of respectability.

I pleaded, "I want to go home."

My shoulders hurt and the private parts between my legs burned. Anger gave way to shock, and I had the fleeting sensation that this wasn't really my life—that surely, I was dreaming. *I've become the Bride of Frankenstein.*

Squeaky walked toward the parking lot. I followed a few steps behind, like a zombie. We got to the car and climbed in. He drove me home without a single word. The minute I saw my street corner I opened the car door before the car came to a stop and scrambled out.

The Skillet Gets Hotter

Bacon and eggs

I T WAS ABOUT ten when I got home from our "date." Harvey heard me walk into the house. "What's wrong, Gab?" he asked, meeting me in the living room.

"Just a minute," I said, then headed to the bathroom where I pulled down my undies to check if there was blood. There was.

Harvey lightly tapped on the door and whispered, "Hey, Gab, you okay?"

"I'll be right out," I whispered back through the door hinge.

I washed my hands and glanced in the mirror. The person staring back at me looked disheveled—and unspeakably sad.

"Oh my God, Harv. Let's go in the living room so we don't wake up Dad," I directed, stepping back into the hall.

My words, like a multiple-car pileup, poured out of me in a hushed squeal.

"You aren't going to believe what happened tonight. I lost my virginity and it was, well, awful, and now I'm worried that I'm pregnant. I was a virgin. I have blood in my panties to prove it—but he still wouldn't believe me."

My fourteen-year-old brother had no idea what in the hell I was talking about and could give me no words of consolation. I had none for myself. I felt like the biggest fool on the planet—scared shitless and utterly mortified.

I stayed up most of the night tossing and turning, unable to sleep. I couldn't think of a single person to confide in, not one who would keep my secret, anyway. I was far too embarrassed to call Elaine. Wait. I had a hopeful thought: *Nan. Maybe she can help me.* Nan and I were classmates at Lee High for a year after she moved from San Francisco. Her family relocated to St. Petersburg after sophomore year, a few hours away. I'd always thought of her as my beatnik friend—made wise by her years in California. *She probably has experience with these kinds of matters...I doubt she's a virgin, anyway, people from California mature earlier.* I decided to write her a letter in the morning.

I lay in bed, vacillating between flashes of memory from the incident hours before, the desperate desire to talk with someone about what had happened, and a general feeling of terror I'd thrown away my life by becoming a teenage mother. The ping pong ball of thoughts bounced rapidly off the walls of my distressed mind.

A letter will take forever. There's no way you can wait that many days for her to write back, I thought. *Crap. I should call her.* But I was afraid Dad would see the long-distance call on our next telephone bill and throw a fit. *Dang. And Nan's father probably won't want to accept a collect call from me.*

I was up now, pacing the bedroom floor, trying my best not to awaken ten-year-old Paulina. I huffed an exasperated sigh, took a deep breath and tiptoed to the kitchen. With all the strength I could muster, I grabbed the kitchen phone and dialed Nan's number—hoping her father, who was a radio D.J. happened to be working the night shift. Luckily, Nan answered and accepted the charges.

I hurriedly explain to Nan what happened and Nan's reaction was surprisingly blasé.

"First of all, calm down—it's no big deal," Nan said. "Come down here on the Greyhound. I'll give you a couple of quinine pills and throw you in a hot shower and, viola, instant miscarriage."

"Seriously?" I asked.

"Yeah, seriously," she replied, calm as a cucumber.

"Uh, okay, I'll ask Dad. Call me back tomorrow, about five-thirty? He'll be home from work by then."

"Sure."

The following day, as Dad pulled into the driveway, I ran to the backdoor to meet him. My words tumbled out too quickly, without a pause between them.

"Hey, Dad. How did your day go? Would you please give me an advance on my allowance so I can buy a bus ticket to visit Nan?"

In my desperation, I'd momentarily forgotten that Dad had never, once in my life, given me permission to do anything, right off. Stringing out his decisions was one of the tactics he regularly used to exasperate me.

As I figured, his answer was a stiff, "N-O."

The only approach I had left was to start begging mercilessly, a pitiful method I'd successfully used in the past to wear him down. I'd forgotten that if he didn't end up saying "yes," that I was the one who ended up worn out. Nevertheless, I pressed on.

"Nan needs to know, because if I'm not coming her Dad wants to take her to Miami for a few days," I blurted out, tossing him a curve ball.

The phone rang. It was Nan.

"Gab, you've got to get here soon, or it'll be too late for the treatment to work," she urged through the receiver.

I stretched the phone cord into the living room so Mom couldn't hear. "I understand. I think I may have better luck after dinner, can you me back at seven?" I asked, buying more time.

"Yeah, okay. But you're running out of time," she replied, with a twinge of resignation at the edge of her voice.

Mom was bustling around the kitchen setting food on the table when Dad commanded in a deep, angry tone, "Come here, Ruth! And you, too, Gabrielle!"

He angrily marched down the hall to their bedroom. Mom and I followed. Once inside, he slammed the door.

"Ruth," he began, "our daughter is a whoourr."

Mom grabbed my hand, pulling my face toward her. Then she looked intently in my eyes, but I couldn't read her expression because her lazy eye wouldn't focus. Suddenly I felt struck by an overwhelming sensation that every bit of blood in my body was gushing out of my toes, creating a massive red puddle under my feet.

"She had sex, Ruth. Now she thinks she may be pregnant. Call Dr. Lillian, at home, right now."

Flabbergasted, my mind spun. *How could Dad possibly know this? Oh no, he must've listened in on my phone call.*

Dad turned and stomped back into the kitchen where he handed Mom the turquoise wall phone, hovering over her as she dialed. Our sweltering kitchen was so small it barely held the table for six. I glanced toward my brothers and sister, seated on the yellow-grey duct taped Naugahyde chairs, and for a moment they looked like orphans.

I eased into the chair next to Harvey, trying to steal a glance from him. He turned away as if to say, "Don't look at me. I don't want them to think I knew anything about this."

"She wants us to come in tomorrow at eleven, Max," Mom said, as she took her seat at the table.

The little kids sensed the discomfort in the air and kept their heads down, while quickly cleaning their plates. Dinner conversation was sparse, limited to, "Can you please pass the chicken," and other words needed to keep food circulating. I ate a spoonful of Mom's mashed potatoes mixed with spinach—which for many years I would believe was the only way anyone in the world tolerated eating the soggy green vegetable. The green-white lump lingered in my mouth. It, like my worried thoughts, seemed to expand, transforming from a small bite into a mass too enormous to swallow. Staring into space, I sat stunned, worried, and frightened, dreading the next sound that would inevitably slice through the silence.

The kids asked to be excused and scrambled into the living room to turn on the TV. Mom scurried after. *Smart move.* So as not to provoke Dad, I didn't ask to be excused from the table—instead, I waited for him to finish his dinner. With each remaining bite, his cheeks reddened, appearing to grow bigger and crazier looking with each movement of his jaw. When he finally stood, I felt myself shrink in his presence. Dad, the thermonuclear weapon. I felt I'd only witnessed the fission of the first stage of the incendiary device of him. Panicked, I tried to think of a way to brace myself against the second stage that would soon detonate.

"Follow me," he said.

Shit. Here we go again.

Once in his room, he handed me a clipboard.

"Write down the name and phone number of the boy who did this to you," he demanded.

I refused.

Next, in an unusually deep voice, he yelled about lying to him about going to the dance with Elaine.

Then, in measured words, "Go-to-your-room-I-don't-want-to-see-you-the-rest-of-the-night-you-understand? Good. See."

As I headed for the door, his hand landed on my back, and half pushed me into the hall.

The following morning, Mom woke me with a flat, "Get dressed. We're going downtown."

Thankfully, Dad had already left for work.

Mom and I shared the kitchen, silently consuming our breakfast. Mine, a small bowl of Cheerios, without the usual banana slices, and jelly jar of orange juice. Mom's, a cup of coffee, black.

"C'mon," she said, as she stood up from the table and rolled her eyes. I could almost hear her thinking, "You pain in the ass."

We walked to the bus stop, as we'd done plenty of times before, but this time we didn't stop at the juice stand to get fresh-squeezed piña coladas, our tradition. This time we are not headed downtown for a girls' shopping trip for back-to-school clothes. Instead, I'd become the prisoner in the movie *Good Day for a Hanging*, led through the dusty streets to gallows waiting in the center of town.

At the red brick office building, we stepped into the elevator with a nod and, "Good morning" to the uniformed Black man who delivered us to floor five. Walking down the cool, narrow corridor toward Dr. Lillian's office, I realized that I'd been there before, many times, with Mom when she was pregnant with all three of my younger siblings.

Dr. Lillian didn't leave us waiting long. She whisked us into an examination room, with a welcoming smile and warm demeanor. The same height as Mom, Dr. Lillian was a bit chubbier, with perfectly round, rosy cheeks that seemed to glow with a perpetual smile—for which I was, at this moment, incredibly grateful. She handed me a thin pink gown, told me to tie it so the opening was in the front, then pointed to a curtain hanging in the corner. I stepped behind it, emerging moments later clutching the gown closed around me.

I sensed that I was not the first teenage girl she had ever known to have been caught in this kind of predicament. The only piece of furniture in the chilly grey room was a rectangular stainless-steel examination table with drawers underneath. The two long appendages growing from one end of the table were menacing, like something out of a Frankenstein movie. Dr. Lillian motioned for me to lie on my back on a flimsy sheet of crinkly paper as she placed a white cotton sheet on top of me, covering the area from my neck to just below my knees.

"Put your feet in the stirrups, scoot farther down the table, and try to relax."

Seconds later, her hand on my abdomen, then the push of an ice-cold speculum deep inside my vagina. As she opened it inside me, a painful pinch threatened to make me jump right off the table. But instead, I clenched my teeth hard, and inhaled an eight count breath, then held it for eight seconds, exhaling for eight counts, then inhaled for eight counts and repeated this act, over and over—a technique that I'd created for distraction when trapped in compromising situations.

Lying on my back, helpless as a roach, a thought made its way through my mind: *I should have used my breathing technique the night Squeaky screwed me and maybe it wouldn't have hurt so badly.*

Then I felt something warm inside me and stretched to raise up on my shoulders so as to get a peek at what she was doing. A flashlight. The heat felt good. Then she abruptly yanked the speculum out as a solitary tear rolled slowly down my cheek. I imagined my vagina exhaling and saying, "Whew, thanks."

"In case you bleed from the exam." Dr. Lillian said as she handed me a sanitary pad—her kindness making the shameful experience less soul-crushingly dehumanizing than it might have otherwise been.

"Meet me in my office when you're dressed, Gabrielle," she added.

"Ruth, follow me," she quipped as they both headed out of the exam room.

I dressed quickly, joining Mom in the office and taking a seat behind the desk.

The doctor reached over, handing Mom a little manila-colored envelope. "Give her two pills today, one after each meal, and another two tomorrow. You can wait in the other room, Gabrielle, I need to talk to your mother for a moment."

Once finished and outside the building, I asked Mom, "What are those pills for?"

"We better hurry or we will miss our bus," she replied.

Juvie

The long drive

THAT EVENING, WHEN Dad got home from work, he asked Harvey to look after the little kids, directing Mom and me to get in the car.

"But, Max, we haven't eaten dinner," Mom argued, gently.

"I don't care, Ruth. Harvey, make tuna sandwiches for yourself and the kids."

Mom knew to not counter Dad a second time.

As we headed out the door, Dad picked up his clipboard, tucking it under his arm.

Passing through the San Marco neighborhood, I gathered we were headed back downtown. Dad crossed the Main Street Bridge then up and over a few more blocks until he stopped in front of a nondescript concrete-block building painted government green. The building, set back from the street, had a set of wide brick stairs that ran half the width of it, with no-nonsense tubular railing framing the sides. The day was blustery, and the wind off the river blew random garbage about—empty paper sacks, cigarette butts, and paper cups rolled along the deserted sidewalk.

Then Dad thrusted the clipboard into my hands as I stared out the backseat window, demanding, "Write the name of the guy you were with Saturday night—and a list of everyone you know at high school."

I paused and looked at his big, red face. Mom sat silently, staring forward, averting eye contact.

"Do you know what this place is?" he asked next.

"No."

"This is where girls like you end up when they don't follow the rules at home," he replied. Then he looked at his watch, "Hurry up—we have an appointment."

"I don't want to talk to anyone," I urged.

"I don't give a damn what you want," Dad shot back. He exited his door, then walked around the vehicle to open mine.

"Ruth, wait here, we'll return shortly," he commanded.

I refused to move. With a swift grab and tug, he yanked me by the arm out of my seat then half pulled me across the sidewalk and up the stairs to the building as I fought him, screaming, "Let me go!"

My breath was wasted. Once at the wide metal door, he turned to the uniformed guard inside, "Which way to Judge Weingart's office?"

"Last door down the hall on the left."

Painted on the door in gold and black script was The Honorable Judge Beauregard Weingart.

After entering the waiting room, we sat down on a couple of old oak chairs. I looked to the window frame, out at the concrete sky, as Dad pondered his watch. Five very long minutes passed until an office door popped open and a stout, balding, heavy set man in a dark grey suit and tie signaled for us to enter.

"Mr. Mack, do you mind if I speak with your daughter alone for a few minutes?"

"No sir," Dad replied, with a tone of relief that someone else was taking over.

"You can sit here, Gabrielle," the judge said, motioning to a heavy oak captain's chair sitting in front of his huge oak desk.

I surveyed the room. On the desktop sat a thick black book splayed open—lined pages scribbled with notes filled both sides. Old mahogany bookshelves enveloped the wall behind him and stacks of manila legal files exploded across the lower shelves. Higher up, burgundy law journals and other thick important looking books gave the sense this was a place seated at the intersection of authority and history.

"Do you know Donald Cutshaw?" he asked, breaking the silence.

"Yes," I replied, timidly.

"Did you have sex with him on Saturday night?" He wasted no time seeking an answer to the only question he was truly after.

I had no idea that I was stepping into a bear trap from which there was no return and was so frightened it didn't even occur to me to try and lie. "Yes."

He scribbled something in the book, slammed it closed with a big whump, bang, then stood up, opened the door to where Dad was seated and said simply, "I got what I need."

We made our way down the glaringly bright corridor.

As Dad huffed his way to the outside stairs, I followed behind, noticing a sign as we exited: Jacksonville Juvenile Detention Center.

Oh, this is what Juvie looks like. I'd heard about kids being sent there for stealing—but I hadn't committed a crime.

Mom has been dutifully presiding over the clipboard in the

sweltering car. Upon our return Dad grabbed it from her lap, then in his perfect block-printed lettering, wrote something near the page bottom, turned and handed it to me. It read, "I, Gabrielle Mack, agree never to see Donald Cutshaw, or the others listed in this document, again in my life."

The names of all my closest friends, like Marsha and Elaine, filled up the list. An echo, "forever and ever, amen," jangled in my mind.

Dad had signed and dated the bottom.

"Now you put your signature and today's date under my name," he said without so much as looking at me, through what sounded like clenched teeth.

"No!" I yelled, turning away as the clipboard dropped to the floorboard with a loud rattle.

Dad hopped out of the car, ran to my door, and attempted to pull me out—but I fought back like an caged animal while screaming, "I will not! Take your hands off me!"

"It's simple, see. You either agree to my rules, or I'm leaving you here," he said, with a calm, stern tone that made clear that no amount of fight would get me out of the situation.

He shoved the clipboard in my face one last time.

"But—Mom," I eeked, but for how little she offered help, I could have been talking to the wind.

Like a cigar store Indian statue, she stared straight ahead, ignoring me completely.

"All right," I whimpered.

As I grabbed the pen out of his hand, scribbling my name on this most devastating contract, a singular thought passed through my mind: *I've gotta get the hell out of here.*

The Last Gasp

Cocktail hour

T HE FOLLOWING MORNING, just as soon as Mom and Dad pulled down the driveway headed for work, I threw a change of clothes, nightie, toothbrush, and bathing suit into my beach bag, and jumped on the bus to the beach. Squeaky's friends, Lyle and Peaches, lived half a mile from the bus stop, so an hour later, I was off the bus, strolling along the sidewalk toward their apartment.

The August day was heating up. Still, ninety with the ocean breeze felt tremendously better than ninety inland. I inhaled, filling my lungs with a long intake of salty air. I loved the smell of the sea, and noticed I felt strangely relaxed. *Probably because I've left the worries of Jacksonville there.* As I hurried down the sidewalk, on a mission to connect with someone who might understand what I was going through, adrenaline and anger overtook me. I kept remembering Dad's voice calling me a whore. And couldn't make sense of the fact that my parents were blaming me for being forced to have sex with Squeaky. It was as though all the years I'd spent loving my family vanished in an instant. I'd become a pariah, an untouchable, an orphan—my innocence snatched away because I was forced to do something against my will. Surely Peaches, who got pregnant in the middle of her senior year, would understand. *There it is—finally.*

The small brick 1950s fourplex with its white shutters was perfectly charming. Remembering they lived on the main floor, I peeked in some windows until I saw Peaches through a front screen door, wearing an apron over a flowery muumuu, doing something at the kitchen table.

"Hey, you!" I yelled.

"Oh, hi, Gabby, what a surprise! You're the last person I expected to see today. I'm just making lunch to bring Lyle at the lifeguard station."

She'd really ballooned up since last time I'd seen her—it looked as if her baby might pop out at any moment.

"Can I help?" I asked.

"Sure, how about you cut up some carrot and celery sticks. What's been going on?" She asked, a friendly tone to her voice.

"Well, I ran away," I began. "Last night Dad drove me to the juvenile detention center and threatened to lock me up if I ever saw Squeaky again," I continued.

"Oh, wow. Okay, let's get this food in a basket and you can tell me all about it on our walk to the beach," Peaches replied.

We layered a couple of bologna sandwiches, the stack of vegetables, a small bag of potato chips, and a cold Coke into a basket lined with a red-checked cloth.

As we walked the half mile to the beach, words spilled out of me—it was only the second time I'd told my story to anyone—and two weeks since confiding in Nan. After spending most of the day visiting, I realized sharing my worries seemed to lighten them. Feeling a little better, I dug in even more, explaining my concerns about being pregnant, to which she laughingly replied, "Don't feel like the lone stranger. I should warn you Squeaky often stops by here on his way home from work—you know he's on a construction job just down the road."

"No, I didn't know," I replied, a twinge of anxiety rising across the edges of my mind.

I wasn't sure I wanted to see him.

A few hours later Lyle returned home and got the charcoal briquettes going while we girls played patty-cake with the ground beef. Lyle had been outside grilling burgers for half an hour when Squeaky let himself in and walked to the back yard with an open can of Schlitz in one hand and the remainder of a six pack in the other.

"Whoa, Gab, what're you doing here?" he asked, surprised.

"Come here and I'll tell you," I said, motioning to join me in a room in the far end of the apartment.

He followed me down the hall.

"Squeak, I'm worried I might be pregnant. Dad took me to juvie and made me confess to a judge that I had sex with you. Then he made me sign a paper agreeing to never see or talk to you again—and threatened to throw me in the juvenile detention center jail if I do."

Squeaky didn't say a word. Instead, he crunched up the now-empty beer can, stuffed it in his pocket, then opened another and damn near guzzled the entire thing in one long swig. I stood there waiting for him to say something, anything—to hug me. He wrinkled his brow and twisted his mouth to the side as though he was assessing the situation for one long minute, then said, "C'mon, let's get something to eat," and headed for the back yard.

How stupid to think he would have any advice, or kindness, to offer. I stared at the barbecue pit, wishing to disappear into the smoke.

"So, how's work going, man?" asked Lyle.

"Uh, okay," said Squeaky, part of his burger falling out of his mouth.

Watching him wolf down his food disgusted me. He wouldn't even look in my direction. He didn't give a damn and it hurt.

As the rest of them made small talk, thoughts spun wildly in my mind. *What a mess I am. I've run away two weeks before the beginning of senior year. I can't believe I thought Squeaky loved me and could offer a more peaceful life than the one at home. And here he stands, this fine specimen of an immature guy who won't even give me eye contact. Jesus, what a disaster.*

Peaches set down a bowl of potato salad, then signaled to follow her into the house, "So what're you gonna do, Hon?"

"I don't know, but I don't want to go home. Can I spend the night here? So I can have some time to think?"

"Of course," she said, offering me the couch.

Four beers later, Squeaky left to drive home.

The following morning, Lyle went to work. Peaches and I made fried chicken and potato salad, then put on our bathing suits and walked to the beach. I was exhausted to the bone. I stretched out on the blanket and fell asleep straightaway. When Peaches shook me awake, I was disoriented, unsure of both place and time. *Oh, the beach. Had it been one hour or three?* I shook my head, feeling as if I'd woken from a terrible dream. Did I really have sex with Squeaky, who I now mentally referred to as Squeaky the Horrible? And fought with my parents over it? Run away? Got called a whore for being tricked into doing something painful? It was too much to take in. I shook my head again and looked around. Sure enough, I was at the beach, with one hell of a sunburn.

"We need to get home," said Peaches. "The boys will be finished with work in an hour or so."

I shook off the blanket, folded it, and we hurried home, took showers and set the table.

Squeaky strolled in first.

"Gab, you have to go back to Jacksonville tonight," he said, an urgency in his voice.

"I what?" I said, perplexed. Who the hell was he to order me around?

"Yeah, or they are going to arrest me for statutory rape."

"What?" Peaches and I chimed in unison.

"Police came to my job site today with an order from a judge. They said they'll arrest me for statutory rape if you don't get home by tomorrow morning. Get your things, I'll drive you to the bus station."

"What does that mean, 'statutory?'" I asked.

"It means being over eighteen and having sex with someone under eighteen," Peaches explained.

"Well, actually, if you think about it, it kind of was rape, Squeaky. I tried to get you to stop and you wouldn't," I said, loudly enough to have Peaches as a witness.

Squeaky didn't reply. He grabbed my arm and pulled me into the living room. I burst out crying.

"Get your stuff," he demanded.

My whole body shook, and my heart went crazy in my chest. I struggled to take a breath as I reached to pick my crumpled beach bag off the floor. *Okay, slow down, exhale, take a breath. What am I forgetting?* I ran into the bathroom, grabbed my toothbrush and wet bathing suit and threw them in my bag.

"Thanks for the visit, Peaches. You too, Lyle. I'll call you guys."

Squeaky reached for my arm again. "C'mon," he ordered.

I smacked his hand. "Don't touch me," I hissed.

When we arrived to the bus station, he handed me bus fare and muttered a casual, "See ya." Then walked to his car and drove away.

I watched him, seething.

The bus wouldn't arrive for another hour, so I relived the scene at Peaches' and Lyle's, all the while blaming myself for what Squeaky had done. *Nobody understands me. I should never have agreed to go on a date with him. I shouldn't have danced with him at The Jay Notes. Why did I leave the dance with him? I should have known better than to let him touch me. I'm such an idiot.*

On the ride home, my interior voice continued—the inside of my head a war zone. Each ensuing thought felt as though a bullet had hit my heart. It was black outside. There was nothing to look at or distract from stumbling around the enemy territory that had become the inside of my mind. I was my own terrorist.

Finally, the bus pulled in front of the Florida Hotel, my first stop. Being so very tired, and not wanting to trip down the stairs, I lowered my head, paying close attention as I placed each foot on the metal steps to disembark the bus. *I wonder how long it'll be until the Lakeshore bus comes*, I thought. Once on the sidewalk, I lifted my head.

Standing there in front of me, was Dad—tears rolling down his cheeks. He walked over, put his arm around me, and we walked toward the car in an embrace. *Oh gosh, I made Dad cry!* I felt terrible. In that moment, every pent-up emotion broke through—I began sobbing mercilessly.

We didn't exchange any words on the ride home, then tiptoed through the back door so as not awaken the sleeping family. I quietly grasped the handle to the bathroom door and paused. Dad reached for the door to his bedroom.

"Thanks for picking me up, Dad," I said, as our eyes met across the distance of the hall. "Goodnight."

I stepped into the bathroom, pulled down my pants, sat on the toilet, and glanced down. I had started my period.

The Fruit Bowl

Love, Max and Martha

ONE HOT EVENING a few weeks after the Squeaky frenzy, I went to the living room intending to lay down on our lumpy couch and take advantage of the lovely cross breeze from the two open screen doors in the kitchen and front room. But Dad had beat me to it and was already stretched.

"Can't sleep," he said, as he saw me walking toward the sofa.

"Me, either," I commiserated.

Since we were alone—a rarity those days—I used the opportunity to strike up a conversation.

"Dad," I asked, "have you ever been in love with anyone else—before Mom?"

I'm not sure why I felt confident broaching such a personal subject that night—especially given how tired and irritable we both were from the heat. But it was a question that had rolled around in my brain for so long I figured I'd give it a shot. I was so sick of Dad's controlling who I could date that the anger I'd been hauling around must've needed a place to go, and, I figured, maybe I could learn something about what he valued in romantic pairings that would make it easier for me to find an acceptable boy.

"I mean," I said, "you really don't seem like you love Mom all that much."

There it was, out in the open, the elephant standing squarely in the middle of the living room. I had finally given shape to the emotions I'd felt my entire life—the obvious strain and disconnect between Mom and Dad—and blurted out the words for God and everyone to hear. As they tumbled from of my mouth, even I was stunned. That was it. I was suddenly sure of it—he didn't love Mom. I jumped up from the couch and backed into the wall, bracing myself for a smack across my face.

It didn't come.

Instead, Dad shocked me with the phrase, "Wait a minute."

He jumped up from the couch and hurried from the living room to his bedroom, where he carefully opened the door so as not to awaken Mom.

I followed him down the hall and glanced into his room—he was rifling through the top drawer of his dresser. I scurried back to the kitchen, poured myself a glass of milk, and kept watch on the living room for his return. A few minutes later, he came back holding several stacks of yellowing envelopes tied with faded blue ribbons.

"Come heah—let me show you something," he said in his deep Bronx accent, patting the place next to him on the couch.

I stood frozen for a minute, assessing whether it was safe to come closer. Upon determining it probably was, I slunk over, nervously plopping myself down on the couch next to him. I wrapped my arms around myself like a pretzel.

Could he, for the first time in my life, be about to confide in me? I held my breath as he began to unpack a secret which would, in turn, become the key to understanding a great deal about our life.

He began, "I was in love once. I never told you this before, but I do know what it is like to be in love, really in love. Her name was Martha."

My mind zipped back to the wooden fruit bowl I'd found in the garage, years earlier, with the carved inscription that read, "To Mom and Dad, Love Max and Martha, 1937."

Dad went on, stumbling and pausing, trying to gather his thoughts. Beads of sweat appeared on his forehead and the few remaining strands of hair on the top of his head grew wet.

"She was my first wife," he said, inhaling several short spurts of air then exhaling for what seemed like forever.

Whoa, I thought, *this is the last thing I ever expected to hear. Is Martha my real mother? That would surely account for why Mom is so cold and distant toward me.* I looked down and noticed my right hand was shaking.

"How old were you when you got married, Dad?" I asked.

"We were both nineteen. It sounds young, I know, but it was not so unusual for those days, given the war and all."

He paused. I was at a loss for words but found myself making connections, thinking, *I knew that the ghost I thought I saw sometimes was not a figment of my imagination.* Like Topper, Dad had a Marion Kerby of his own. I pondered, *I wish I had known then, it might have been easier for me to understand why Dad seemed so aloof at times—and Mom so frustrated. The ghost finally has a name: Martha, Dad's first love.*

"What happened?" I asked, in an attempt to move from the realm inside my wonderments back to the reality unfolding on the couch.

"It's complicated to understand," he said, continuing the story, "but I'll try. Only two years into our marriage I was awakened in the middle of the night by Martha's distressed voice. When I looked up, she was standing over me, wielding a butcher knife yelling, 'Max! I'm going to kill you!' I called the police, they called an ambulance, and they put her in a straitjacket and drove her to Bellevue Hospital, the public psychiatric facility in Manhattan."

"Oh, my God, Dad." I reached over with my shaking hand and put it atop his. He sighed deep and slow, then his shoulders slacked as though they were weighted down by the grief of his memories.

"In the back of the ambulance, on the way to the hospital, she vacillated between telling me how much she loved me, and screaming she wanted to kill me." He went on. "I waited faithfully and visited her almost every night after work the first few months. But month after month went by and she made very little progress. I prayed to God to please heal her—to please heal my love," he sputtered.

"How long was she in the hospital, Dad?"

He inhaled deeply. "More than nine years," he said, then gave a deep sigh. "We were perfect for each other. She played the recorder and I the clarinet. She, too, was an artist, and we both worked for Warner Brothers in Manhattan. She was tall and athletic and endlessly kind."

Mom is neither tall nor athletic. She's not musical or artistic, either, blipped through my mind.

"During the years I waited for Martha to recover, my parents closed their grocery store in New York and moved to Florida with my two brothers and sister to open the family business. My siblings were all getting married and having children. I stayed behind, alone in New York, waiting for Martha to get better, hoping she would finally be released from the hospital. I just couldn't let go of the belief that one day she would walk out of the hospital and we would be together again."

I was gobsmacked. If there was something I was supposed to say, I surely didn't have a clue as to what it was.

Dad continued, "I used to look out of my sixth-floor apartment window at night onto the snowbank below and watch it turn into the figure of a woman, with outstretched arms, reaching up to me, beckoning me to jump. 'Come on Max,' she'd say, 'you know you want to join me. Open the window and fly like a bird to me. I'm waiting for you.'"

The ghost again, I thought.

"Jesus, Dad, what did you do?"

"I thought I was losing my mind. The only thing I could think to do was run. So I'd run down the six flights of stairs into the dark, snowy night, and jog up and down the streets until I was so exhausted that I couldn't move another muscle. I felt trapped. I couldn't do anything to help her, but I couldn't let go. I'd made a promise to love her in sickness and in health and I had to hold on so that when she got well, we could resume our beautiful life together. But each year that went by with no progress made it more difficult for me to keep from giving up. One day, I realized that each night, when I ran out into the snow, I was trying to outrun my devastation, which had transformed into suicidal thoughts."

I squeezed his hand, spellbound, staring into his soft, brown, watery eyes, frozen with a barrage of emotions.

"Did she ever recover?"

"That's another story," he said. "My parents urged me to have the marriage annulled so I could get on with my life. They felt I had waited long enough. They wanted me to move to Florida and join the family. Finally, I agreed. It was the hardest thing I had ever done in my life, but I knew that I really wanted to have children, and I would always worry that Martha might go berserk and harm one of our kids. So, after all those years, I finally agreed to go through the legal proceeding to have the marriage annulled. Shortly after, I met your mother and we moved to Florida."

That night my heart broke for Dad. My feelings toward him began to soften, and I hoped that by unpacking this most important part of his life and sharing it with me his feelings toward me might also begin to soften. I was glad to have these new puzzle pieces, while also knowing better than to totally let my guard down. When it came to his moods, he'd shown that nothing was predictable.

A number of years later, my Aunt Rudy shared that no sooner than Dad had married Mom and brought her to Florida, Martha was released from the hospital. To Rudy's knowledge, Dad never did try to find her.

I couldn't fathom how hard it must have been for Dad to hear of Martha's recovery only shortly after he had married Mom. I'm sure, without a doubt, that it added another layer of anguish to the complexity that was his life. I wondered: *What other family secrets are there?*

Movin' On Up to the Southside

Date night

I'D BEEN HOLDING my breath for a year, knowing that if Dad didn't find people to move into his rental houses, we might one day lose our house. I also worried that my parents wouldn't be able to afford to have Willie continue to work for us. As the weeks progressed, I overheard conversations ranging from Dad emphatically telling Mom "I feel like I'm drowning in debt!" to whispers of, "I think we may have to consider the possibility of letting Willie go."

I was struck and strained by the stress of the impending outcomes—knowing nothing would be easy. More, I couldn't imagine our household without Willie—she was the glue that held our family together and the calm voice of reason amidst Dad's mood swings and Mom's emotional distance.

To his credit, I could see Dad was trying everything possible to reconcile the financial situation, but due to the two nearby naval bases closing—a situation out of his control—he simply couldn't find new renters for the houses in the adjacent neighborhoods. He and Mom were just plain not making enough money to cover payments on the loans he'd taken out against our family home to try to save the rentals.

One by one, nearly all of his fifty houses was getting foreclosed on and, as they did, Dad's retirement dream vanished with them. It was a particularly bleak period for Dad. He had, in the past, spent time skulking in his bedroom when he was upset—but now he was in there so much I worried that he'd simply given up. Whenever the phone rang, figuring it was a bill collector, he'd yell, "Tell 'em I'm not home!" The only way out seemed to be selling our house to pay off his debt, then moving into a rental—Dad, it seemed, was about to trade our family home for his good name.

The demise of Dad's dream felt like it moved at light speed. *How*, I wondered, *can it take such a short time for a dream to crumble when it took so long to build?*

One night, Dad said, without explanation, "I've made a decision. We are going to move our family to the Jewish side of town."

Living on the Jewish side of town meant nothing to me. I glanced at Mom, who stood silently by, catching her rolling her eyes.

He didn't mention they were broke or say anything about being forced to sell the house to pay off piles of debt. Just "We're moving," which, to me, equated to one thing: he didn't care that he was going to uproot us without warning and ruin my senior year of high school.

My mind spun into a panic. Everyone I had gone to school with since kindergarten would be on the other side of town. I would now spend my senior year with complete strangers, graduate, and most likely, would never see my new friends again since Dupont kids were wealthy, and would leave for college, unlike me and my friends from Lee. At least in Lakeshore we had a decent home and a nice big yard, even if our furniture was old and taped up and Dad's car was a mess. Now, we would be the poorest people living among a lot of rich folks with the same beat up belongings. I was devastated, and embarrassed.

As time passed, Dad continued to justify the move saying things like, "Well, it will put Harvey geographically closer to the Bolles School." Bolles was a private college preparatory school and since Florida schools were having accreditation problems, going to Bolles—which was extremely expensive—would assure that Harvey could get into a good university. Here he was Dear Old Dad—we were losing our family home and almost all of his rentals—and he was focused on his son's education.

As the move got closer, each of us kids had a different emotional reaction to the shock. Little Benny, at six, started wetting the bed and became so distracted in school he had to repeat a grade. Poor little guy just didn't have the wherewithal to grasp the reality of leaving the only house he had ever known. Worse yet was the fact that soon Willie would also be gone, along with Raymond and Marvin, who Benny considered his brothers, something that would shake him to his core.

Harvey, on the other hand, worried over what his baseball team was going to do without him and whether he'd find another place to excel in sports.

Paulina, at ten-and-a-half, didn't seem to struggle as much as the rest of us, something I envied. She rarely shared her feelings, so I didn't really know how this move would affect her.

I felt like the rug I'd been standing on my entire life was being yanked out from under me, shattering my foundation.

Harvey and I knew that our lives were about to change in a big way—the brick house on Bayview Avenue was all we'd ever known. We'd been living there since we were three and five. While life was far from perfect, we loved our yard, our refuge at the swamp, our beloved Lakeshore Theatre, the Twin Hills Drive-In, and Pritchett's Kitchen.

Worse still, we were banned from seeing our aunts, uncles, and favorite cousins. This left us with our least favorite aunt and uncle. And, since they lived on the Southside, Dad decided that we should start spending Passover with them each year. Before the feud, Passover had been a holiday we looked forward to spending with our favorite relatives. Now, it was about to become yet another dreaded part of our lives.

When we had Passover at their house, the moment our aunt opened the front door and ushered us into the living room it was obvious, by her body language, that she looked upon us with the same disdain given to the orphans in *Oliver Twist*, and her husband displayed the same attitude. We were riffraff to them and we knew it.

All of us could sense that Aunt and Uncle thought we were going to steal or break one of their fragile glass tchotchkes, which they should have had the good sense to remove from their glass coffee table. Try as we might to please our parents, we collectively held our breath and bumbled through the Seder, doing our best to pronounce the Hebrew correctly when it was our turn to read from the Haggadah. Still, invariably, one of the four of us knocked something off the table or broke something accidentally.

Prior to the family feud, we'd had Passover at Uncle Sid and Aunt Bertie's house. Sid, Dad's oldest brother, was handsome, gregarious, and reeked of men's cologne. He went to Las Vegas often and always had a pillowcase filled with silver dollars he'd won to pass out to us kids. Aunt Bertie was our family's version of Auntie Mame. Their house was ultra-modern with a big open floor plan and a built-in fish tank in the entryway. Each room was awash in dramatic indirect lighting. Everything in the house was painted turquoise or purple, including the baby grand piano and curvy turquoise couch.

While the adults were upstairs imbibing Mogen David wine, we cousins were downstairs raising hell, playing, "Bang Bang Booby Trap," a ridiculous made-up game which was a combination of hide and seek and doctor. The only real rule was that when the first one of us to spot a hiding cousin yelled, "bang, bang, booby trap," the kid that got caught had to do whatever the cleverer cousin told them to do. This pretty much had to do with pulling down your pants or the like. We always had a grand time together but, by the time we moved to the Southside, five years had passed since we had enjoyed a Seder at Uncle Sid's house.

Fortunately, I had a few acquaintances on that side of town because I belonged to B.B.G.—B'nai B'rith Girls—which was a bit like a Jewish sorority, and had attended several Sweet Sixteen and pajama parties at their homes.

Harvey was almost old enough to join A.Z.A., the boy's version of B.B.G., and a few years later would make a spectacular metamorphosis from the orange-headed nerdy-looking kid with glasses to being appointed the year's B.B.G. heartthrob. This surprise event occurred after he threw a smart-ass kid who called him "four eyes" over a desk at Sunday school and nearly punched his lights out in front of an audience of B.B.G. girls standing nearby, swooning.

I was also fortunate that Charles, who I had dated a little the year before, lived on the Southside. He also attended Bolles, and he was still very interested in dating me.

I told myself, *It could be worse, try to think positive and look at the bright side. Hell, it's only one year.* Still, as I struggled to convince myself that these things should help me to make the move easier I couldn't fool my body. My stomach clenched and I felt like someone had kicked the air of me.

The Bloodiest Month

Selma to Montgomery March, 1965

MARCH OF 1965 would go down in history as one of the bloodiest in the fight for civil rights in the South. In Selma, Alabama, the Selma-to-Montgomery marches, also known as Bloody Sunday, and the two marches that followed, marked the political and emotional peak of the American civil rights movement. All three were attempts to march from Selma into Montgomery, where the Alabama capital was located.

The marches grew out of the voting rights movement in Selma, launched by local African Americans who formed the Dallas County Voters League. The first march took place on March 7, 1965, when 600 marchers were protesting the death of unarmed Jimmie Lee Jackson a few weeks earlier.

On that fateful day, twenty-six-year-old Jimmie Lee, his mother Viola Jackson, and his eighty-two-year-old grandfather, Cager Lee, ran into Mack's Café behind the church to escape the Alabama state troopers chasing them. Police hit Cager Lee with clubs until he fell to the floor in the kitchen. They continued to beat the cowering old man, and when his daughter Viola attempted to pull the police off, she was also beaten. Jimmie Lee attempted to protect his mother, leading to a trooper throwing him against a cigarette machine, then a second trooper shot Jimmie Lee twice in the stomach. Although shot twice, Jimmie Lee escaped the café, ultimately collapsing in front of the bus station. His mother, Viola, was able to make a statement to an attorney in the presence of FBI officials stating he was "clubbed down" by state troopers after he was shot and had run away from the café. Jimmie died two days later.

During the standoff between police and the protesters, streetlights mysteriously went out. Rumor had it, they were shot out by the police to make it easier to attack the protestors. In the scuffle, two United Press International photographers' cameras were smashed and the two were beaten, and NBC News correspondent Richard Valeriani was badly injured by an ax-wielding protester leaving him hospitalized.

The second march was held the following Tuesday, in which 2,500 protesters crossed the Edmund Pettus Bridge, then turned around, in keeping with a court order refusing them permission to march any further. They marched in good part to protest the killing of the Reverend James Reed, a Unitarian Universalist minister who had, along with two other white ministers, gone to Selma to support the march on Bloody Sunday. The evening after the march, he was beaten with clubs by the Ku Klux Klan. Reverend Reed was rushed to Selma's Public Hospital, where he was refused treatment and had to be driven to Birmingham's University Hospital, two hours away. The following day, he died.

Meanwhile, the race riots in Saint Augustine continued to gain steam. In Jacksonville, they also reached a fevered pitch. To make matters worse, Mother Nature started kicking up her heels—in the midst of unprecedented violence and destruction, Hurricane Dora, which was battering the coastline of Saint Augustine, began working its way north toward Jacksonville. Before the third march in Selma began, Hurricane Dora was already clobbering Jacksonville.

Though the Dallas County Voters League had begun its registration campaign in 1963, it had become obvious that the organization had still not overcome white resistance to Black voter registration, so a third march was formed. Marchers averaged ten miles a day walking along Route 80. 2,000 U.S. Army soldiers and 1,900 Alabama National Guards people protected them, along with federal marshals and agents from the FBI.

One of the places they marched through in the chilling rain, Lowndes County, had a population that was 81% Black and 19% white. Despite the large numbers, not a single registered voter was Black. Meanwhile, 2,240 whites were registered to vote there, a number that represented 118% of the white adult residents, highlighting the corruption that permeated the South. It was commonplace to allow white voters to remain on the rolls even after they had died or relocated. On March 24, the marchers arrived in Montgomery and at the Alabama state capitol on March 25. There they were met by a line of Marion City police officers and sheriff's deputies.

At the same time the third Selma-to-Montgomery March was taking place, Jacksonville was experiencing its worst race riots in the history of the city. The unrest started outside New Stanton, a Negro high school, where the Blacks, frustrated by the lack of improvement in their lives, threw bottles, bricks, and stones. A car carrying three white reporters was overturned and set on fire. One of the reporters from *Life Magazine* was cornered and beaten. By the time it was over, 260 people were arrested.

The same day, across town in another area of Jacksonville, Johnnie Mae Chappell, thirty-five-year-old maid and mother of ten, was walking down the highway after work, carrying a bag of groceries. She arrived home to find her wallet was missing from her grocery sack, so she went out again, retracing her steps to see if she could find it along the highway. At the same time, four young, racist white men were joyriding around town, drinking beer when one of them said, "Let's go get a nigger," and, spotting Mrs. Chappell on the side of the road, shot her in the stomach.

When she didn't return home, her husband went on a search to find her. He eventually encountered her body on the side of the road, still alive, but having nearly bled to death. In the ambulance on the way to the hospital, she died. Her death sent shockwaves through the Black community of Jacksonville. Despite the violence happening in other parts of the South, this incident hit far too close to home to ignore. Her family was torn apart, children sent to live with relatives and in foster homes, their lives forever altered by this senseless act. These men robbed Johnnie Mae of the rest of her life, but it's the ripple effect that impacts the children and the husband that's easy to overlook. All in all, twelve people were impacted by this one act of hatred. To make matters worse, only one of the four men was arrested and charged and he served only three years in prison.

Willie worried for her and her family's safety constantly. Everywhere I looked, life seemed unjust and unfair.

The Unthinkable

Vietnam

BECAUSE THERE WAS little reported in the newspapers about the riots, my teenage friends and I didn't know many details about the appalling events playing out around us. Still, it was impossible to ignore the tensions from these injustices happening in our world. And, while there was an undercurrent of sadness and frustration, being young as we were, the need to enjoy ourselves bubbled to the surface of the prevailing angst. The Jay Notes and Lemon Twister dances were still well attended. But, as we bopped along with The Supremes, The Temptations, and other Motown favorite recording artists, in an attempt to distract from the fact that it felt as though the world might break apart, another new musical style was beginning to make its way across the ocean from England.

I reckoned that if I was going to survive my last year of high school, I better start focusing on making new friends. Sally, another senior girl I was hoping would become a friend at my new school had her own car, a vintage MG Roadster convertible, with running boards along the sides. She lived in an A-frame house, something entirely modern and unusual for Jacksonville. Sally was being raised by a single mother who was gone a lot, so she had access to the car most of the time.

A whole lot of shakin' was going on in my world, so I turned to the tried and true things I'd done in the past to have fun. Where the Crystal Burger had been the hangout on the Southeast side of town, now, on the Southside, my new friends and I cruised over to Lou Bono's Barbecue on Beach Boulevard for ribs. If Lou's wasn't hopping, we'd drive over to Frisch's Big Boy nearby, where we'd spend our hot evenings swilling down milkshakes, munching on French fries, and scanning the parking lot for the opposite sex.

Meanwhile, in Washington D.C., it appeared President Johnson was going to support the Civil Rights Act that President Kennedy had been promoting before he was gunned down, appearing on national television talking about his plan to make the USA "a great society." I'm not sure who he thought was buying this line of rhetoric delivered with his Texas twang. Initially, his speech may have given Blacks a momentary sigh of relief, but they'd been tricked enough throughout history that when it came to simple words and empty promises, they weren't easily convinced. It was over one hundred years from when President Lincoln delivered the Emancipation Proclamation, and very few Blacks felt emancipated—especially in the South. Once the KKK got wind of the planned Civil Rights Act, it served as fuel to enflame them, ultimately inspiring them to step up efforts in promoting their evil agenda.

As if that all wasn't enough, there was Vietnam. Several thousand military advisors were in Vietnam along with 11,000 troops, then Johnson announced the United States would send over an additional 5,000 U.S. soldiers, bringing the total number of U.S. forces in Vietnam to 21,000. Military spokesmen and Washington officials insisted that this didn't represent any change in current political policy, noting that new troops would only bolster existing U.S. efforts.

However, in August 1964, the situation changed when North Vietnamese torpedo boats attacked U.S. destroyers off the coast of North Vietnam. The Gulf of Tonkin Incident, as it came to be known, resulted in the Gulf of Tonkin Resolution, which passed near-unanimously in the House and the Senate, resulting in empowering President Johnson to, "take all necessary measures to repel an armed attack against the forces of the United States and to prevent further aggression."

In short order, Johnson ordered the bombing of North Vietnam in retaliation for the Gulf of Tonkin incident, and 1964 became the year the first U.S. military person was killed in Vietnam. As the years pressed on, thousands of young men were blown to bits or suffered injuries that would change their lives forever.

Among my friends, relatives, and classmates preparing to graduate from high school, tension constantly hung in the air around us. The boys were consumed with worry about being drafted and sent to war. Charles, who I had first met at a dance for Jewish kids when we lived in Lakeshore and who I was hoping would become my boyfriend, and some of his friends decided to enlist in the Coast Guard Reserves so as to ensure they could remain stateside. Soon so many boys, including Harvey, were signing up that it became dubbed, "The Jewish Navy" in Jacksonville.

The Civil Rights unrest continued to move at a fevered pace until the unthinkable happened. At the end of June, my first summer living on the Southside of town, three Civil Rights workers in their twenties were brutally murdered when Michael Schwerner and Andrew Goodman, both Jewish New Yorkers, and James Chaney, a Black native Mississippian, were killed by a KKK lynch mob near Meridian, Mississippi. They were all members the Congress of Racial Equality (CORE) and were working to register Black voters in Mississippi.

The three were returning from a trip to Philadelphia, Mississippi, where they had been registering Black voters all day, when Deputy Sheriff Cecil Price, a Klan member, pulled them over for speeding. He threw them in jail and waited. The three activists were later released, only to be chased down in their vehicle and cornered in a secluded spot in the woods, where they found themselves surrounded by Klan members. Moments later, they were shot and killed, then buried in graves that'd been prepared in advance. James Chaney, the only Black man, was brutally tortured before finally being shot to death. Forensic evidence later showed that Andrew Goodman was still alive when the KKK members buried him.

The murders garnered international attention—primarily because, this time, the Klan had killed two white boys. The search to find their bodies took forty-four days and involved local, state and federal resources including a group of Navy Seals who dove and explored a nearby river. By the time Michael, Andrew, and James's bodies were found, searchers had discovered two Black college students who had disappeared the month before, a fourteen-year-old boy, and five other unidentified Black individual's remains in their search for the three civil rights workers.

All in all, eighteen Klansmen were arrested. At trial, they appeared before an all-white jury and most of them walked free. Edgar Ray Killen, who initiated the night's events, would live decades as a free man before finally being brought to justice forty long years later.

From where I sat, 1964 appeared on a trajectory to cram in as many horrific events as one could possibly imagine.

California Dreamin'

Golden Gate Bridge

DESPITE DAD'S WISHES that I cut off all communication with friends, I stayed in touch with Nan. Because she still lived in Saint Petersburg I figured he was unlikely to find out. Hailing from San Francisco, Nan had opened my eyes to an entirely new way of looking at the world, one in which people lived free and easy—nothing like the rigid roles of Florida and the East Coast—and knowing I would soon be finishing high school, my thoughts often traveled back to her description of life in Northern California as a kind of *Brigadoon* fantasy to look forward to discovering one day.

Nan identified with the beatniks—and with her straight, long black hair, beret, mini-skirt, and knee-high boots, she sure looked the part. Her father was a D.J. on a radio station in San Francisco, which meant she knew all the latest songs and international hits.

Nan was as worldly a person as I'd ever met. She introduced me to the Brazilian Portuguese Bossanova sounds of Astrud Gilberto and the jazz of Stan Getz and their popular song, "Girl from Ipanema." She loaned me a book called *The Way of Zen,* by Alan Watts, a British-American philosopher who adapted Eastern philosophy for the Western audience. I became fascinated by contemporary new-wave poetry, learning about the City Lights Bookstore in San Francisco, founded by Lawrence Ferlinghetti, whose poetry, along with Richard Brautigan's, I adored. I lost myself in Jack Kerouac's road trip across America, set against a backdrop of jazz, poetry, and drugs, and dreamed of one day when I, too, could leave Jacksonville and find my own adventures.

I took a class on comparative religions at my synagogue, which included visiting various churches. I studied the Unitarian and Lutheran doctrines and found myself left with more questions than answers.

I reflected on the long hours Nan and I had shared, where she chain-smoked while telling me of the charm of the City by the Bay. As she described the steep hills, cable cars, and Chinatown, I could almost imagine myself there. The more stories she told me about Golden Gate Park, the drag queens, and coffee shops in North Beach, where folk music rife with political dissent and something called "Cool Jazz" were played every night, the more my heart stirred with longing. Her description of nightly recitations of beatnik poetry performed with the musical accompaniment of one or two instruments on stage, such as a flute or an upright bass playing dissonant sounds behind the performer, tugged at my creative soul.

My bland and difficult life in Jacksonville, contrasted against Nan's animated stories of California, began to make my life seem like one not worth living. By senior year, I had a thick file in the back of my mind labeled My Trip to San Francisco. But for a sixteen-

and-a-half-year-old girl who'd never traveled farther than Daytona Beach, San Francisco seemed far, far, away. And though the dream of ever actually finding my way there seemed impossible, still, with each continuous hurt and disappointment, my dream began to grow wings.

South Alcatraz

Mom looking glamorous

I T WAS SUMMERTIME and we had made the move to Southside. We were now officially living in "the rental," which was so small that Paulina slept in a roll-a-way bed in the living room because my bedroom was too small to share. There was only one bathroom for all six of us. The kitchen was tiny. The front screened porch was stacked floor to ceiling with the extra belongings we couldn't fit inside. There was no front yard to speak of and the back yard was the size of a postage stamp, mostly taken up by a small detached garage Dad used as a sign-painting studio.

Each day he came home from job hunting, poured himself a glass of iced tea, walked into the bedroom, and asked Mom "Ruthie, can you wake me up in fifteen minutes?"

Upon awakening from his power nap, he'd mutter aloud, "Okay, Max, shwit, shwit, back to the salt mines, shwit, shwit," while pretending to whip himself over the back. Then he'd go out to the little sign shop and work until the sun fell to the horizon.

Dad's behavior reminded me of the movie *Birdman of Alcatraz*, specifically the desperation of Burt Lancaster's character, Robert Stroud, a man sentenced to life on the prison island. Whenever Dad went into his faux back-whipping rendition of misery, I pictured Burt Lancaster singing the Tennessee Ernie Ford miner's lamentation, "Sixteen Tons."

As always, Dad, never one to suffer in silence, let all of us know just how miserable he was.

Conversely, our move to Southside meant that Mom had an excuse to leave her management position at The Vogue Shoppes, which she hated. She found a job nearby at an exclusive ladies clothing store called Bolen's, settled in quickly, and enjoyed working there.

Each morning, when Mom donned one of her designer dresses and took off for the air-conditioned, upscale shop, she looked stunning. This set me to thinking, *It's as though she's performing in a play, where she's the wife of a well-to-do husband and only works at Bolen's as a hobby to fill her days.* I wished it was the truth.

As refreshed as she looked when she walked out the door, at evening's end—after serving dinner in our hot, cramped kitchen— she was equally deflated and frazzled, only to be renewed again the following morning at work. I was happy she was blessed with at least part of a life she enjoyed, out of the house, with other people and away from the stifling heat of our cramped cottage. I knew in my heart that the role she was playing was her salvation and, I thought, a well-deserved godsend.

We were simply too many sardines packed in the hot little tin can of the rental house. We got on each other's nerves without the slightest provocation. We didn't have a big yard to retreat to anymore. Desperate for nature, Harvey and I took to schmoozing over to the cemetery nearby—a lovely open space next to a deep creek, with weeping willows growing at the water's edge. It reminded us of our beloved swamp, and became our new refuge to walk among the tombstones, smoke stolen cigarettes, and air grievances to one another, away from the pressure cooker of life in the rental.

I slowly began to grasp the fact that Mom and Dad would probably never again have the security of owning their own home—a thought which brought me immense sadness.

The Hope Chest

ATTRACTIVE MODERN CHEST in blond oak. Model #1132. $599.95*

Give her the graduation gift that gathers _more_ gifts...
A LANE CEDAR CHEST

Lane Cedar Chest advertisement, 1955

O NE SATURDAY, A couple of months after we moved into the rental, the doorbell rang. I peeked out the living room window to see a man dressed in a cheap black suit carrying a large satchel. Willie answered the door, exchanged a few words, then left him on the porch.

"Mr. Mack," said Willie, "he asked if the lady of the house is here."

Mom was still at work. Dad walked to the front door and opened it.

"Sir, I understand you have a daughter living here who will soon be graduating from high school, is that correct?"

This was the poor guy's opening line.

"Yes," responded Dad, perturbed.

"Well, Sir, I can almost bet you a dollar to a donut that your daughter has a hope chest, correct?"

Dad stood there speechless for a very short minute and before he could take a second breath the salesman continued, "If you'll give me a moment of your time, I would like to show you the fantastic buys I can offer you on dishes, silverware, pots and pans. After all, you want your daughter to have everything she'll need to set up housekeeping once she finds that lucky fella to marry, isn't that right?"

Dad's neck started to flush, the red color working its way up toward his cheeks. Dad was gearing up for one of his famous slow-motion fits of rage.

When he finally spoke, saying, "Buddy," in his fake nice voice, I shuddered.

This is not going to go well.

"Why don't you come inside, I want to show you something," Dad said, ushering the man into our small house.

Once Dad had successfully cornered the salesman in the kitchen, he pointed to the duct taped yellow Naugahyde upholstery of our chrome and Formica dinette set. Miraculously, at that moment the bolts keeping his head screwed to his neck were holding, but just barely.

"See this dinette set?" said Dad, trying to suppress his urge to yell at the top of his lungs.

I took a long deep breath.

The man looked embarrassingly at the chairs. They were so covered with grey duct tape almost no original yellow color showed through.

"Come here," Dad continued. "Let me show you something else."

Dad and his blazing cheeks walked the salesman over to the closed rollaway bed standing in the corner of the living room.

"See this bed? Here in the living room? This is where my youngest daughter sleeps." Dad motioned again, "Come heah."

The salesman followed Dad to the jalousie front porch they'd passed through to get inside the house. With the exception of a narrow entry path, the porch was jammed from floor to ceiling with cardboard boxes.

"See these boxes?"

This time, the salesman silently nodded.

"Before I'm going to spend one red cent on cookware for my daughter's future, I'm going to buy my wife a new dining room set and a house with a bedroom for my youngest daughter and—"

He stopped mid-sentence to let the salesman bolt out the front door.

I was mortified.

Nearly every day after our move into the tiny rental, our lives were rife with a kind of pandemonium bordering on chaos that felt as if at any moment the ground underneath us might crumble and swallow us whole.

We still had the security of Willie for the moment, but her presence, too, was on an invisible chopping block, and I worried that might change soon enough.

Another Secret Suitcase

I finally learn the biggest secret in Dad's suitcase

BOUT A WEEK after Dad chased the hope chest salesman out of our house, I bumped into my Aunt Rudy at the San Jose Shopping Center. It was so great to see her. I asked if she had time to get an ice cream with me and we walked over to Baskin-Robbins together.

In part, I felt I was betraying Dad, by talking with his sister, who our family was banned from seeing but, I reasoned, now that we were living on the same side of town, Dad had to know we would run into our "other relatives" every now and again. Also, he seemed to be mad at me so much of the time that I figured it wasn't any added risk to seek her counsel.

"Aunt Rudy," I began, "Dad scares the hell out of me. I think there might be something wrong with him. He has such a temper and can't seem to control himself. I don't know what to do."

"Oh sweetie," Rudy said, shaking her head slowly and looking at me with pained eyes. "Yes, honey, there is something you need to know."

I took a deep breath.

She began, "Five years before your father met your mother, he was in a terrible car accident. Grandpa Ben had driven up to New York to see the mishpocheh (extended family) in Rockaway, something he did every summer. He and Grandma were in the front seats and Aunt Bea, the wife of one of Grandpa Ben's brothers, was in the backseat sitting next to your father. Well, another car plowed into the back of their vehicle and the door where Aunt Bea sat flew open. Your dad reached over to grab her and try to pull her back in the car. When he did, the car door swung back and hit him in the face, knocking out most of his teeth, and he fell out of the moving car and hit his head on the pavement. Sadly, Aunt Bea died at the scene."

"Oh my God," I uttered.

Rudy continued, "By the time the ambulance arrived at the hospital, your dad was in a coma. We didn't know if he would ever regain consciousness, or—if he did—if he would ever recover and live a normal life again. He remained in the coma for three weeks. In fact, he was in such bad shape that when Uncle Uly went to the hospital to visit him, the receptionist was typing up your father's death certificate. Miraculously, he regained consciousness. But he was not the same person he had been before the crash. He suffered a traumatic brain injury and went on to exhibit most of the behaviors associated with such a problem."

I sat spellbound, completely dumbfounded hearing this story flow from my trusted aunt's lips. This was it—the final secret Dad brought into his marriage, spilled open. I couldn't speak. I felt faint.

Aunt Rudy looked at me. "Are you all right?"

"I'm not sure."

In a flash, it all came rushing back—the nightmare I'd had of Dad telling me he was going to die in a car suddenly made sense. And the ghosts...Dad's Aunt Bea was one of them. *I bet she's been in the car with us on trips to Daytona,* sailed through my head.

"Can I get you an ice cream?" she asked.

I was so engrossed in our conversation that I didn't even register her question, so she continued talking about how easy-going Dad had been before the accident.

"Even though he was broken-hearted over Martha being institutionalized, he had always had a lot of hope and optimism. But after the car accident happened, he fell apart. So, ten years later, when Mom and Dad, your grandparents, died—also in a tragic accident—it brought those terrible memories flooding back to your father. In fact, he had to see a psychiatrist for a while. I wish I could do something to help, but your Dad doesn't want our family to have anything to do with yours."

"Thank you for telling me the truth," I said, "I love you," and threw my arms around her and planted a kiss on her cheek. *Finally, the truth.*

"I love you too, Gabrielle," she said, squeezing me tight.

Then I watched as she used her cane to limp toward the car, wondering if I would ever see her again.

The Third Terrible Trouble

Demonstrators taunt the police during the Harlem riot of 1964

E ARLY ONE MONDAY morning a few weeks after my talk with Aunt Rudy, Willie showed up to the house for work. I walked into the kitchen just as she was saying to Mom, "Miz Mack, remember when I told you that I had an aunt in New York?"

"Yes, Willie."

"Well, Missus, just yesterday, I received a letter from her with three train tickets in it. I'm taking my boys to New York on Friday."

Willie had told me more than once that if her aunt ever sent her the money to move to New York she would go, in hopes of giving Raymond and Marvin a better chance in life. But I never really believed it could happen. *Then, again,* I thought, *I never imagined our president would be murdered, either.* My heart sank. I couldn't fathom life without Willie. In my seventeen years, I'd never lost anyone I loved as much as her, except maybe Tippy.

"I'll stay here with Benny until Harvey or Gabrielle get home from school," Willie said to Mom, then she picked up a basket of wet laundry and carried it outside to hang on the line. "Is there anything else you'd like me to do today, Miz Mack?"

"Just the usual things," Mom replied. Then she cast a casual, "See you later, kids," to us and walked out the door for work.

Looking back on it, I wish I had begged Willie not to leave. Or told her how much I—we—all loved her. I wish I had run into my room and gotten the allowance I'd been saving up for the movies and given it to her for her journey. I wish I had asked her to write to us when she got settled.

Why didn't Mom ask her to stay in touch? I wondered.

All I can figure is that the news was so surreal—so unbelievable—that neither Harvey nor I thought of saying anything except, "Bye, Willie," as we headed out the door to school.

Soon after we had missed our window of opportunity, I began wondering what Willie must have thought. She'd been with us twelve years, most of my lifetime, and not a single one of us wished her well or asked her to stay in touch. All I could think is that we were all so taken by surprise that her leaving didn't seem real.

We were all devastated, but none as much as little Benny. He was so young and considered Willie his "real" mother. Now, he was in a new neighborhood and school where he knew nobody, and his best friend would no longer be there to joke around with and to love him. My heart sank. I felt terrible for him.

Poor Benny was still wetting the bed and failing in school. For many years after Willie left, Benny would say, "Every time I see a Black woman, I want to follow her home."

When the reality of Willie's loss settled in, in order to cope, we made up a fantasy that we used to help each other when one of us would felt overwhelmed with remorse over her departure. The conversation went like this:

"Don't lose hope, because one day Willie will contact Bob Barker of *Truth or Consequences* and arrange for him to invite us on the show. And when we walk out on the stage, Willie will be hiding behind the curtain, just like she used to when we tried to take her photo."

Then Mr. Barker will say, "And now, kids, I have an old friend who has been waiting to see you after all these years."

Then all four of us will run across the stage to meet her and we will spend the rest of the show hugging her and thanking her for having blessed our lives."

But as the years rolled by, we never did go on *Truth or Consequences*—nor did we ever see or hear from Willie again.

Senior Year, Supercar, and Vietnam

Supercar

NOW A SENIOR in a new high school, I finally gave up my attempts at trying to date non-Jewish guys—it just wasn't worth the battle with Dad. Charles had become my steady boyfriend. He was ruggedly handsome and, though he was a year younger than me, he looked older. Like me, he was the oldest of four children, two boys and two girls, though his mother was raising her children alone. Dad finally got his wish: I was dating a Jewish boy and Harvey began attending the Bolles School, the same school Charles went to, and they became fast friends.

In a clever maneuver, Harvey managed to turn a disadvantage—our family car—a huge, winged, flesh-colored beast, a 1959 Dodge Coronet, designed at the apex of the fin era—to his advantage. Along with its huge fins, it sported ginormous tail lights, which stuck out several inches off the back of the car, making it look like a huge anemic tuna, with the retrorockets a superhero might have on their spaceship. Brilliantly, Harvey turned his poverty into a novelty by dubbing our car "Supercar."

None of the boys in their navy blue blazers with the Bolles coat of arms on the pocket would have ever driven a piece of junk like our car onto the circular driveway of the school's estate, much less have the nerve to park it in front of the stately stone and brick school that practically reeked of old money. But whenever Harvey came driving up, whoever spotted the car first would yell, "Supercar!" and a big group of boys would all run out yelling its name, and surround the banged-up clunker, as though they were greeting royalty.

I'm sure the other students thought it was Harvey's very own car but, in truth, it was really the only car our family had. Supercar had a trunk that was tied down with a piece of rope but still made a banging sound as we bounced down the street. Unable to get the trunk completely closed, the stinky fumes were drawn from the exhaust pipe through the trunk into the inside of the car, making it impossible for the passengers to avoid inhaling the toxic carbon monoxide.

My favorite feature of the car was its speedometer—a long rectangular strip that turned colors from blue to green to yellow then red once you were speeding. I always enjoyed stomping on the gas to watch the colors change.

While Harvey rubbed elbows with the upper crust, I was just managing to complete my senior year. A few months before my high school graduation, the Civil Rights Movement grew stronger and more focused—it was 103 years since President Lincoln signed the Emancipation Proclamation freeing the slaves and yet, in most states in the union, Blacks were still unable to vote.

It didn't seem to me that much of anything had changed in the

Deep South. I witnessed continued injustice and hatred directed toward Blacks. Once it came to light that Stanley Levinson, a Jewish attorney, was Dr. Martin Luther King Jr.'s right-hand man, it further stirred the ire of the rabid racists determined to keep the Black community down. This news, coupled with the fact that most folks pretty much knew that of the three civil rights workers slain in 1963 in Mississippi, two were Jewish, fueled the fire of hatred toward the Jews in the South. Even though we were now living on the "Jewish side of town"—which was really a misnomer considering how few Jews there were compared to Gentiles—the fact that the media could point to Jewish people being supportive of the Blacks in a definitive way caused me to feel that I should still continue to be cautious about revealing the fact I was Jewish to my new Gentile friends.

The era of the folk song was in full swing, and God only knows there were plenty of things to sing protest songs about. I figured if I could learn how to play the guitar, I could become part of the collective voice against prejudice. Charles and his friend Steve played guitar and banjo on the weekends at a trendy coffee house, The Jongleur. The venue, opened by a couple of progressive Jewish schoolteachers, gave folk singers a place to perform. We thought we were very grown-up, sitting at the little tables drinking ginger beer in the small, dark café. Their debut song was "The Lion Sleeps Tonight." Charles had mastered the yodel part of the song and they sounded great.

Charles bought me a Goya nylon-stringed classical guitar and began teaching me how to play. I practiced songs by Bob Dylan and Peter, Paul and Mary, trying to emulate Mary's voice. I didn't have long blonde straight hair, so I began ironing my naturally curly red locks. Charles and I went to see Peter, Paul and Mary live and got to go backstage and meet them, which was quite a thrill.

Protest songs were all the rage, so the first songs I learned on the guitar were "Blowin' in the Wind" and "The Cruel War."

Barry Maguire's tune "The Eve of Destruction" was the most popular folk-rock song of 1965—its direct and powerful lyrics propelled it to continued popularity throughout the Vietnam years.

"The Times They Are a-Changin'" by Bob Dylan combined the folk protest movement of the 1960s with the Civil Rights Movement and would soon become the hippie lamentation. In Florida, boys didn't have shoulder-length hair yet, but I had a feeling that in California they did—and were singing Dylan's lyrics to their conservative parents. The lyrics became a manifesto that emboldened us to the challenges that lie ahead.

We were a generation that had witnessed the threat of nuclear war, seen our president assassinated, and observed continued, blatant, racist cruelty. That these shocking events invaded our living rooms via our television sets only served to magnify them. Bob Dylan, along with others' iconic lyrics, spoke to the insanity of war.

Anti-Vietnam war protests were gaining popularity. Hundreds of students demonstrated in New York's Times Square and marched to the United Nations building, while twelve young men burned their draft cards as a publicity stunt. At the memorial service of the three civil rights workers slain in Philadelphia, Mississippi, one mourner used the media coverage as an opportunity to speak out bitterly against President Johnson's use of force in Vietnam, comparing it to the treatment the Blacks had suffered.

Television broadcasts of the first American combat troops arriving in Vietnam served as a momentary distraction from the happenings of the Civil Rights Movement. I watched spellbound as 3,500 U.S. Marines arrived at China Beach to defend the American airbase at Da Nang which was broadcast on the nightly news. They joined the 23,000 American advisors already there. The

U.S. was definitely in a war now, and everyone I knew worried how it was going to affect them or their children. More casualties were reported from Vietnam every day, even as U.S. commanders demanded more troops. Under the draft system, as many as 40,000 young men were called into service each month, adding fuel to the fire of the war. *What a mess,* I thought, although the Vietnam War hadn't hurt anyone I knew personally, at least not yet.

Jackie Gleason

June Taylor Dancers

O NE EVENING WHEN Charles and I were sitting on his bed at his Mom's house practicing guitar, the phone rang. It was his father, Will, who Charles hadn't spoken to in many months. His handsome father was beginning auditions for the musical *Gypsy*, which was to be performed at the Little Theatre, our community theatre in San Marco, across the street from Bolen's Dress Shoppe where Mom worked. Both Will and Jeanie, his second wife, auditioned and got parts. Jeanie played a stripper and sang the song, "You Gotta Get a Gimmick," in which she appeared on stage scantily clad, sporting a horn.

She did a fantastic job. Will played Herbie, the manager of the original vaudeville stage act. Watching Will perform was like seeing an older version of Charles strutting across the stage. He was a talented actor.

Because Jeanie had been in the June Taylor Dancers, Charles and I were invited to spend a weekend at Miami. The first evening we went to a live recording of *The Jackie Gleason Show*. The next two days were spent dining at the famous Art Deco hotels on the strip, like the Fontainebleau, the Delano, and the Raleigh. We spent our last day on a huge yacht sailing around Biscayne Bay. Charles and I felt like royalty, rubbing elbows with the rich and famous as they hobnobbed and shared inside gossip about *The Gleason Show*. Our biggest thrill was meeting Mercedes Ellington, Duke's daughter.

I liked Jeanie, but at the same time felt conflicted in that I had become very good friends with Charles' mother, Marsha. I felt sorry for her having been replaced by a much younger woman, especially in light of the fact she had to work full-time at a thankless bookkeeping job and was raising her four kids alone. Even so, she was fortunate that there was money in the family, which enabled her to send her boys to Bolles. Charles' family was also blessed to live in a nice big house within walking distance from the school.

Their home became a refuge for me, especially on the weekends. Charles's wealthy elderly grandmother had recently moved in with them. She left her big, beautiful estate home and grounds behind, a place she'd lived most of her life, which continued to be maintained by a gardener and pool boy. This gave Charles and me an opportunity to enjoy skinny-dipping in the pool, something we did often.

I had finally gotten the Nice Jewish Boyfriend, and Dad relaxed his grip. Still, the concern over what would become of me after high school was never far from my mind.

One night, I got to thinking that since I'd been caring for my younger siblings and animals most of my life, I might make a good nurse, and I shared the idea with Dad who, for once in his life, had nothing to say. I found his silence more disconcerting than hearing him rant.

The following evening after dinner, he instructed me to get in the car. "We're going to visit a friend," he said.

We sat at her dining room table, sipping iced tea while she talked for over an hour about bodily fluids, bed pans, and every other disgusting aspect of nursing. On the drive home he returned to his mantra, "See, I told you, the best thing for you to do is to learn how to type."

Truth was, I didn't really want to be a nurse, but it sure sounded more interesting than being a dang typist or a secretary. In my desperation to come up with a future plan, I'd forgotten about the time I fainted in the parking lot of a hospital from the sight of a young boy being walked into the emergency room with a bandaged arm leaking blood.

I wanted to be an art teacher, but Dad would hardly look at my art and often recited his old saw, "Art is fine, but it is no way to make a living. Just learn how to type good, see."

With each passing month, I grew more nervous. I couldn't talk to my new friends about my dilemma—they didn't want to hear about my worries when their biggest concerns were choosing a prom dress or what university to attend. Deep down inside, I knew that my life was never going to become anything that vaguely resembled an Elvis movie. Hollywood was not going to discover me. My parents didn't think it was important for girls to go to college and wouldn't have had the money to send me even if they had.

Mom and Dad hadn't even graduated from high school and knew nothing about navigating a system of financial aid or applying for scholarships. Somehow, they had gotten the mistaken idea that if a kid was a straight-A student, the Good Fairy of Scholarships would fly down and wave her wand and a huge pot of money would fall from the sky that would cover every conceivable expense one needed to flourish in college. They simply didn't know that many folks got partial scholarships and used work-study or loans to supplement the remainder of the university expenses. Our only family member who'd gone to college was Uncle Uly, compliments of the G.I. Bill.

One evening, after the little kids went to bed, I decided to try to reason with my parents, one last time.

They were sitting on the couch watching TV when I approached them. "Mom and Dad," I said, "I'd like to go to Daytona Beach Junior College."

I knew that I could easily get into DBJC, as only a C average was required, and my average grades were above that.

"You're not college material!" Dad barked. "Learn how to type."

If he had kicked me in the stomach and knocked the air clean out of me, I couldn't have been more devastated. I knew that I was smart, certainly smarter than some of the cracker teachers I'd had throughout my life. I wasn't a straight-A student, that was true, but my grades were good enough to get in DBJC.

I didn't know how to explain that school bored me—not because I "couldn't keep up," rather because I wasn't interested in science and math, but was fascinated with the humanities, theatre, art, and music, courses that our cracker high school offered very little of.

Mom was a little more supportive. She tried to convince Dad that he should let me take an entrance test they offered to prove to him that I was, in fact, "college material," though her next comment, "But most girls only go to college to get their MRS degree, you know, to get married," negated the support. The MRS degree was a well-vocalized opinion of the times and one Mom considered witty.

As if the fire in my brain wasn't already sufficiently stoked, she poured fuel on it by saying, "It's really more important for your brother to get a college education because he is going to have to support a family someday."

Then Dad repeated again, "Just learn how to type, see."

I ran out of the room in tears.

How can he say I'm not college material? My Dad thinks I'm too stupid to attend higher education.

His words bruised my soul, and would go on to haunt me for years, sowing such havoc to my self-esteem that, from that moment on, the driving force of my life became proving that I was, in fact, smart and capable. *And,* I promised myself, *one day I will go to college and get my degree and then we'll see who's college material.*

That night sleep would not come. I tossed and turned, trying to think of something to tell myself that would help me, until finally an Elvis tune bubbled into my brain: "Didja' ever get one of them days?" The song chronicles the kind of day where nothing goes right from morning till night. He's at a picnic and it starts to pour, he runs away and into a poison ivy patch. It culminates with ants carrying off the sandwiches. It was from the movie, *G.I. Blues,* which I loved.

The last thing I remember thinking before sweet sleep came was *most of my days lately feel like "one of them days." Still, I'll figure something out.*

The following morning, I still felt like I was in a bad dream. Dad and I had been through our share of rough patches, but his notion that I wasn't suited for college was undoubtedly the most painful thing he had ever said—a statement that even managed to trump being called a whore earlier in the summer. The person I loved most in the world had told me I was stupid. I was devastated. No, more than devastated, but there were no words for this flavor of grief.

Telling me I wasn't college material felt like a well-calculated design to rob me of all hope of a promising future. I felt panicked and frightened to my core. Graduation was coming up and I was filled with complete and utter dread.

Pomp and Circumstance

Our senior photos

ON JUNE 9, 1965, my skinny, red-haired self stood waiting in the freezing air conditioned corridor of the Jacksonville Coliseum, twisting and turning under my heavy black graduation gown. The audio portion of my brain replayed the worries that would plague my mind all evening and, in the name of drowning them out, I became distracted by meaningless observations: *Boy, they really turned the air conditioning up high. Look at these folks, they all know what college they're going to after they get their diplomas. They don't have a worry in the world.*

Fact was, I was nervous. Even if the temperature had been perfect, I would have found something to trouble me. This was supposed to be an important day.

From the vantage point of the acoustic-tiled ceiling where my disembodied spirit floated, most of the smiling students seemed happy, or at least that was how it looked to me. Friends elbowed and joked with one another. Teenage couples held hands, drawing one another close, trying to calm their raging hormones.

I felt so incredibly alone, a stranger in this scene I was supposed to be part of. For the rest of the students, this would be only one of the many joyous and important days of their lives.

Why is this taking so long? I wondered. My stomach grumbled. I'd only gone to Dupont one year prior to graduation. A year that had, so far, won the "worst year of my life" award. *What the hell am I going to do with the rest of my life?* I began mentally counting the horrible events:

We'd lost our family home and moved into a tiny rental.

Dad lost his job.

I was forced to leave all my friends on the other side of town.

We lost our beloved nanny, Willie.

I got date raped.

Shit, shit, shit.

All painful events, but even those paled in comparison to my plea to go to junior college to study art.

My father's words about college echoed in my mind and cut through me.

I didn't know most of the other black-robed kids wearing mortar boards on their heads. The few I did know were definitely going to college. In fact, they all were. After tonight, they would resume their happy lives with wonderful futures. They would live in beautiful homes and drive fabulous cars and, like their parents, they, too, would make plans for their kids to go to the best colleges before they could walk.

I would not be joining them.

I didn't know what would become of me. Nor did I know that years from this day I would learn that a college degree was not a guarantee for a long, happy, and healthy life. But at the moment of my high school graduation, it sure seemed that is was. I was seventeen, scared, and lacked the knowledge I needed to make my dream happen. The Good Fairy of Scholarships was not going to stop at my house, not ever.

As the graduates waited, joking with one another, I felt jealous. For them, this was a night of parties and congratulations. I felt my face turn red as envy turned to rage. *I'm the first person in our family to get a high school diploma, including Mom and Dad. Why is it, then,* I asked myself, *that my family isn't even in the audience?*

I was a ghost going through the motions.

My spirit screamed. *Why aren't they here, God dammit!*

This night, like many events over the last few years, was devoid of logic. But this experience, of graduating with no plan ahead, with no family support, brought it all to a head in equal parts humiliation, anger, and utter bewilderment. *What was the point of anything?*

The dark, cavernous coliseum at the end of the hall was a whale, and I was Jonah, spiraling toward the black hole of its huge open mouth. There would be nothing left for me after I grabbed that piece of rolled paper—"the sheepskin," as Mom liked to call it. There was no celebration, just the quick step off the edge into a bleak future of nothingness. My knotted shoulders broadcast loudly to my nervous brain the same message it had been repeating endlessly for the last few weeks: *You have no idea what the next stage of your life holds, do you?* The internal interrogation found no reply—anxiety had become my closest companion.

My thoughts ran rampant in a frightening circle. *I can't think about this now. I must focus,* I told myself in a vain attempt to quell the paralyzing reality, if only for a moment. The inner voice continued, *Just breathe and keep standing.* That was the answer. *Keep breathing and hold yourself up, shoulders back, that's it, breathe. Wait until you see people moving, then put one foot in front of the other until you make it to the stage and pick up the meaningless scroll. Then it will be over. You will be able to escape this shame and run away from this dark worry that has been stalking you for years. Focus on something else: San Francisco, San Francisco, San Francisco.*

The Rotten Apple

My favorite teddy bear

FTER THE GRADUATION ceremony I went home. All I wanted to do was go to my room and sleep. The last thing I wanted to do was talk to anyone—least of all Mom or Dad. Truth was, I didn't want to hear Dad's damn voice. His words had wounded me so deeply that I couldn't imagine that he could say anything that would hurt me more. But, like so many things I'd learned I couldn't control, this desire was another on that list. I creaked open the front door and padded into the living room. Dad was on the couch.

I wanted to ask, "Why didn't you and Mom come to my graduation ceremony?" But, I decided, it's too late. *It's over, just go to your room.* Instead I figured a simple, "Hi, Dad," would get me a pass through the living room and on to bed. But boy, was I wrong.

"Congratulations on your graduation," Dad said. "You have two weeks to get a job and move out."

"Uh?" was all I could manage.

He continued, "You see, it's like this. If you have a barrel full of apples and one of them is rotten, you've gotta' get rid of the rotten one or it will rot all the other apples."

There are no words to describe the feeling of the knife, already in my heart, being twisted.

I ran out of the living room, fell onto my bed, and unraveled. Tears fell like a torrent. I couldn't catch my breath, my chest heaved and hurt. I wrapped my arms around my pillow and held tight like it was a life raft. *Jesus Christ, he's kicking me out.*

As I lay in my bed, I watched a slideshow of a life that I would never be a part of again. Paulina wasn't even twelve. She'd been practicing cheerleading routines in the yard every day after school in hopes of becoming a cheerleader in the upcoming tryouts for junior high next year. I will never see her tryouts. Little Benny had been working on robots—he was barely nine. *I won't see the little guy grow up. Harvey is my best friend—he will be gone too. I will no longer be part of their lives. Period. End of sentence. Dad's taking away "my kids." I hate him. He wants me to go. Then, god dammit, I'll go. And not in two weeks—Monday. I will apply for a job. That's what I'll do.*

Songs had always served as guides for me—so I found a new one that would provide strength during the dark, lonely days ahead. The lyrics to "California Dreamin'" became my mantra as I imagined happier days ahead—sometime in the future, past Dad and the little house and the fear of the unknown.

Someday, I promised myself, I'll find the courage to forge my own path forward and move across the world to my dream of San Francisco, San Francisco, San Francisco...

Epilogue

Dad and me in New York, 1972

A T THE AGE of seventeen, living in the Deep South, I had no idea that I wasn't the only young person who felt disenfranchised, confused, and at complete odds with my parents. In only a couple of years I'd discover there was a huge groundswell of young people just like me who felt called to take action over the injustices that loomed over us—like the young men who were being used to stoke the war machinery of Vietnam—but for now, I was on my own, and had to figure out the next steps.

I told myself I'd use my steely resolve to find my own apartment, but first I had to get a job.

The very first Monday morning after the "Rotten Apple" speech I got up early, put on my Sunday Go-To-Meetin' clothes, walked past my parents seated at the kitchen table, and made my way to the bus stop toward downtown Jacksonville to apply for a job at Prudential Life Insurance Company. I had heard through the grapevine it was easy to get hired at the seventeen-story home office, just past San Marco down the river.

I had also recently learned that Jacksonville was about to open its first Junior College, which was to be located in an abandoned high school only a few blocks from Prudential. If I could get a job there, I could start taking some night classes and work toward a degree.

I marched in, applied, was hired on the spot and told to report to work the following Monday. I had no idea what my job was, but heck, the pay was $52.50 a week with free lunch in their cafeteria and free health and life insurance. The only thing that mattered was I would earn enough to move out and stand on my own two feet.

I called Aunt Rudy to share the good news. Although I rarely saw her, she too appreciated art and we shared a bond over our love of painting.

We celebrated the start of my new chapter and then with a sigh, she said. "I need to tell you something. I feel terrible saying this—but it seems to me you deserve the truth."

My emotions balanced on the edge of her words for what felt like a long while, until the sentence that followed knocked me over the edge.

"It wasn't your father's idea to make you move out." Pause. "It was your mother's."

I gasped. A feeling of shock overtook me. "Are you sure?"

"Yes."

"Wow." It was the only word I could utter.

Dad and I had our share of disagreements over the years, sure, but I knew he loved me. He wasn't a quitter—this was evidenced time and time again throughout his life. My last year at home had been utterly uneventful if measured by the frequency of conflict I'd previously created by challenging him. Heck, I even brought home a nice Jewish boyfriend. He may not have supported of my desire to go to college—but it was because he believed that boys would one day have to support a family, whereas girls could get married and receive the support of their husbands. In the 1960s in the South, his was the prevailing sentiment.

I imagined Mom, who had never made it past tenth grade, struggling to make ends meet, thinking, "Gabrielle is a high school graduate—hell she has more education than me." To her, I represented just another mouth to feed. For many years I felt I had to protect Mom and the little kids against Dad's crazy, and here she was the one responsible for a massive betrayal, meanwhile allowing me to believe being thrown out of the house was Dad's doing.

A new kind of pain seared into my heart.

Then a thought: *Well, isn't this a crock of shit? I have a job now and, I'm going to get my own damn apartment and a dog. I'll show both of you.*

And finally: *Prudential thinks I'm smart.*

This was it—finally—the end of living in the powder keg that our family had become, and the beginning of my dream of eventually finding my way to college and San Francisco. I climbed aboard the bus and started humming, "California Dreaming."

On the bus home my shoulders relaxed and I realized that I'd grabbed ahold of something I hadn't felt for a very long time—hope.

GABRIELLE BRIE

Opposite: Extended family (before the feud); Grandma Paulina in NYC; Mom & Gabrielle; Mom, Dad, Gabrielle & Harvey; Harvey, Mom, Gabrielle, Benny & Paulina; Dad, Gabrielle & Blackie.

This page: Gabrielle; Dad & Gabrielle; Harvey; Paulina; Benny; Mom & Gabrielle.

Opposite: Dad & Mom at the Valentine's Dance; Grandma & Leon; Dad working out; Gabrielle & Marsha; Aunt Rudy & her granddaughter, Sharryse; Mom & her brother Jack in New York.

This page: The Redheads in Oregon; Benny & Paulina at Disneyworld; Marsha & Gabrielle with Marsha's mom; Gabrielle & Tramp; Harvey & Gabrielle at the red brick house, 1995.

Acknowledgements

San Miguel Writers' Conference Summer Residency, 2015

I WOULD LIKE to thank the following people:
Hunter Sunrise, my child and writer extraordinaire who championed me in the creation of this memoir through its many drafts.

Marico Fayre, for her unconditional love and encouragement, and who designed the interior and cover of this book.

Louis Marbe-Cargill and Libbe Dennard, my two faithful writing partners, for the years of lovely meetings at Louis' home and the many wonderful, intimate breakfasts at Libbe's and her husband Lee's home where a small, select group of friends celebrated our writing every few months for many years.

Nate Feuerberg, Maia and Wyman Williams, and Susan Page, whose contributions to the San Miguel Writers' Conference and the Literary Sala gave me a platform to perform the stories in this book at their many venues over the last eight years. The faithful friends who attended my readings including Joey Merrifield, Toby and Gerri Baruch, Jane Dill, Jocelynn Sunrise, and Isobel Kramer.

The many years of our Sunday "Not Dead Yet Poetry Share" meetings at Barbara Poole's Casa de la Noche.

My tough and loving beta readers and editors: Bill Cloud, Mark Saunders, Libbe Dennard, Kristin Masters, Nancy McCurry, Heather Snow, Beverly and Chris Wood, and Michael Wright.

My siblings and parents who brought these stories to life, and the many furry friends who have accompanied me on this journey including: Pepper, Zoe, Sanjay, Suki, Diego, Corazon, Lupita, Birdie Boy, Kitty Boy, Sylvester, Bunny Boy, and Stinko Luigi Magoo Mack—a gift from my brother Harvey who talked a magician into selling him baby bunny Luigi for fifty cents to take home to me, his sick sister, who had missed the Magic Show. And the many rescue dogs of Mexico who have taught me the truest meaning of grace.

The many others who encouraged me along the way to keep going when the memories felt too painful to continue.

Finally, to San Miguel's Poet Laureate, Rick Roberts, whose laughter and wisdom provided the glue for many of my stories— and the loudest applause at every reading.

About the Author

G ABRIELLE BRIE IS a literary writer, fine artist, and poet who explores themes of cultural tension and the growing pains that result from opposing beliefs across the various mediums of her work. She had a successful entrepreneurial career in California and Oregon while raising her two children.

When Gabrielle is not traveling the world, she and her three rescue dogs, Lupita, Diego and Corazon make San Miguel de Allende, Mexico their home.

Gabrielle spends her days fully dedicated to art and writing and operates Rescue San Miguel, an organization she founded that has saved the lives of hundreds of street dogs. Gabrielle's art, poetry and current writing, can be seen at her website *gabriellebrie.com*. To learn more about her rescue work go to *facebook.com/RescueSanMiguel*.

PHOTOGRAPHS

Most of the photographs are the author's own. When needed for cultural context, the following licensed images are used.

Lights Out, Empty Seats, and a Kiss in the Dark: *Lakeshore Theater from Cinema Treasures*

Music: *Old accordions with a book lie on a retro sofa by Andrii Siryi / Shutterstock. Contrast was adjusted. Image converted to black and white.*

Gillette Presents: *Sugar Ray Robinson, 1947, ACME, public domain via Wikimedia Commons & Gillette logo*

Giant and Midget Wrestlers: *Little wrestlers Beauer and Tiny Tim, in costume before a fight. Jan. 29, 1957, Paris, France. Keystone Pictures USA / Alamy Stock Photo*

Freedom Riders and Lee High: *"Freedom Riders" by Seattle Parks & Recreation, licensed under CC BY 2.0. Image was cropped.*

James Meredith: *Integrating Ole Miss, 1962 by Marion S. Trikosko (public domain)*

The Love Machine: *Felixstowe, Suffolk, England, May 07, 2017. Classic Blue Grey VW Beetle Motor Car Parked on Seafront Promenade by Martin Charles Hatch / Shutterstock.com*

Scrambled Eggs and Civil Rights: *Advertisement for Freedom Riders Anniversary Event at UMW by snakepliskens, licensed under CC BY-NC-SA 2.0. Image contrast was adjusted.*

Miss Sue from Alabama: *Four black college students sit in protest at a whites-only lunch counter at a Wollworth's in Greensboro, North Carolina. From left: Joseph McNeil, Franklin McCain, Billy Smith, and Clarence Henderson. (public domain)*

The Day Time Stopped: *"Toni Frissell: John F. Kennedy and Jacqueline Bouvier on their wedding day, 1953" by trialsanderrors, licensed under CC BY 2.0*

The Bloodiest Month: *"Black History Month" by US Department of State, licensed under CC PDM 1.0 (public domain)*

The Unthinkable: *Vietnam War, US Soldier Wounded, 1967, by FotoshopTofs on Pixabay. Image was converted to black and white.*

ATTRIBUTIONS

California Dreamin': *Golden Gate Bridge by Tae Fuller, pexels.com. Image was converted to black and white.*

The Hope Chest: *Lane Cedar Chest advertisement, 1955. Image was converted to black and white.*

The Third Terrible Trouble: *Demonstrators taunt the police during the Harlem riot of 1964, Library of Congress*

Senior Year, Supercar, and Vietnam: *1960 Dodge Matador 2 door hardtop by tapztapz, licensed under CC0 1.0 (public domain). Image was converted to black and white.*

Jackie Gleason: *Promotional photo of Jackie Gleason and the June Taylor Dancers from 1975, Wikimedia Commons*

SONGS IN THE PUBLIC DOMAIN

"By the Light of the Silvery Moon," Gus Edwards & Edward Madden, 1909

"Has Anybody Seen My Gal," Leo Fiest, 1925

"Oh You Beautiful Doll," Nat D Ayer and Seymour Brown, 1911

"Go Tell it on the Mountain," John Wesley Work, 1865

"It's Raining it's Pouring," *Little Mother Goose*, 1912

"Dayenu," ancient Jewish song over one thousand years old

"Row, Row, Row Your Boat," Eliphaet Oram Lyte, 1811

"Skidamarink a Dink a Dink", Felix F Feist and Al Piantados, 1910

"Fishing Blues," Henry "Ragtime" Thomas, 1928

"Hello! Ma Baby," Joseph E.Howard and Ida Emerson, 1899

"She'll be Coming Around the Mountain," 1899

"Drink to Me Only with Thine Eyes," Ben Jonson, 17th Century

"Fascination", Fermo Dante Marchetti, 1905

"The Bridal Chorus," Richard Wagner, 1850

"Miss Sue from Alabama," jumprope rhyme from the early 20th century

"Pomp and Circumstance Marches," Sir Edward Elgar, 1904

21

Made in the USA
Columbia, SC
07 April 2021